INAYAT KHAN

INAYAT KHAN

A Biography
by
Elisabeth de Jong-Keesing

EAST-WEST PUBLICATIONS FONDS B.V.,
The Hague
in association with
LUZAC & CO. LTD.,
London.

Translated from the original Dutch edition *Golven waarom komt de wind* by Hayat Bouman and Penelope Goldschmidt.

Copyright 1974 by East-West Publications Fonds B.V., The Hague and Messrs. Luzac & Co. Ltd., London.

ISBN 0 7189 0243 2

Contents

Acknowledgements

Thanks are due to the many who have helped to make this book a reality.

In the first place the family of Inayat Khan: his sons Vilayat and Hidayat Inayat Khan, who gave me introductions to old disciples and relations in America and France; his grandson Fazal Inayat Khan, who put the unpublished *Biography* and other documents in his possession at my disposal; his sisters-in-law Madame Maheboob Khan-van Goens and Madame Musharaff Khan-de Koningh, who found more and more memories, papers, photos and tape-recordings; and above all his nephew Mahmood Maheboob Khan, who untiringly checked and provided with supplementary comment each chapter and told me in many conversations and letters all the memories of his father and his uncles he had so often heard from them. Thanks also to Tez Mohd, great-grandson of Maula Bakhsh, who helped me in Baroda, and showed me round the old family house.

For their willingness to be interviewed I thank Miss A. W. Henny LLM, the Dutch poet Adriaan Roland Holst, Mario Montessori, and very especially Raden Aju Jodjana and Kismet Stam, who with great patience repeatedly answered my questions about the periods 1914-1920 and 1925-1927.

Hayat Bouman in Delhi I cannot thank enough for her hospitality, help, enquiries and introductions in India. Through her I received information, advice and corrections from Syed Awsaaf Ali, Faiz Abu Sahar, Muzaffar Husain Khan and Yunus Husain Khan, and from B. P. Shinglu, invaluable for the explanation of *Minqar-é-Mu-*

siqar; of Rayhane Behn Tyabji, who gave great moral support; of Mahmood Nizami, descendant of singers in Hyderabad who, as a child, had heard about Inayat and passed on what he remembered with the remark, 'If I had known he was to become so famous, I would have listened more often.' Through Hayat I made the acquaintance of Professor Khwaja Ahmed Faruqin, who opened the way to his friends in Hyderabad. There, especially through the hospitality of Professor Abdul Mahmood and his wife Professor Rafia Sultana, I met so many people that I cannot possibly mention them all. I shall never forget the interest, the readiness and the advice I was given in Hyderabad. Bishop John Subhan, however, I want to mention with special thanks, as also Ghousinisa Mir Maqbool Sultana, the grand-daughter of Inayat's spiritual teacher. In Baroda Tez Mohammed took me to see Inayat's oldest living admirer, Shri Vibukumar Desai and, his kind, helpful family. Baron van Lamsweerde of the Royal Institute for the Tropics in Amsterdam gave me an introduction to Professor Premlata Sharma in Benares, who answered all my questions about music and even bought a book to trace the author of the song Inayat sang before Gandhi. I also thank Mrs Shobarani Basu and Dr M. R. Gautam in Benares.

Than Europe and America. I owe special thanks to M. Marcel Dietschy, biographer of Debussy, for an extract of his recent discovery: a letter from Debussy to Walter Rummel; to Manfred Kelkel, biographer of Scriabine, for the translation and evaluation of Scriabine's remarks on Inayat Khan; to the nephews of Sergei Sergeiev Tolstoi for relating his memories; and to Sam Waagenaar, the biographer of Mata Hari, who supplied me with data from Mata Hari's scrapbooks.

For the translations from Hindustani and Russian I thank respectively Dr M. K. Gautam in Leyden and Madame I. Van Leeuwen-Reuvekamp in Amsterdam; for checking the D'Annunzio translation thanks to Dr F. Musarra in

Nijmegen. And I greatly appreciate the work of the young people who, with exemplary accuracy, did research for me: Miss Ulla Renquist in Helsinki, and Miss M. Chalmers and Mr William J. Foley in New York. Further I am indebted to my correspondents Bryn Beorse in Seattle and Paul Reps, wandering; also to the officials of New York Public Library and the Vedanta Society in New York.

Three helpers have passed away, Madame Rycklof van Goens-van Beyma in The Hague, Dr O. C. Gruner in Canada and murshid Samuel Lewis in San Francisco; all the warmer thanks therefore to the Maheboob Khan family, Mrs Edna Gruner and Mr Lewis's secretary Melvin Meyer.

In England I thank Jean Overton-Fuller and the officials of the Public Record Office, the Indian Office Library, the British Museum Newspaper Library and the Royal Asiatic Society; in France Mlle Giteau of the Bibliothèque Nationale and Mlle Maria Scriabine; in Brussels Madame Chkliar Morello; the T'Serclaes families in Paris, Brussels and Canada for identifying the author of the first biography; in Sweden Ingmar Berild; in Switzerland the Marquis de Breteuil; in Amsterdam Madame J. van Otten-van Warmelo, mr. H. J. Bosman of the Theatre Museum, the officials of the Institute for the Near East and of the International Institute for Social History; in The Hague the first Secretary of the Finnish Embassy and the Librarian of the Indian Embassy.

Among Sufis in the Netherlands my thanks for support, co-operation, memories and rare material go to Madame K. W. Blaauw-Robertson, mr W. A. Carp, Miss P. Fürtner, Miss R. H. Klaassen, Madame S. J. Smit-Kerbert, Miss C. C. and C. G. Voûte.

Finally I thank my husband, Dr H. W. van Tricht, and my daughter, Madame M. S. de Jong, who shared each discovery with me and severely criticized each chapter.

For the western reader I have restricted the use of Indian terms to the minimum. If unavoidable the translations occur in the text; failing that they have been included in the Glossary and Personal Notes.

The book was originally written in Dutch, the author's native language, but the English version could not be a mere translation. So the indefatigable Hayat Bouman made the first draft for most chapters, Penelope Goldschmidt did the same for chapters VII and X, and the final text resulted from close consultation between the author, the original translators and British-born controllers: Mrs Mary Vilayat Inayat Khan for the first two chapters and Mrs A. Kalkman, née Bowie for the rest. Dr R. Jamshyd Tillinghast, Sufi, poet and English scholar, very kindly did the final editing.

Ellecom, January, 1974   E. de J.-K.

Chapter I (1882-1896)
The House of Maula Bakhsh

Inayat's earliest memory was of distant singing he heard
before dropping off to sleep,[1] the sound drifting over the
courtyard from the main building where all the grown-ups
were gathered together: parents, grandparents, uncles,
aunts, servants. He slept in a little room in one of the
daughters' houses at the end of the garden. His father and
grandfather were musicians. When he was still a small child
his grandfather, Maula Bakhsh, used to come into his room
in the early hours and awaken him. Then they went to the
big house in front and Inayat stayed listening to the singing
and practising. He was, of course, destined to become a
musician himself. Soon his father, Rahemat Khan, wished
him to study until late at night, for what would become of
the boy if he didn't? Twelve hours' practice a day is quite
normal for Indian students of music, but Inayat's mother
thougt a child should rest, not work at night. 'He'll make his
way, you'll see,' she said.

Years later, in the West, Inayat used to tell stories of his
childhood to disciples who travelled with him, in England,
or France or Italy or Sweden or Illinois or California. He
and his brothers never stopped reminiscing about Baroda
and the charm of their childhood, which spanned two eras.

The West was remote and hardly figured in their young
lives, though it was always there, on the fringe. When
Queen Victoria was crowned Empress of India, Maula
Bakhsh played before the Viceroy and this was proudly
remembered. In directly ruled areas, like Calcutta and
Bombay, the British were always conspicuously present,

11

but in a princely state such as Baroda only the maharaja had any direct dealings with the foreign rulers. About 1870 the British Raj began to select very young royal successors, educating and influencing them. They were particularly successful in the case of the next to last maharaja of Baroda, usually called the Gaekwar.

Because this maharaja was an exceptional prince and the house of Maula Bakhsh a centre of Indian culture, the children had no need of outside interests. The palace and its splendour were always there, in the background. Their grandfather's visitors fascinated them. And everybody, father, grandfather, aunts, guests and servants, had wonderful stories to tell: stories of the past, of heroes and holy men and faithful lovers, but also stories of real and recent adventure. There were two mysterious persons in the house, called retainers or vassals, who had come with Maula Bakhsh's first wife, Inayat's grandmother. Her ancestry was only whispered about, and not until the children were grown-up did they learn that she was related to Tipu Sultan, the last Moghul king who resisted the British on a large scale. The mysterious retainers had arranged her marriage to Maula Bakhsh, because he was one of the few men this princess could have married. His fame as a musician had gained him royal rank.

Maula Bakhsh's own life story is picturesque and full of adventure; moreover his personality and ideas influenced Inayat deeply. His original name was Chole Khan and up to his fifteenth year he was just a cheerful boy whose most remarkable quality seemed to be his proficiency in wrestling. Then a dervish, whom he had helped, discovered his talents, advised him to use them and gave him as a blessing the name Maula Bakhsh, which means 'the gifted one,' gifted by God. This is how he started to study music. He learnt most by secretly listening to the famous singer Ghasit Khwan. Traditionally a master passed his knowledge only to chosen pupils, but Ghasit Khwan never accepted any one

Maula Bakhsh.

pupil. When he unexpectedly heard his own ragas sung by Maula Bakhsh, he forgave him the furtive way in which he had acquired them and taught him all the mysteries of his art and all his knowledge of northern, Indo-Islamic, music.

Soon Maula Bakhsh became an itinerant musician. In between his own concerts he listened everywhere and learnt what he could pick up. The most remarkable thing was that he also mastered the southern style. This so called Carnatic music belonged to the Brahmins and Maula Bakhsh was a Moslem. But he was gifted, not only with a lovely voice, but also with a fine ear for music and great perseverance. The first master he approached refused to teach him: 'he would first have to be re-born as a Brahmin.' This was in Mysore. With hurt pride he left, did not wait for another birth, but began to search. In Malabar, the centre of southern music he found a Brahmin willing to entrust his art to him. Triumphantly he returned to Mysore in 1860 and accepted the next challenge. Singers were invited to come from all over India, and for ten months a great competition went on. By the end Maula Bakhsh has conclusively proven himself superior to any others and the maharaja endowed him with the royal insignia: a jewel in his turban, a sceptre, a gold chain and golden umbrella. He actually went about in all this splendour, in spite of envy and intrigues.

He wandered through the country with his wives, children, servants, camels and tents, like a patriarch from the distant past. But in his outlook he was far ahead of his time. Not only was he a great artist, but he used systematic methods and was fully and clearly aware of the changing world around him. He collected Indian music from everywhere and classified it to preserve this cultural heritage for posterity. He wanted to take it out of the hands of the hereditary guardians of music in the palaces and temples and bring it to the people. He invented a system of notation, whereby the ragas, which had hitherto been passed on orally, could be recorded. Meanwhile to carry out his ideas he was dependent on royal patronage. His wish to establish a music academy as a public teaching institution could not be fulfilled till 1881. This was shortly before the birth of Inayat, when the exceptionally good Gaekwar came to the throne.

This prince, too, lived and worked in an atmosphere of transition. He modernized the administration, even spruced up his court a bit, seriously reformed the system of justice and of course encouraged new industries. He embellished his town with broad boulevards and opened parks for his people who lived in suffocatingly narrow lanes. 'We all like fresh air.'[2] For himself he built baroque, western style palaces, but he still knew and honoured his own culture. That is how, among other institutes, Maula Bakhsh's Gayanshala, school of music, was started. Today it is the faculty of music of Baroda University, which any Barodan can show you.

In the Yaqudpura quarter they still know the house of Maula Bakhsh. His name is carved above the gate, but little is left of the glory of former times. The ground-plan of the large complex is still intact, but the buildings themselves have changed beyond recognition. The expanding town has been encroaching upon the compound for years. When Inayat was a child it stood alone, on the edge of the town, with fields at the back. In front a wide gate with studded doors gave access to the house and the courtyard. To the left of the gate were the stables. The place bristled with visitors and guests. Pilgrims arrived on foot; gentlemen came in riding or driven in elegant horse-, ox-, or camel-drawn carriages. Supplies were carried in on porters' heads. Occasionally even an elephant stopped there.

The elephant was a royal mount. Once a year Inayat and his brothers were treated to an elephant ride.[3] But when young Maula Bakhsh was in the South he used to go to concerts in full regalia, riding an elephant. Once, when he came home, the servant who helped him to descend asked

15

him what he had sung and what it all meant. There and then, in the middle of the night, the master gave a demonstration for his servant. It woke up the whole household, but nobody objected.

Whatever Maula Bakhsh did or said was accepted. An ex-resident of Baroda says, 'Maula Bakhsh, ah, what a man. If he so much as sneezed, the whole house trembled.' Yet they all loved him, the women, the children, the servants and the guests who lived with him around the courtyard.

Beside the gate, facing the road, was the two-storeyed main building with the large rooms where he sat with his guests. Behind stood the enormous, high-ceilinged kitchen, centrally placed, between the courtyard and the women's quarters. During Maula Bakhsh's life-time meals for forty or fifty people were cooked every day in this kitchen, which still stands as it stood. The mud floor, the rafters, the mud and bamboo walls — not a nail used — the dark red paint work, the piles of brass and the enormous fire place remained unchanged.

Between the kitchen and the women's quarters a staircase lead to the servants' rooms downstairs. All along the right side of the compound stretched the vast hall where the women spent their lives and from where they ruled, watching everything. On the opposite side, behind the stables, were the sons' houses. The daugthers' residences which looked out over the fields at the back, completed the square of the courtyard. Four small white houses, each with a dark door-opening, they stood three storeys high, topped by a terraced roof. In summer people sleep on these terraced roofs, in winter boys fly their kites there and all the year round good Moslems can say their prayers in this quiet spot five times a day.

Rahemat Khan was such a good Moslem. He came from the North, from the Punjab. He, too, could tell wonderful stories, of his own wanderings, and especially of heroes of the past. His ancestors were Turki, heads of clans and tribal

16

priests.[4] They had come to the subcontinent in the four-teenth century, either with the armies of Tamerlane, or fleeing from them. In India the Brahmins, the priests, are the highest caste and the most respected. Therefore the family never forgot its tribal priest ancestors, even though they had ministered to a primitive people, long ago, even though the descendants of these Shamans had embraced other, greater religions, and even though in the Punjab they had acquired a considerable amount of Persian, Pun-jabi and other 'Aryan' blood. Rahemat Khan's portraits could well be those of a European. He looked like Gounod, or any other nineteenth century gentleman, with his beard, moustache and side-burns, and his expression of suppres-sed sensitivity. He had such a fair complexion that he could blush. What we know of his character sounds like many nineteenth century fathers — a strict man, both a rationalist and a puritan, with a strong sense of honour and manliness.

But his lot in life was not Victorian. He had to wander and search, as Maula Bakhsh had done in his youth and as many other Indians had to do in that age of struggle and change. After the death of his father his elder brother, according to custom, had brought him up. On one or two occasions, when his sister-in-law had spoken to him harsh-ly, he had run away from home. But his brother, a kind and mystically inclined man, had always managed to bring him back. When Rahemat Khan's musical education was completed, he set out into the world for good. Later he often recalled that a holy man standing along the road looked at him and made a gesture in a certain direction.[5] Following this indication Rahemat Khan came to Baroda, where he found shelter in the house of Maula Bakhsh, as many musicians had done.

It was part of Maula Bakhsh's work to judge the profes-sional abilities of travelling singers and musicians. Rahe-mat Khan proved to be an excellent dhrupad singer. Soon he was invited to perform and teach at the Court. He was made the ustad, music teacher, of Maula Bakhsh's eldest son. And the grand old man of music gave him his daughters in marriage. First the eldest, who died after giving birth to a girl; then the second, Khatijabi. Rahemat Khan was thirty eight when he married her, and she was fourteen. But fourteen was not too young for a girl to run a household, certainly not for Khatijabi, who was a descendant of rulers.

With all customary modesty, Khatijabi also brought self-confidence and a sense of dignity to her marriage. She had been brought up with Persian, which for ages was the official and fashionable language in India, as French was in Europe. She read Persian poetry, and knew Arabic as well as the colloquial Urdu. Certainly she had received more schooling than most Moslem girls.

Her greatgrandfather, about whom one only spoke in whispers, had married an Ethiopian wife. There were many Abyssinians in old Mysore. They were held in high esteem and their daughters were much sought-after as brides. Traces of this strain can be recognized in a portrait of Khatijabi and some of her descendants. Maula Bakhsh's own ancestors were originally Brahmins of the Vyas-caste and did not embrace Islam till the eighteenth century. Maula Bakhsh's second and third wives were Hindus, one a Brahmin, the other a Kshatrya.

Amongst so many influences, cultures and traditions, from so many different fathers and grandfathers, fair, dark, Moslems, Brahmins, musicians, soldiers, holy men, priests and princes, Inayat Khan was born, on July 5th 1882.[6]

The family treasured many anecdotes of his childhood. Some of these tales seem contradictory, but all his life Inayat showed many sides of his being. He was a lively child, but sometimes very quiet. He loved to leap and bound from great heights and alarmed his parents by running through pools and puddles when the country was flooded. Once he jumped into the river, because some other boys had challenged him, though he could not swim. He admired courage ('if it is courageous to swallow nasty medicine without making faces, I'll do it.'). But he thought wrestling, a national sport, silly and cruel, not because of the fighting, but because it was humiliating for the loser.

He was generous, chivalrous, and much too fascinated by all he saw to be very obedient. On summer afternoons, when the hot wind tore across the plain, he was not allowed to go out, but no lively child can be kept indoors for a siesta. Inayat preferred to climb the pear tree, even if there was only one ripe fruit to pick. From his father he learned self-control and self-respect. Rahemat Khan's stories always ended with a moral and the boy never stopped asking questions of how, why and wherefore. In his grandfather's room he was allowed to sit and listen to the conversation of philosophers and musicians. Sometimes Maula Bakhsh took him to see a Brahmin friend of his, who was the first to notice something exceptional in this restless child whom one found profoundly serious one moment and playfully adventurous the next. If there was a dervish in town, or a man with a dancing bear, Inayat would come late for dinner, or not at all. The holy man as well as the bear fascinated him.

One day his brother Maheboob, who was five years younger, came home in tears. The big boys, Inayat and his friend Sadanand, were on their way to the South to set up a new school, and they would not take him with them because he was too small. All the men of the house swarmed out to look for the runaways. They found them outside the town, sitting under a tree, seriously discussing how they should go about starting their school.

One can well imagine that Rahemat Khan worried about Inayat's future. What would become of the playful child, who reacted so intensely, whose character was so difficult to grasp, who disliked school, but who clearly was a born leader? How could he use this talent for leadership in a country ruled by foreigners? And what possibilities were there for a Moslem boy who would not inherit any land? The younger sons of the landed nobility, like Rahemat Khan, had to attempt to make a respectable profession out of a respectable hobby.

After careful consideration Inayat was sent to a Hindu school, the best one in Baroda, whose modern curriculum, it was hoped, would lead to an opening in modern society. But the methods were not that modern. Between the teacher and the pupils there was no contact at all and no effort was made to develop insight. Geography and history lessons had to be repeated parrot-fashion, and a pupil whose attention strayed was struck with a stick.[7] Inayat's bare legs were often rapped. This lifeless way of teaching was alien to all in him and to all he knew. When his father or grandfather taught him something, they explained and there was always a warm, personal relation. In class he started to dream of things that puzzled him, or he drew on his slate, cane or no cane. He spurned arithmetic and herein he was not the only one – the serious Gaekwar did not care for it either.[8] Doing sums was good for merchants and moneylenders, not for artists and aristocrats. Consequently Inayat always did badly in some subjects, but he was brilliant in languages, philosophy and composition.

India is a country of many languages. Inayat had to learn the regional Marathi and Gujarati, the wider spread Hindustani, and Sanscrit, the Latin of India. At home he heard the Arabic Quran and Persian poetry. The family spoke Urdu. The boys could not understand their father's Punjabi, and Rahemat Khan was at a loss when his sons made up their own secret language by using Marathi words back to front. English was taught only in top standard and Inayat, because of his aversion to part of the curriculum, barely reached that grade.

If anything interested him, he would do it very well.

When he was eleven, he started a debating club, to which he contributed most himself. This did not surprise anybody at home. Even as a small child he had thought out his games in detail. When the boys played at circus, Inayat told everyone what animal he had to be and how he should growl or jump. Once a travelling theatre group staged a play about Harish Chandra, the king who kept his promise. For months afterwards the boys, too, performed it. Inayat prompted them from behind.

He was, of course, an artist's child through and through. He sang from memory every raga he heard and tried all musical instruments. One day a singer who was an opium addict came to visit Maula Bakhsh and proudly claimed that he only sang new compositions by his great master in Jaipur. Inayat immediately picked up the tune, quickly made up new words and said teasingly, 'But this is not a new raga!' and he proceeded to sing the same melody with his own words and variations.

When he also began to write poetry his parents felt very troubled. It was not practical, they said, and took away his poems and his drawings. In general people of their class had great respect for poets and poetry in those days. Rabindranath Tagore was the youngest in a big family, and nobody paid much heed to him, until they found out that he was writing poetry. Then he suddenly became an important person.[9] But Rahemat Khan and Khatijabi worried because Inayat was becoming more and more inclined to withdraw in thoughtful silence. They tried to keep him 'normal' by giving him toys and even a pony of his own. Their worry was increased by their own uncertainty, especially the father's. Unconsciously their ideas and sentiments were as old-fashioned as could be, but they liked to think themselves modern and they wanted to arm their children in the struggle for modern life. Rahemat Khan's brother was a mystic and so was his music teacher, but he did not encourage any tendency to mysticism in his sons.

21

He shared the belief of all Indians, that the presence of a sage or dervish is a blessing in itself, so he did take the boys to see holy men. But eventually he wanted a worldly occupation for his sons and he emphasized his dislike of superstition. That was in the air. Both Hindus and Moslems had their enlightened reform movements. Among the Hindus it was the Brahmo Samaj, which aimed at social reform. Among the Moslems the strict and rational reformers were the Wahabites. Both movements fought against superstition.

Surely, Rahemat Khan's attitude towards mysticism may have had something to do with his fear of his own emotions. Outwardly he was severe and admired manly self-control, but he was hot-tempered, and at heart an extremely sensitive person. If one of the children hurt himself, tears would come into his eyes and the child had to comfort the father — 'it is nothing, really.'

A man of this character shuns poetry, which means expressing one's feelings. But when it became evident that Inayat's writing could not be stopped, they found him a teacher. If he had to do it, then he sould know the rules.

Inayat's parents may also have been embarrassed, because his first poems were the result of his enquiries after the origin of babies. In proper nineteenth century fashion this information was not given. Even Maula Bakhsh put him off with 'later, when you are older.' Whereupon Inayat consulted the books in his grandfather's library and when he had found what he wished to know, he wrote a love song and a poem to his mother.

The grown-ups ought to have known that he would not be satisfied with an evasive answer, for they knew how he used to go on and on asking questions. They also knew how he could sit, lost in thought, when something painful had happened. In an Indian community illness, poverty and death are visible facts, even for a child in a safe and sheltered home. Inayat accepted nothing that came his way without questioning, except the cultural background against which he grew up.

Of course he asked all the questions any intelligent child asks about God: where is God? how old is God? what happens to people when they die? why must I pray? For whatever the Hindu seasoning of the family, Inayat had learned to say his Moslem prayers five times a day. He had seen pictures of gods and goddesses, of Krishna playing the flute and dancing with the milkmaids, and he liked them. But he had also been taught that it was far superior to pray to Allah, the One of whom no effigy could be made. So he prayed to the Invisible, until the moment of doubt and rebellion, which comes in the life of every serious seeker after truth. One summer evening he was kneeling on the familiar terraced roof to say his prayers, when the thought came to him that though he had been praying with all devotion and humility 'no revelation had as yet been vouchsafed to him; and that it was not wise to go on worshipping one whom he did not see or know.'[10]

It was evening, the sun was setting, the roof still warm. Soon the fields behind the house lay in darkness, Inayat ran down the narrow stone staircase, crossed the courtyard to his grandfather's room, and told him he would not offer any more prayers to Allah, until He was seen or known: 'There is no reason why one should follow a belief and do as one's ancestors did without knowing a proper reason for it.'

Maula Bakhsh smiled, was silent for a moment and then quoted a verse from the Quran. 'We will show them our signs in the world and in themselves, that the truth may be manifested to them.' It appears that the grandson, still rather impatient, said something like 'Oh, well.' For years later, when he himself told this story, he added, 'And then he soothed my impatience and explained, saying, "The signs of God are seen in the world, and the world is seen in thyself."'

These are ancient words of wisdom. They were used in Egypt, in Canaan, in Persia. And they are used today by philosophers and psychologists after a life-time of reasoning and searching.

Inayat was still young when, in a flash of enlightenment, these words entered deep into his soul and he knew that he had found the way he had to go. He would seek God in the world around him, in his fellowmen, and in himself.

In his memoirs he does not tell how old he was at that moment, but he cannot have been more than fourteen, for in 1896 Maula Bakhsh died.

Chapter II (1896-1900)
Worlds outside Baroda

The son of one of the mysterious retainers had taken up a modern art, photography, and he made a picture of Inayat as a boy of eight or nine years: a trusting child's face, cheerful, yet with an expression of attentive listening. His eyes are intent, not on the man under the black cloth who told him to sit still and watch for the bird, but on some inward memory, felt but elusive.

About 1891 Maula Bakhsh's youngest son Alauddin Khan left for England and on that occasion many photos were taken, even of the women. Some Hindu ladies, friends of the family, took the opportunity to join in this thrilling adventure. Women led very secluded lives and hardly ever went out. The public parks observed special ladies' days when no man was allowed to enter the gates. The photographer belonged to the family, but he made the uncovered faces of old women, young mothers and little girls visible for any one who might see his pictures.

An old lady stood in the centre, she was eighty, but her blazing eyes made her look no more than sixty. Everyone called her grandmother, though actually she was the aunt who had brought up Maula Bakhsh. She was the first lady of the house; the second in authority was Maula Bakhsh's Brahmin wife with her proud, beautiful face, and then came young Khatijabi.

Rahemat Khan did not like photos of women and girls who did not modestly lower their eyes. Either Maula Bakhsh or the old grandmother must have given their consent for the ladies to be photographed. The women had a considerable voice in family matters. It was only after long deliberation that Alauddin Khan had been given permission to go and study in England. He refused to take training in Indian music, for he thought the conditions under which he would have to work would be humiliating. His elder brother was to be their father's successor, and he did not see much future for Indian music anyway. The family council sanctioned his departure. In 1893 Maula Bakhsh was invited to perform at the World Exhibition in Chicago, which could have added world fame to his national fame. But the women would not hear of it, they said he was too old. Of course Inayat, who had wished to go with his uncle as well as with his grandfather, stood no chance, for he was far too young.

'Europe' — whether it was called Chicago or London — attracted and repelled. The West was hated and admired, desired and envied. Anyone who went there could either show 'them' what he and the culture of India were worth, or he could acquire the knowledge from which the foreign rulers seemed to derive their power. Alauddin Khan was the first of this thoroughly Indian family who went to the West. When Inayat went abroad for the first time, five years later, his route lay eastwards. Not long after Maula Bakhsh's death he accompanied his father to Nepal.

1896 was a year of famine and plague, even in fertile Gujarat, which had not known such disasters for years. The family had sufficient means to go and live outside the town, to help others, and to take in children of poor victims. Still, the famine brought problems for the household. Maula Bakhsh wanted to economize and conserve their stores; the old grandmother said that growing children should be fed properly. 'And when we run out of food?' 'Then I'll catch you by the ear and sell you in the market,' said the vigorous old lady. This bit of banter, which was also a compliment — a Maula Bakhsh will fetch a good price — must have been one of the last conversations between the two rulers of the

Baroda, 1896. Inayat, fourteen or fifteen years old, playing the jaltarang.

house. Maula Bakhsh died, sixty three years old; his aunt lived till over a hundred.

There is a picture of Inayat, taken in this sad year: a thin boy, looking down miserably, though he is playing a gay percussion instrument, the jaltarang. He had not only just lost his grandfather, but also his best friend Sadanand, the boy with whom he had once run away to start a school in the South. He was so unhappy and had become so quiet, that the family council decided he needed a change. His entreaties to travel with his father were granted.

The king of Nepal had invited well-known musicians from everywhere to add to the splendour of his court. Rahemat Khan went there in place of Maula Bakhsh. The Nepalese court, magnificent though it was, would disappoint Inayat in some respects. But apart from that he would always remember his first long journey with joy.

It started in Gwalior, also one of the better princely states. For music-loving Inayat this was above all the town where Tansen, the singer at Akbar's court, is buried.[1] Tansen was a magic word for him, an ideal. When Tansen sang his firesong, so the legend goes, the torches lit up by themselves. His singing moved the emperor to ecstasy and there was one story Inayat especially loved. The ruler, disguised as a servant, travelled to the wilderness to hear Tansen's teacher sing — to the wilderness of the Himalyas where Inayat himself was now going.

After Gwalior, a city of Moghul culture, they came to the holy Hindu city of Benares. Enchanted, feeling as if he were being initiated, he walked by the river and temples. An orthodox Moslem may frown at this, anyone reading today's newspapers, full of Hindu-Moslem strife, may find it difficult to believe. But in those days Hindus and Moslems lived together in peace,[2] though there was a definite line of demarcation between Moslems, Christians and Jews on the one hand, and Hindus, Buddhist, Sikhs and Jains on the other. It was almost a difference between East and West right there in the East. But difference of tradition did not mean coming to blows. The bitter hatred and fighting began later, when influences from the outside forged lines of political divisions between the old socio-religious identities.

In the East reverence for holy places is taken for granted. Durga Das, the journalist, relates how the boys from his Hindu school used to pray for success in their examinations at the tomb of a Moslem saint and vice versa, Moslems used to go to Hindu shrines. Certainly this adaptation to all kinds of worship is more a Hindu than a Moslem trait. Even today memorial services at the tombs of some Moslem saints are performed by Hindu priests.[3]

At a high level, that of the mystic, all distinctions between religions fall away, but that is different. Inayat was destined to become a great mystic and this essential unity of all religions was to be an important part of his teachings. Perhaps his feeling of initiation in Benares suggested that already; besides, he was the grandson of Maula Bakhsh, who took him to see Hindu priests, his best friend had been a Brahmin boy, he was educated at a Hindu school, and the Brahmins called him by a Hindu name: Vinayak. From childhood he had listened to and been taught South Indian, Hindu, music. His first musical composition was on a Hindu theme: when he was about ten years old he wrote a simple, playful song about Krishna stealing the butter. And a song about Ganesh, the elephant God, brought him his first public honours.

He did see the Ganges: the sunrise above the wide river, the early morning bathers, the stillness of the afternoon. He saw the high river bank and the point where the pilgrimage palaces of the rajas made it look even higher. Not far from there, on a small, rarely used cremation ground, he saw the hut of Harish Chandra, the king who kept his promise, and he remembered the play he had seen and later acted over and over again with his friends. In the town he saw vivid paintings on the white-washed walls, like enlargements of old miniatures. And temples everywhere, large ones towering above trees and house, others so small that they fitted into a hollow trunk. In the monkey temple the monkeys jumped on the swinging bells while below the priests received the offerings of the devotees. And then there was the narrow street where he saw the silver doors of the gold-topped temple. But he, a non-Hindu, was not allowed to enter there.

From Benares they went to Sigoli, which was as far as the railway ran in those days. So there they alighted, Inayat, his father, the servants and other travelling companions. Before them rose the Himalayas.

He saw the snow-capped mountains. He knew their names, names of gods and goddesses and he knew that here was a scene of epic battles. It was a world for gods and giants. Nothing resembled the landscape he was familiar with: friendly groups of shrubs by a pond, planted by the hand of man, or solitary shade-giving trees in the vast expanse of the plains. Here he stood before thick jungle, full of strange odours and secret sounds. They climbed and descended the winding paths, sometimes they could smell a tiger, higher up bears lived in freedom. Fragile looking bridges were slung across splashing streams. The higher they climbed the more unfamilar were the trees: oak, fir and cedar. He saw the abundant flowering of orchids and rhododendrons and bare rock where nothing could grow. In the jungle near Nainital he saw elephants being captured. They passed the lake, now blue, now green, and centuries' old temples and shrines, lost in the wilderness. Forests in the distance which should have been green, looked black or dark bluish. In the evening the setting sun glowed on the snow caps in every possible shade of red and purple. Every moment was different and new.

Years later he was to use his memories of this journey as a metaphor. 'The joy of life is the joy of the journey. If one could close one's eyes and be put immediately on the top of the Himalayas, one would not enjoy it as much as the one who climbs and goes from one peak to another, and sees the different scenery and meets different people on the way. The whole joy is in the journey.'[4]

Palanquins were waiting to take the party across the mountains, but Inayat refused to be carried. He wanted to feel this rugged nature under his feet and with his hands, to smell, see and hear it. He also wanted to show his youthful strength. And then there was his innate respect for others: he could not let himself be carried by another human being, a rare scruple in the East. On the last lap of the journey the palanquins were replaced by panniers, carried by the Sherpas on their backs, for there was no longer a path and they needed their hands to climb the mountain face. Even here Inayat insisted on managing by himself. It was not without some risks, but he was ready for adventure and enjoyed the challenge.

This year away from home remained with him as a glorious memory, even though it was in Nepal that he discovered how remote most people were from the ideal behaviour he had been taught and which he had seen in practice. As long as he had met musicians only in the house of Maula Bakhsh it had seemed to him that they all shared his grandfather's dream of saving the music and the culture of the country. And the exceptional Gaekwar was for him the standard by which he judged all other rulers.

No doubt the king of Nepal had grandeur and royal manner, but also certain foibles with both surprised and disappointed the grandson of Maula Bakhsh. He discovered that His Majesty knew nothing about music and had invited the musicians only to satisfy his vanity. The majority of the musicians were no better, it was not music they worshipped, but their own fame. They elbowed their way to the top, scandalmongering among their equals, bowing and bending before the rajas.

31

Inayat had seen illness, death and starvation, these were all part of life. But petty meanness, jealousy and vain stupidity besmirched his image of a king, who should be an ideal man, and of music, which was his ideal cultural heritage.

He had to digest this disillusion. To do that he had time, freedom, nature and his veena. Besides, some of the musicians present did come up to his standards. He learned many new ragas and made some new friends: boys of his own age at the palace, and an old Sufi from the Punjab with whom he could talk as he used to with his grandfather. He avoided the elbowing clique, which did not make him very popular with them.

He had, it is true, set himself a very high ideal. Tansen was his dream, the unparalleled, who evoked a vision of heaven for Akbar. When praised, Tansen always replied that his art was nothing compared to that of his master. 'He is not a musician, he is music.' That is why the emperor went with Tansen into the wilderness, although Tansen's master sang only for God and not for mere mortals. But Tansen drew him out by starting a raga and deliberately making a little mistake. Whereupon the master corrected him and went on singing. 'When he sang it seemed as if the trees of the forest were vibrating, it was a song of the universe.'

Was Inayat thinking of Tansen's master when, to escape the palace atmosphere, he rode into the jungle on horseback? He did not find a singer, but a muni, that is a holy man who never speaks a word. This muni sat there 'untouched by earthly contact, ambitions and environments, he seemed to be the happiest man in the world.'[4] These are the words in which Inayat describes the saint, the absolute opposite of what he had seen in the palace. Later, in the West, when he himself was a teacher, he used to warn romantic dreamers that one should not search in far-away places for what can be found at home and that holy men are everywhere, not only in the silence of the Himalayas. But he was an Indian boy visiting Nepal and he happened to be in the Himalayas. Dreaming of Tansen was his romanticism. He sat before the muni and sang; on his next visits he took his veena with him. The saint did not move, he said nothing, he seemed unaware of Inayat's presence. But: 'he revealed to me the mysticism of sound and unveiled before my sight the inner mystery of music.' These secrets of sound and silence and the mystical power of music pervade Inayat's whole development and later work. He had been shaken by loss through death and by the disillusionment of life, now this discovery gave him new confidence. Around the muni there reigned absolute silence; even the trees and plants did not stir and seemed to be listening 'as if the everblowing wind had lost its power in this perfect silence which came from the peace of his soul.'

This encounter in the wilderness and the silent contact made a deeper impression on Inayat than the new influences that awaited him in Baroda. When he and his father returned by the end of 1897, uncle Alauddin, too, was home again. He called himself Dr. A. M. Pathan now and apart from a European-style surname, he had also brought from the West European clothes and European musical instruments. And bitterness.

Among the many family portraits in Maula Bakhsh's house there is, even now, a picture of an elegant couple in an elegant carriage in a Londen park. They might be Soames and Irene from the Forsythe Saga. But they were the Indian Alauddin Khan Pathan and the daughter of his British music teacher. The English family had no objection to a marriage. In those days Indians were looked upon as romantic and interesting, they were no longer so unfamiliar and remote as to be considered strange savages, and not yet close enough to be thought a menace. London could still recognize a handsome and talented young man when it saw one.

But the women of the Indian family vetoed the union.

They had plenty of motives: one ought not to choose one's partner, match making was family (read: women's) business; such a foreign person would never feel at home in the women's quarters, she would criticize and make all kinds of changes. Besides, the British were enemies.

Actually, Dr. Pathan, too, considered them as such. His choice of a surname shows that. The Pathans were the brave mountain tribes in the North West Frontier Province, who never stopped fighting the British. To call oneself Pathan was a challenge, absurdly if applied to something so western as a surname.

Introducing western musical instruments, too, was a challenging imitation: 'anything you can do, we can do too.'

Wearing western clothes did not have the same emotional value as it has today. Durga Das[5] tells how he and his schoolmates flocked to the house of an Indian who went around bareheaded and wore western clothes. A few years later a boy in an English suit and solar topee 'was for some time an object of goggle-eyed curiosity and not little envy'. Today wearing western costume is no longer defiant, but a form of adaptation, though in some circles it gives a certain prestige. The ambiguity of this kind of adaptation soon became obvious. In Calcutta, the capital, where everything happened before it happened anywhere else, Tagore's elder brothers tried to find a solution in a most funny compromise, a half Indian, half western costume.[6]

In Baroda, in 1897, it created quite a stir when Dr Pathan dressed his nephews in European suits. He fitted them out with high collars − the photos will make any Westerner laugh − ties − which Indians for some reason considered as a symbol of Christianity and the cross − but no headgear which must have given Moslems a feeling of being naked. Covering the head is generally a sign of respect in India. But the alien costume was a demonstration of independence. If anyone commented on it, he would get the peculiar reply, 'we are playing western music and have to conduct.'

That was accepted and the jacket and trousers came to be called the 'musician's garb' by some people. Actually, as the trouser legs had a habit of riding up, it was a hindrance for Indian musicians who play with their instrument on their crossed knees. Tight, tailored clothes are not very suitable in a hot climate, for conductors as little as for veena or sitar players. But then, one does not wear protest clothes to be comfortable, but to protest.

Uncle Alauddin, now Dr Pathan, founded a department of western music at the Gayanshala, and the maharaja was enriched with an orchestra of strings and woodwinds, and a western military band. For some time all the nephews were under Dr Pathan's influence. Inayat learned to play the harmonium and the violin, and even wrote manuals for these instruments. Later he was to detest the harmonium. His experiment with western music did not last long, for soon he chose to return to his veena and his ragas.

He started teaching while he was still at school and in training. From childhood he had learned the northern as well as the southern music at home. At the Academy of Music he followed the evening course and sometimes, just for fun, he taught other classes what he had learned the evening before. The teachers did not mind; it was hot. In 1899, another year of famine, Inayat was officially appointed lecturer in music, and soon became a professor, whereas his father always remained a lecturer. The titles professor and lecturer belonged to the modern system of teaching a class, while as ustads they would have taught only a few individual pupils. As late as 1913 Inayat's brothers adressed him as 'Professor' when they wrote to him. Their westernization did not include calling their respected and much admired eldest brother by his name.

They can all be seen in a group photo taken in front of the Academy of Music in 1900.[7] Two boys, the youngest brother and his friend, are sitting on the ground in front.

35

Enthroned in the centre is the painted portrait of Maula Bakhsh. On the left the representatives of eastern music, among whom Rahemat Khan in a great turban. On the right sit those who have had a taste of the West. First Dr Pathan and next to him Professor Inayat Khan Rahemat Khan Pathan, a strong young man in a high collar and neatly parted but rebellious hair.

Chapter III (1902-1903)
Professor Inayat Khan Pathan

The young professor was over-energetic and full of plans. He wrote a textbook[1] for singing instruction, the contents of which were extremely varied. The theoretical part was followed by 75 songs in different languages and different styles, from very simple to highly classical, on religious subjects, Moslem and Hindu, interspersed with love songs, a wedding hymn, seven English songs, including *Home Sweet Home* and *Dolly Darling,* and finally a national anthem for Baroda. The ghazals which form the main part of his later, great book on music, are already in the majority. The introduction is significant: 'Music was in decline in our country, but by the grace of God it is recovering.... The notation system of Maula Bakhsh and the Gaekwar's Academy of Music make instruction for boys and girls possible; we Indians had never thought about this before.'

Inayat was engrossed with these two innovations: music for everyone including singing instruction for girls. He even thought about so modern a subject as general education for girls and could vividly explain how that should be done. One day he talked enthusiastically about all this in the presence of his father, who thought both the subject and Inayat's behaviour improper. 'Be silent,' Rahemat Khan said curtly and severely. His son, the professor, got up, bowed low before his father and left the room.

Because of this correct reaction Rahemat Khan forgave him. Sometimes, indeed, Inayat was a son to be proud of, for instance when he composed a song on the lotus-girl, the ideal of modest and noble womanhood. This composition was so beautiful that it must on no account be printed, but, according to tradition, remain the property of the family.

Yet it is understandable that Inayat, whose head was full of ideas and who had a keen sense of his possiblities, did not remain at home for long. 'Leaves home for the national Cause' is the heading of a paragraph in the oldest European biography.[2]

Inayat would never be a political fighter but the fate of his country weighed heavily with him. In 1900, when he became a man in society, the Indian resentment against colonialism was still searching for a form. Gandhi, for tactical reasons, supported the British in South Africa with Indian soldiers. Other future leaders were still professors, journalists or civil servants under the British. Naoroji, later called the grand old man of India, was a member of the House of Commons; Tilak, the most vehement among the politicians, advocated an India for the Hindus, not the kind of thing that could attract a young Moslem full of Akbar ideals.

Inayat's image of the real India resembled most that of Sarojini Naidu, the Hyderabad doctor's wife, who wrote poetry in English and was at the same time an ardent freedom fighter. In her earliest poems and in her most eloquent speeches she portrayed a grand national unity, the Akbar ideal: peace and co-operation of all creeds and communities.

This same ideal rings through Inayat's earliest songs and his first appearance in public. He wished to make the many different peoples and faiths aware of their common and interrelated culture. That is why in the preface to the above mentioned book of songs he stressed his hope to serve the country with his music. Having been for some time subjected to western ideas he knew that copying European accomplishments soon lead to forgetting one's own. He always warned against blindly imitating everything western.

Madras, July 1902. Honoured after his first public performance far from home.

He did continue to go about in European costume – that was emancipated and distinguished. In 1899 he thought of demonstrating the marvels of Indian music at the World Exhibition in Paris. Maula Bakhsh had not been able to go to Chicago for this purpose in 1893. The family council was prepared to let Inayat part. At 17 he was no longer considered too young. But he did not leave because of his mother. Those who went to Europe often did not find their parents alive on their return.

Indian women, imprisoned within their rooms and closed gardens frequently died young. A doctor was rarely allowed to come near a female patient and had to make his diagnosis from a distance. In a short poem Inayat describes the fate of a beautiful young girl, modest, as was expected of her, eyes downcast, head bent, as delicate as a flowerbud on a slender stem. 'But clouds arise, the shadow of the years, Dewing her gay saree with rain like tears.' This might have been a conventional memento mori, but the experience was painfully real and the tears were his own. Within a year he saw his mother and two brides die.

Khatijabi died at the age of 34 or 35, in the middle of the preparations for the marriage of her eldest son. Two years earlier she had lost one of the younger boys, Karemat Khan, a lively child of eight, and she had never quite got over that. Inayat's marriage to his cousin, Dr Pathan's daughter, was for her the fulfilment of a long cherished wish. When she died, after a short illness, the family's first impulse was to postpone the wedding, but because she had set her heart on it, it took place as planned.[4]

She had been a remarkable woman, with a great deal of strength under her gentle submissiveness. Like her father she loved gaiety and she, too, possessed natural authority. In spite of her youth everyone intuitively respected her. People recognized in her, as in Inayat, an 'old soul.' When Maula Bakhsh died, Khatijabi had refused to accept her inheritance. 'It is enough if my children inherit his spiritual gifts.' The refusal may also have been tact on her part. During her short life Khatijabi had always tried to keep peace in the crowded house. It is even possible that Inayat's marriage to his cousin was meant to maintain the unity of the family.

But this was not to be, though the wedding took place, a great feast for a short marriage. Musharaff Khan, who was only 7 in 1902, describes the festivities and the sad ending as a dream: the bride gentle and graceful, shy, but with shining eyes, in her beautiful clothes against a background of flowers. 'Everything happened just as it should... the bride and bridegroom seemed to be the very ideal of young happiness and love. But a few days after the wedding the bride died.... Wise old people said that a different date should have been chosen for the wedding.... Some alter-ations should have been made, something done to keep back the rhythm. Everything had been too intense, the beauty had been too much, the perfection too complete, the rhythm too swift. A reaction of some kind was inevitable.'

That was what the wise old people said. Of the bride-groom it is only recorded that he left, because the shelter of the old home no longer existed for him. What he thought or said is not mentioned, for one did not discuss the women of the family. In the biography the loss of his mother is stressed, a mother could be talked about with love and gratitude. Inayat did that all his life.

His first journey alone was to the South, to Madras where there was a centre of Carnatic (southern, pure Brahmin) music. He had an introduction there. The for-mer prime minister of Baroda, whose children he had taught, was now inspector-general of the registration (whatever that may have been) and he wrote a warm letter of recommendation. Evidently, he thought Inayat young, as indeed he was, but he liked and recommended his man-ners and the way in which he roused his pupils' interest. Finally, Mr Ayengar would always be happy 'to hear of Inayat Khan's success in life.'

That success, it seemed, began at once. In the hottest and wettest time of the year, 13° above the equator, still wearing a stiff collar, Inayat gave a concert followed by a lecture on the state of Indian music. What he said can be concluded from the address his appreciative audience presented to him, together with a gold medal. They said it was very good of him to consider promoting the cause of Indian music his task in life and to try and introduce a uniform system of notation for the whole of India 'so that a kind of friendly understanding might be created between northern and southern music.'

From these words we can gather that Inayat advocated Maula Bakhsh's system of notation. He also carried his work further. Maula Bakhsh collected and classified Indian music to save it. Inayat could now spread it, make the unknown known, create a better understanding between North and South. This was already in line with his later work. Like his grandfather he needed schools and he always sought to found one. His sympathetic but sceptical audience in Madras referred him twice in their brief address to the 'princes and potentates.'

The next one to further his ideals was indeed a maharaja. Mysore, the state where Maula Bakhsh had become famous, invited his grandson to sing at a state festival. Whatever sorrow he had just past through in his private life, this was a dream come true. In Mysore he heard the most famous singers of that time, and, as he had done as a child, he managed to sing a southern raga after hearing it only once. This not only required a good ear and talent for improvisation, but also the ability to identify with the style as well as the emotional background of Carnatic music. Though he did not have Maula Bakhsh's perfect and beautiful voice, it seemed that he would be able to continue his grandfather's work.

Before wandering on, he returned home, most probably

because of the new marriage that had meanwhile been arranged for him.

In the South he had been given a kind but sceptical hearing when he pleaded for more understanding between northern and southern music; at home more complicated distinctions and differences awaited him. A musician from Jaipur, whom everybody liked very much, stayed with the family in Baroda. He had suggested that Inayat should marry his sister. But he was a Shia and Rahemat Khan and his family were Sunnis. They were all Moslems and though difference in sect was no obstacle for friendship, it was for marriage.[5]

If a Hindu woman marries a Moslem she loses caste in the eyes of the Hindus, but to her new family she will be a new Moslem and as they consider their faith a kind of supercaste, they see such a change as an honour. All Indians, even non-Hindus, think and feel in terms of caste. Losing caste makes one nameless and makes self-identification, respect and correct behaviour impossible. A marriage between two different Moslem sects seemed like a marriage between two sub-castes. Rahemat Khan with his strong sense of honour did not want to inflict confusion and namelessness on either his Shia or his Sunni friends. Already at that time there were progressive minds who had risen above these old standards, but the Shia friend understood and appreciated Rahemat Khan's objection. He was so keen on an alliance with the Maula Bakhsh family, however, that he now offered them the daughter of a Sunni friend in Jaipur. That girl became Inayat's second wife.

The family went to Jaipur for the wedding. Inayat met famous musicians there, he always recalled memories of this visit with pleasure, but nothing is known about this marriage, except that his second wife, too, died within a year. When in 1903 Inayat began his mystical training his father no longer troubled him with marriages.

After his journey to the South he had wanted to start

work in Baroda again, but he had become too important to be content with a secondary position. His eldest uncle was head of the Oriental Department, Dr Pathan ruled over the Western; the former lacked the power, and the latter the noblesse of Maula Bakhsh. Professor Inayat Khan Pathan went away again.

Not too far from home at first, only to Bombay. But there he found a world, totally different from everything he had, until now, taken for granted and considered normal.

Bombay, on the west coast, was Europe's gateway to India. Sir Stanley Reed, for years editor of *The Times of India,* enthusiastically describes the town as he saw it: a good place for sports, with a beautiful hinterland, for hunting, and marvellously cheap horses. At the end of the book he writes about India's problems. He strongly believed in the British way of life and expressed his indignation if a club closed its door to nice, anglicized, Indians. In short, he was a sympathetic Westerner, who had the country's welfare at heart, but had only British standards to go by. Industrialization for him was a panacea, though he realized that 'Industrialization in a subtropical country can never be a lovely thing; ... in India [it] can be the breeding ground of discontent and revolution.'[6]

Inayat, too, described Bombay. He was shocked. In this town the westernized leading citizens no longer knew their own culture. For the first time he heard vulgar light music, a mixture of eastern and western elements at their worst. He calls it an almost physical pain to hear this nonsensical, soulless music in his country. He suffered even greater torture when he himself gave a concert and found that the audience could not respond to his music.

An Indian musician plays sitting down, for hours on end. He needs time to warm up and the participation of the audience plays a significant part. But Bombay's anglicized merchants could not react. They hired a musician for an evening out, because background noises seemed to be called for. But pompous talk, well-bred exemplary smoking, drinking and having fun in the foreign manner were much more important. The rich did not know the music of their own country.

This was not altogether their fault. For centuries the old music had been played only in temples and palaces. Inayat knew, as Maula Bakhsh had known, that the old civilization was dying. That was why they stressed the necessity of schools, where men and women of all creeds and castes might receive and preserve this music and all it meant. That was why Inayat gave his lecture in Madras, and why the not very far-sighted but polite élite referred him to the princes and rulers. There was no point in appealing to Bombay's merchants and industrialists, the kings of the new age.

He was young and the events of the past few months had probably made him oversensitive. For the first time the artist in him had been hurt. But that was not all. Inayat believed and always would believe that music was necessary for the development of character. What would be the result if his countrymen lost this art of forming their personality? A town of factories, stinking slums, noisy funfairs full of money grabbers without any identity of their own. The foundation of his view of the world, centred round a good and dignified India, was shaken. He felt helpless. He wanted to do what his grandfather had done and, at the age of twenty, he failed. 'Once, in my utter despair at my futility in comparison with him, I broke down completely, crying, "Allah! If our people had lost their wealth and power it would not have been so grievous to bear, since these temporal things are always changing hands in the mazes of Maya. But the inheritance of our race, the music of the Divine, is also leaving us through our own negligence, and that is a loss my heart cannot sustain!" I invoked the name of Sharda, the goddess of music, and prayed her to protect her sacred art.'[7]

It was the most painful crisis in his life. Singing before the smoking businessmen was so frustrating that at a certain moment he could not utter another note. He struggled through, imagining that he was singing only for himself. But from then on there are no more merry stories of Inayat singing a raga he had heard only once. Later, in India and in Europe, it was said that his singing sounded more beautiful at home than in public. It was one of the few things he never got over.

As to his ideal, there was something inconsistent in the effort to give classical music, lock, stock and barrel, to everyone. Handing it down directly from teacher to pupil was essential. Schools and manuals produced 'textbook-musicians,' who were looked down upon by the real musicians. Inayat was not the only one who had to face this inconsistency. A later musician, S. K. Chaubey, has not a good word to say about textbook-musicians. Yet both wanted classical music to spread. Possibly this could not be done so simply. This art belonged to a vanishing culture. Years later Inayat came to the conclusion that a new form had to develop from the old, that a new music might even adopt something of the western harmony, but should never imitate. In those later years he also thought the European notation, with the addition of a few directions, sufficient, for the so-called micro-tones and the very personal variations and improvisations of Indian music cannot be written down in detail. But that was not until 1916.[8] As long as he was in India he sometimes defended notation, as being indispensable for the spreading of music, and sometimes he defended the importance of the improvising artist, because only he could make the raga come alive. To Tagore who often stressed the purely Indian tradition, he maintained that notation was useful; speaking to another well-known Indian musicologist, Bhatkande, who adopted and augmented Maula Bakhsh's system about 1920, he spurned book knowledge. He met Tagore in Calcutta in

1909 and later several times in Europe; the discussion with Bhatkande took place in 1902 during the painful Bombay period. Bhatkande began with a critical question: 'According to what shastra (treatise, law, rules) do you prove that your ragas are correct?' Inayat retorted, 'According to my shastra the shastra did not create man, but man created the shastra.'

Inayat would often expand on a one-sided point of view and give quick-witted repartees like this, working in the West. But he was not going to the West yet. On the contrary, from corrupted, westernized Bombay he travelled to the most traditionally Indian state, Hyderabad.

Even for Sarojini Naidu, who was born and brought up in Hyderabad, this colourful city, a living antiquity, was like something from the Arabian Nights, a fairy-tale. It was the capital of the largest and richest princely state and the ruler, the Nizam, considered himself and his court the last heirs to Akbar and his Moghul empire. He was a Moslem, but 80% of his subjects were Hindus. Like Akbar he ruled with pomp and show and put great emphasis on the harmony of religions. 'The peoples whom your laws embrace/in brotherhood of diverse creeds/and harmony of diverse race,' wrote Sarojini Naidu, emancipated woman, freedom fighter and daughter of a Brahmin. And in another poem remains the warm sensuality of this world, now gone for ever. 'Sweet, sumptuous fables of Baghdad/The splendours of your court recall/The torches of a Thousand Nights/Blaze through a single festival.'[9]

Hyderabad was a town full of sound, movement, fragrance; and stench. Minarets, domes, bridges, palm trees in the transparant morning air, against the warm glow of the sunset sky, or in the merciless, glaring light of day. Streets swarming with carriages, oxcarts, camels, horses, elephants, richly dressed courtiers and half-naked beggars. Women in brightly coloured saris, with hennaed fingertips and palms, and eyes outlined with kohl, lived

47

hidden behind latticed windows. Birds sang in trees laden with flowers of overpowering perfume. In this atmosphere Inayat was to receive his training as a mystic, and live as an ascetic for four years. Here he would be happy.

He did not live in Hyderabad proper, but in the twin-city, Secunderabad. The Parsis had a centre there and many of Inayat's friends were Parsis. He had again planned to found a school but his other vocation began to demand time and attention. He meditated a great deal, but did not speak about it much. He had pupils, gave concerts in people's homes, composed for the Parsis and philoso-phized with his friends about Persian poetry and the fate of India, as young men full of plans and common interests do. Once he casually mentioned that he would like to play for the Nizam. His friends simply laughed. The Nizam was unapproachable.

The Nizam, like the Gaekwar of Baroda, had been put on the throne as a boy and he, too, though in a different way, was a remarkable ruler. When in 1890 an Englishman wrote about the most important princes and had them photographed, the Nizam was the only one who was not decked out in jewels and embroidery, but wore a simple jacket. His picture shows a melancholy, introspective face. Later he grew a fantastic handlebar moustache, but few people had the chance to see it. He kept himself aloof with the result that all kinds of legendary stories about him were circulated. In spite of his English education he was inter-ested in mysticism. At night he sat alone in his vast palace, meditating — as did the young musician in a small bunga-low in Secunderabad. With his Hindu minister Krishna Prasad he discussed the affairs of state, and in their leisure hours both of them wrote poetry, or philosophized about Persian poets, as did the young artist somewhere in his kingdom.

Hyderabad knew how to relax and make merry. The country is rocky and hard, but the lines of the hills are lovely and the banks of the lakes made for picnics. People loved boat trips and on Mount Moula Ali they used to combine the sacred with the sociable. A Moslem saint was buried there and the day of his death was commemorated every year. Pilgrims from the town used to stay there for four days, camping in tents or summerhouses.

In 1903 this day fell on April 8th.[10] Inayat made the trip with his friend Deen Dayal, court photographer. Another friend of Deen Dayal's the court physician Luqman Dowla, dropped in for a chat. Luqman Dowla, too, was an adept in Persian poetry, he was writing a commentary on Rumi. They became fast friends and Luqman Dowla took the two young men to the camp where he was staying, that of the prime minister. Inayat was invited to sing and Krishna Prasad who had not been feeling well, recovered and shared in the animated conversation. Then the guest began to speak fervently of that which was closest to his heart, the condition of Indian music. He told them of the miserable situation in Bombay and of his great plans to uplift the country and its music. In the middle of this conversation between congenial men, the Nizam sent word that he wished to call on his minister.

Inayat and Deen Dayal withdrew. But Krishna Prasad told the ruler of the engaging young singer whose visit had done him good, and the improbable happened: the Nizam sent for Inayat to hear him.

The singer was sitting down, the ruler standing up, three hours at a stretch. This time the artist did get the opportunity to warm up, this listener absorbed and reflected what he heard. Both were carried away by the rhythm, the words and the fullness of their feelings, released from outer troubles. That all this happened far from the palace and near a holy place, must have had a liberating effect, especially on the Nizam. When Inayat finally stopped all remained silent. The courtiers and attendants dared hardly move. The Nizam asked how it was that this singing had such an ecstatic effect. Inayat answered what he had learned from the silent saint in the Himalayas. 'Music, thought and feeling are one.' For him religious feeling and music were one; he did not look for worldly success, but wanted to help humanity.

Night had fallen. The tropical sky, a vast dome, stood full of stars. The singer returned to his camp, but the Nizam, like every ruler accustomed to flatterers and jobseekers, could not sleep. Early in the morning he sent for the obscure young man again. He dismissed his servants and guards, even the Aide de Camp. Inayat had to sing once more and answer questions. 'Why did you come to Hyderabad? What is your object?'

Hyderabad was not a city of pilgrimage, there were few holy places. In the beginning of the nineteenth century some Sufi mystics had gathered there, but they were not encouraged since the government had been modernized.[11] Inayat had come to Hyderabad because of its Moghul tradition. If he could maintain himself there, and establish his modern school on the foundations of the old culture, that would be an achievement. But in 1903 he had already begun his mystical development and was going through a stage of wonderment, in which he took no outer phenomena for granted. In a civilization where rank, honour and saving face governed life, this was almost daring. He was in search of the God-united soul, said to be living in man. Through his music he awakened this distant memory. This he explained to the Nizam.

The Nizam knew just as well as Inayat how Tansen had sung Akbar into ecstasy. Seeing himself as the Akbar of his time he called the young musician Tansen. And in this fairy-tale mood he gave him the ring from his finger and a purse of gold.[12] Inayat was admitted to the palace and became a regular visitor of the unapproachable one, and especially of Krishna Prasad. Later he told how one day he found the richest ruler in the world in an almost empty room, sitting on a mat, meditating. This was a far cry from the forecourt, where four thousand soldiers and attendants scurried about, antlike, and from the state rooms full of victorian and oriental opulence.

Now everyone wanted to hear Professor Inayat Khan. But at the very time that all doors were opening for him and he could have started his school of music, he gave up his professorship and became a pupil again. In a different profession.

Chapter IV (1903-1907)
Disciple

Inayat was still a fervent and impetuous young man. His photos by Deen Dayal do not yet show the tranquillity of later portraits. In one picture he is wearing the Nizam's ring round his necktie; in another he is sitting in a western armchair, in western costume, but his expression suggests that a horse, flowing robes and an enemy to pursue would suit him more.

Yet he had already begun to sit quietly and meditate, as many Westerners do today, and as Easterners have done for ages. Which does not mean that every Indian is a saint. There are many convinced money-makers and status seekers and many poor plodders, just concerned about their daily bread. But an Indian may know that meditation is a spare-time occupation that can lead to unknown joy and freedom, that some people are very advanced in it, but that there are swindlers and deceivers too, who make money out of the need of others.

Inayat the musician did no more than any lawyer, film director or civil servant does, who, at peace in the evening, crosses his legs, closes his eyes and sits in silence. But when he did it this unguided meditation produced results he himself did not immediately inderstand. In the middle of the night when a light shone in his room, at first he thought the sun had already risen; he heard music and voices and finally he had a vision of an impressive old man with radiant eyes.[1]

He dared not speak of these phenomena, for fear of being laughed at. The people in the town were either

Hyderabad, 1903. Inayat with the Nizam's ring round his tie.

'modern' or orthodox. Orthodoxy and mysticism are frequently at odds: the dogmatist reasons, the mystic experiences; the one obeys, the other finds out for himself.

Therefore Inayat sought out a friend who was religious but not orthodox and confided to him what he had seen. The friend concluded: 'Now it is time for you to seek your master.' Inayat took this advice with his usual thoroughness, though the idea was new to him. It can happen that someone, in the course of his life, joins an esoteric order, but such a membership usually remains limited and amateurish. For a member of a family of musicians suddenly to embark upon a full mystical training appears to have been so unusual that when the people of Baroda heard that a grandson of Maula Bakhsh was going to Europe as a spiritual master, there was some incredulous gossip.[2]

But before being a teacher Inayat had to be a disciple. He presented himself to the best-known sages of the town, but each time he was turned away, though the refusals were wrapped in respectful words. 'I am your servant, too humble to be your master.' The initiates saw that his vigour and fire needed a particularly powerful and tranquil guide, not just any quiet, contemplative soul.

Once in his later life[3] Inayat recalled this period before he was 'trained to serve God and humanity.' He says: 'Sometimes a great despair overwhelmed me and I wondered why all things were permissible for others should not be for me.' Was he alluding to his being a childless widower? or to the school of music he still had not founded? or to the fact that every other person seeking enlightenment seemed to find a master, but not he? That he was restless and tormented is evident from the pictures.

Elsewhere in his lectures he recalls that during the tense time of waiting and searching he learned to distinguish between true and false masters. False are the tricksters, alluring admirers with miracle stories and occult performances; the hypocrites who always pray and talk about virtue; the moneymakers; and the vain who cannot do without servile homage. The good masters had this in common that they did not accept pupils until they were sure of their worthiness; some concealed their mastership to avoid the temptation of fame, or to discourage candidate-disciples who came with impure motives.[4]

The master Inayat finally found was more or less hidden. He lived the life of an ordinary citizen and family man, in a cultured, cheerful and hospitable home, as was popular in sociable Hyderabad. Some of his neighbours did not even know that he was an initiate and spiritual teacher.

Inayat was visiting the same eminent theologian who had once, politely, refused to accept him as his disciple, when suddenly the host had the place of honour prepared and personally went across the courtyard to the gate. An old bearded man came in, whom everyone greeted with a bow. The young man in his western jacket remained standing and staring. Where had he seen this new guest before? Gradually it dawned upon him that he was seeing, in reality, the face from his vision. Then the old man looked and asked the host who he was. 'He appeals intensely to my spirit.'

All his life Inayat continued to speak with warmth, reverence and enthusiasm about his Murshid, Syed Mohammed Abu Hashim Madani. For Murshid Madani he became a beloved disciple. Some people could not understand that the old man approved of the nonconformist musician. Indignantly they asked the master to teach his pupil the correct ways of the faithful. 'He wears different clothes from us, he hardly ever goes to the mosque, he associates with Hindus, Parsis, Jews and Christians, and even feels at home with such people. We thought your holiness would change him.' The murshid replied that they should not judge from appearances; he could not tell them what

Inayat was and meant to him, but he was proud of him.

Murshid Madani taught Inayat the methods of the mystics and, especially in the beginning, these were very different from what he had expected. His master first tested him on the qualities necessary for inner development: courage, persistence, patience, faith and self-confidence.

Certainly Inayat the disciple did not lack courage; from childhood on he had always tried the most difficult thing, from unflinchingly swallowing nasty medicine and climbing steep slopes to choosing an exacting town for his sphere of activity. Patience and perseverance he had learned as a musician. But he had to calm down through the association with his master and above all develop self-confidence.

After months of waiting and searching he was put to the test again for another six months. Two or three times a week he rode the long distance from Secunderabad to the domes and minarets of Hydarabad, past the glaring water reservoirs, with here and there on the banks the bright red and loud blue of women doing their laundry; straight across the crowded old town and out again on the road to Golconda where Murshid Madani lived. And then, when he had dismounted, the disciple with his short black beard thrust forward, he could no doubt go and sit quietly with his murshid, but this murshid talked and talked about nothing special. Why? Was that all? He had expected something tremendous. Should he give up? Not go any more?

That was impossible. 'Now that you have received initiation from me, your faith must not change, no matter what great master you may meet,' Murshid Madani had said. In after years, knowing how hurried his own western disciples were, Inayat, amused, said, 'Because I had had a modern education, I did not at first understand why this was necessary.' The blessing Murshid Madani gave him each time on his departure, 'May your faith be strengthened' he also found a little thin. 'As a young man I thought, "Is my faith so weak that my teacher requires it to be stronger?" I would have preferred it if he had said, may you become illuminated, or may your powers be great, or may your influence spread, or may you rise higher and higher, or become perfect. But the simple thing, may your faith be strengthened, what did it mean?"[4]

It meant that the disciple had to be absolutely certain of himself and his aim, and that the relationship with the teacher had to be based on perfect trust. Doubt, vagueness and tension obscure the concentration needed to tune body and mind like fine musical instruments. It began with physical training, similar to Hatha Yoga. He learnt consciously to control every muscle and every nerve reaction. The senses had to function on command: to hold a particular taste, to look, motionless, at one thing or to concentrate on one sound, excluding everything else.[5] Some people concentrate naturally if something interests them very much. But he who can concentrate and open and shut himself at will becomes invulnerable. In Inayat's later European portraits this invulnerability is striking — it is not impassiveness but an imperturbability that is neither cold nor aloof.

For he not only learned the techniques of body-control, and to shut out unwanted influences, but also to open his heart to others. First he had to discover and clear a path in the maze of his own thoughts and feelings. This end was served by memory-control and self-observation; he had to watch his own actions and reactions without attaching the ready-made labels of good and bad to them, but asking himself why he acted in such and such a way and why actions were called good or bad. This was the first plunge beneath the surface and he emerged with insight into our complicated motives and an awareness of the relativity of social values.

Observing others began fairly simple with exercises in empathy: adopting the attitude of a sad person, or a soldier, someone in love, or whatever. He would need a supple and quick empathy during his travels through countries of which as yet he scarcely knew the names and still less the ways of life. Once having arrived there, he soon understood the cultural differences, but the people he met in these countries did not think of his cultural background and seldom realized another thing, that as a mystic he had developed a second personality.

In some respects he always remained the grandson of the great Maula Bakhsh, and the son of Rahemat Khan, the man of honour: an Indian Moslem with many Hindu contacts in a society where kings were still kings. In other respects he became the liberated initiate, the broad-minded, ever more embracing and penetrating knower of all that is hidden beneath the surface of life.

But when he started on his training he was just a disciple − a gifted one, but a curious one as well. He did not like the dull days of first disciplines, when nothing seemed to be happening. At last the teacher began to speak of meta-physics. Inayat the eager pupil, delighted, produced a note-book. Immediately Murshid Madani changed the subject. The disciple understood that he must not record the lessons on paper but, through concentration, in his heart and memory.

Many of his reactions as a beginner resemble those of his own followers later on. Once he asked his murshid if it would not be a good idea to stay awake all night. 'Whom do you torture,' the murshid asked, 'yourself? Is God pleased with it?' Recalling that memory may have been a tactful warning to an over-diligent western disciple. Self-torture is not necessary, it may even be so dear to the self-torturer that stopping it would be an act of asceticism for him. Asce-ticism can be used to strengthen the will-power, but it is not an end in itself, and not a sign of holiness. Breath control is much more important, rhythmical breathing exercises are a permanent activity, while abstaining from certain habits is a temporary task. Mainly in the second phase Inayat underwent trials and tests, and these included abstaining from things he thought he could not do without. In retrospect he called these tests amusing and as an example he mentioned the old story of a Moslem master who confused his disciples by suddenly worshipping a Hindu goddess.[5] Later he himself tested those few who received a complete training from him, for instance by doing something unexpected during a musical performance — surely a good way to test an artist's presence of mind and imperturbability. No need of dark passages or weird noises. Fearlessness came naturally, as another human being was no longer felt to be a stranger and an enemy, and as, through his power over mind and body, he grew more and more unruffled.

The actual receiving, absorbing and assimilating of esoteric knowledge began in the third phase. The main methods are not unknown today: rhythmic breathing exercises with word repetitions, concentration on a word or image, meditation on a special subject. This subject varies according to the school and the personality of the adept. The aim is to develop certain qualities, not always the same for everyone. The word-repetition must not be mechanical, the pupil has to ponder in different ways on the given word, so that ultimately it becomes inseparably a part of him, 'it becomes reality.' In so far as it concerns qualities this method is a form of self-suggestion. Later Inayat shrugged his shoulders about the Coué-method: that was a primary exercise. But he who has made God a reality, who can live in open communication with his fellow-creatures and with other worlds, becomes a greater human being. 'A holy man is not recognized by his words and not even by his actions, but by his atmosphere,' said Murshid Madani.[6]

Inayat's journey towards God-realization can be followed in the book he wrote during his period of training. Parallel with his largely wordless training under Murshid

Madani he studied Sufi literature with a scholar. The result was a 300-page book *Minqar-é-Musiqar*. It is mainly a work on music, a description of ragas, dances and short Hindustani poems, in their outer form and inner meaning. A few poems are his own and the course of his development becomes clear. The book takes most of its inspiration from Islam, but Krishna and the gopis too make their appearance. In one of the introductory poems Inayat tries to describe all seekers after God, 'wonderfully radiant;' 'indifferent to heat and cold;' and so saturated with their longing, that they find God wherever they are, in the temple or the mosque. Just as the poem gathers pace, he interrupts himself in order not to get caught in a cliché or to go on writing, drunk with words. He addresses himself, 'O Inayat, you and this high talk. How dare you shout about truth.'

He guarded against the mistake of immediately taking an enraptured emotion for real ecstasy. He ends with an entreaty, the ardent wish he once expressed on the roof of his parental home: I must really see, really know, really feel. It is not by accident that a poem at the end of the first part is dedicated to Maula Bakhsh. 'The signs of God are in the world and God is in all that exists.' With all his strength and power Inayat tried to turn old wisdom from a conception into a reality. Not only with old formulas such as 'none exists save Allah,' but also in his own poems: 'God exists, God exists, God exists. You, I, we, they, all. All that exists is God, this and that, now, then.'[7]

The beginning of the book shows signs of struggling. Over and over again he calls himself to order. 'Turn away from courts and worldly affairs.' 'Be reverent in the presence of your master,' 'Control yourself, control yourself.'

In the second part, he chooses texts which evoke the divine in everyone and everything, in nature, in the voice of the flute, in a helpful friend, in apparently totally different people. 'He was a man and took the form of a woman, he was a helpless child and an old man; God is in the rich and the poor, in the friend and the foe, everywhere and nowhere, in all forms and formless.'

There are some of his own poems, too, in the second part, different from those in the beginning. He no longer advises himself to abandon the world of rank and reputation — it had slipped away of itself to the edge of his consciousness. This very consciousness is dissolving. 'I am losing all my consciousness and knowledge,' Do we perceive a trace of fear?

Not for long. A new, greater consciousness is born, he has glimpsed a new world and now no longer asks whether he may speak, but he does speak. In one of the last poems he has overcome all uncertainty and focuses on his murshid with unshakeable faith. 'He has made me what I am. My name is the "unknown," my work is love.'

'My name is the unknown.' He has freed himself from the environment where his own and the family's ambition, his feeling of vocation and the whole status-seeking society around him forced him to find fame. Twenty years later Inayat, not without self-irony, told how one day a faqir had addressed him: ' "Murshid, where is such and such a street?" I thought, he calls me murshid, perhaps he sees something great in me. But then I heard him ask a policeman: "Hey, Murshid, is this the way to such and such a house?" and I understood that he said "murshid" to everyone.'[8]

This meeting must have occurred in the beginning of his schooling, for in consequence of it Murshid Madani explained to him the different stages of unification, first with the master, later with all people and then with the Divine. The faqir was in the first stage, where he saw his beloved murshid in everyone.

Love is the first result of inner development and a condition of further progress. One who cannot love another being, cannot love God. Inayat once told his European, often still rather victorian, pupils of a zealous adept who had meditated for years, yet could not reach God-realiz-ation. The master made him stop practising and sent him his food by a beautiful girl who immediately went away. The man wished to detain her, started to long for her, could think of nothing else. When his teacher came, with one glance he inspired him: his heart was now warmed and melted by love.

Being open to others and at the same time inwardly peaceful can result in telepathy. Murshid Madani answered Inayat's unspoken thoughts. At first Inayat thought this astounding, just as his own pupils one day would wonder at him. In the course of his training he discovered that, without trying to, he received the feelings of others. His murshid called this phenomenon reflection; he compared the soul to a mirror which reflects naturally when polished, that is free from agitation. Later Inayat almost apologized for knowing what went on in other people's minds: it might seem indiscreet, 'but a rustless mirror cannot help reflecting.'[8]

Most of the western disciples thought mind-reading a grand idea and they were often more interested in occult side issues than in something as simple as loving one's neighbour. From some stories it appears that, as a disciple, Inayat likewise was not without beginner's curiosity. He sometimes watched a paranormal demonstration and even looked for adventure in a haunted house. But he did not follow the lessons of the Rafai order which specializes in teaching physical insensibility and the performance of miraculous facts.

He belonged to the Chishti order. In this order music and poetry play an important part, while the puritanical orthodoxy of the Arabs forbade music, i.e. music for amusement — for the suras of the Quran were and are sung aloud. Since about 1100 a lively mysticism had been growing in Persia, 'the religion of the heart' as against 'the religion of the book.' These trends had further developed in India, through centuries of osmosis with yoga. The Chishti order was the largest of these Sufi schools.[9]

Inayat, though a Chishti, did learn to reach God-realization through the methods of three other Sufi-schools. This does not happen often, but it is known that Ramakrishna learnt the various ways. Surely Murshid Madani expected something extraordinary. Inayat's own summary of his studies, experiences, experiments and schooling is brief and matter-of-fact. Only when he speaks of his murshid do adequate words of warmth, respect and admiration fail him.[10]

Inayat could be matter-of-fact, but he was never cold. Control was necessary, but so was heart. Agitation made progress impossible, but the first ecstasy is accompanied by great emotion.

For the Chishtyas one way of reaching ecstasy is to sing for nights on end. They sing about the difference between the perfection of God and the limitation of man, but also of the presence of God in man. They create an image of God as the beloved, they see his presence in nature and know that essentially he cannot be put into words. The subject of the song is only a means, the experience is the main thing. The initiates gather within the stone walls of a private courtyard, under a tree in a quiet spot outside, or between the marble screens around a sacred tomb. The one who sings kindles the flame in the others. He who goes through this ecstasy for the first time may burst out into tears or sighs, into swaying or dancing. Inayat comments: 'As... daily life consists of both joy and pain, so the life of the dervish is also filled with both joy and pain in the presence of God. By the help of concentration, poetry and music, joy and pain are felt more deeply. Therefore God becomes living to him: his presence is before him in all his moods. When once his pain has had an outlet in some form or other in the Sama, the musical ceremony, the condition that follows is that of a deeper insight into life... The sighing of the devotee clears a path for him into the world unseen, and his tears wash away the sins of ages. All revelation follows the ecstasy; all knowledge that a book can never contain, that a language can never express, nor a teacher teach, comes to him of itself.'[11]

He who has ever had a glimpse of greater worlds — for in certain circumstances it may come to an untrained person — will probably remember that apart from a feeling of freedom, space and light there is a luminous stillness, not fixed or rigid, nor motionless, though the motion is hardly perceptible. The difference between this state and dreams, day-dreams and drug-hallucination is that confusion, associations and vague memories do not enter into it. Expansion of consciousness through drugs, Inayat says, is mechanically aroused by mechanical means and does more harm then good.

The means for him was his music. Not only in the Sama meetings, but also when he was alone, rhythm and sound helped him. Early in the morning, when everything was too lovely to remain asleep — coolness, silence, a transparent sky, colours slowly detaching themselves from darkness and the first vague light — he would softly play his veena, always the same notes, but always different, more intense. 'No instrument is so suitable as the veena to stimulate deepening and widening.'

During the day he did work and even saw some friends as usual. But he had become a different person, no longer an impetuous young man, no longer ambitious, not yet always perfectly controlled. The highest state of being, which does not bring emotion and joy, but peace and balance, he reached for the first time in Calcutta in 1909. In Hyderabad it might happen that during his singing he deeply moved others, and also himself, so that he could not keep back the tears that come with the first liberation. Twenty years later people in Hyderabad still gossiped about this strange singer. Not only about his being noncon-

formist and absorbed in religion, but also about his voice.
According to the son of one of the court musicians he was
valued more as a veena player than as a singer.[12] That only
applied to the artistic estimation. Inayat himself and his
fellow Chishtis liked his singing for these very tears of
ecstasy. Minister Krishna Prasad wrote that 'Professor
Inayat Khan's voice gave new pleasure to the heart each
time and unlimited joy to the soul.'[13]

Yet, there grew a tension between his two professions.
For himself music and mysticism remained inseparably
linked, but not for those around him. Just as the orthodox
pious people took offence at his friendship outside their
own narrow circle, so the artists did not like him to find
happiness outside their little world. The Nizam, himself
interested in mysticism, did appreciate the change in him.
But the grandson of Maula Bakhsh, who at one time could
think of nothing more wonderful than to be received at
court, had lost most of his interest in this honour. Court life
was child's play, the court a cage. Inayat wanted to be free.
He wanted to go away. What kept him in town was his
teacher.

Murshid Madani was old. What is told about him sounds
very similar to what is being told about his famous disciple,
the friendliness, the naturalness, the sense of humour, the
mind-reading, the fact that in his presence questions were
answered without his saying anything, and generally the
atmosphere of calm, freedom and balance that can be felt
around a real master. It is said that all masters resemble
each other because their inner beings are indeed alike.[14]

In their outer lives there was a great difference between
Murshid Madani and Inayat. Judging from the private
graveyard near the old city wall of Hyderabad, Murshid
Madani was the fourth or fifth of his family line to be born
and bred in this place. He was not a wanderer.

He knew that his pupil was. On his last sickbed — how can
a holy man be ill, Inayat thought, as later his pupils thought

about him — the beloved master gave Inayat his blessing and told him, 'Fare forth into the world, my child, and harmonize the East and the West with the harmony of thy music. Spread the wisdom of Sufism abroad, for to this end art thou gifted by Allah, the most merciful and compassionate.'[15]

On 7th October 1907 Murshid Madani died. His pupil Inayat left everything he had acquired in Hyderabad, said good-bye to no-one and went out into the world. To begin with he wandered through India from south to north and from east to west.

Chapter V (1907-1910)
Robbers, Princes and Holy Men

By now the principal towns in India had been connected by railways, but travellers to distant places joined a caravan, often moving by night as the days were too hot. No night passed, however, without some travellers falling victim to robbers from the jungle. If possible a long caravan of some twenty carts was formed, those in the middle being safest in case of an attack.

When Inayat suddenly left Hyderabad, his ox-cart was the last in a small group of three. He took no notice of his surroundings, his heart was full of the master he had lost. He remembers: 'I had the precious ring of the Nizam with me, and musical instruments instead of arms. All night long I saw the figure of my murshid, vaguely at first, but clearly later, walking beside the cart. The other two wagons were attacked and robbed, the loot was a few bundles of no value; but my waggon was safe.'[1]

This was the beginning of a fascinating journey which brought him more and more recognition as a musician, but which he called especially important because of his constant contacts with all kinds of people, 'of the highest to the lowest classes and from the best to the worst. I associated with the saint and the sinner, and had the great privilege of studying human nature in reality.'[2] All that he knew in theory had to be experienced. This he did till the end of his life.

Escaping from his first robber was followed by coming across his first holy man, and this was a Brahmin, not a

Moslem. Inayat's destination was a Sufi tomb in Gulburga, but on the way he stopped at a Hindu temple.

The first day he remained unobserved – in his grief he did not wish it otherwise. Because he was not a Hindu but, as a Moslem, a casteless barbarian, he was lodged in a stable, full of flies and mosquitoes; a noisy group of musicians in the loft above his head kept on drumming and playing their screeching pipes. He accepted it as a suitable test, but, at the bathing-place the next day, he was recognized by the son of the priest. Pictures of the Nizam's favourite, the veena-player, had appeared in the newspapers and he could not remain incognito for long. The Brahmin's son felt embarassed about Inayat's poor accomodation and took him to his father. The priest asked why he had come to this remote place. A man from the North was not a common sight in the South, neither was a Moslem in a Hindu temple.

This temple of Manek Prabhu was renowned for its music, but Inayat had also reached the stage wherein he sought to recognize his master in all forms, the stage that precedes complete recognition of God in everything. The conversation with the Brahmin developed into an enthusiastic exchange of ideas and an equally enthusiastic examination. The priest asked details about Sufism and Inayat explained with his usual fire, but emphasized that in essence Vedanta and Sufism, though different in form, came from the same source. No doubt the priest knew this, but he could not refrain from asking theological questions. Did not reincarnation make a difference?

During his journeys in the West Inayat was to be asked this question hundreds of times, but never by someone of his own level, as this priest was. He described the purpose of inner development, the liberation of the soul from all outer, transient forms, till it knows its origin again, as he was to do hundreds of times later. But, enjoying the discussion as he would seldom be able to later, he concluded, 'The greatest principle of the Vedanta is Adwaita, which

Calcutta, 1909. Inayat, wanderer and dervish.

means no duality, in other words unity. Is the principal teaching of the Vedanta better served with reincarnation or by leaving it alone? Mukti, liberation, is the ideal of life, rising above various births.'

The Hindu guru was enjoying it too, and when taking leave of the pilgrim who at first had been put in a stable, he honoured him in the Indian way with a scarf of a sacred colour.

When the following night a robber again attacked the caravan, Inayat was no longer passive. He himself discovered the groping hand and chased the thief. He was twentyfive and strong.

Yet, after so many emotions, inward and outward, he was feverish when he arrived in Gulburga in the evening. It nearly cost him his life. A plague epidemic was threatening and as a precaution anyone who had a fever was killed. But by the next morning his youth, his prayers and his strength had cured him.

After these confrontations, as direct and simple as later, in the West, his problems would be complicated and elusive, he interrupted his pilgrimage in Baroda. Home again.

From Hyderabad he had returned to the old place only twice, probably for family affairs. His father had not seen him since his spiritual development and the change struck him all the more forcefully. The difficult child, the fervent young man, had out-grown everybody in maturity and radiated tranquillity. Rahemat Khan who, at one time, had worried about what would become of Inayat, now said, 'If I were young, I would become your disciple.' The son's answer 'Father, don't say that, it embarasses me,' cannot be taken too literally. Inayat, the eldest son, had never been his father's pupil, neither in music, nor in religious thinking, though Rahemat Khan had imbued all his sons with his strict and clear morals. Apart from his severity he had a sense of humour and a Punjabi's ready wit, and was so sensitive that he knew he was sometimes a strain on his surroundings. He was sixty-three now and, with Maula Bakhsh's centenarian aunt, the last survivor of a by-gone world. Though in the past a polite tension had existed between the hot-tempered father and the fierce son, during the final years the relationship was deep and cordial.

As a grandson of Maula Bakhsh, too, Inayat had changed. Not, of course, in his views on India's musical culture, but in his social ambition. Power and position left him as indifferent as possible in the world of castes. Of course a mystic has risen above worldly ambition, but at the same time he is revered and highly respected.

That, compared to others, Inayat was free from Indian pride and prejudice, I suddenly understood from the reminiscence of a fellow-citizen. In 1970 Vibukumar Desai was an old gentleman of over eighty. In 1908, when he was a poor student, he had heard one of Inayat's concerts and had gone to meet him afterwards. 'And he helped me, just like that, he was good to the poor.' He meant that he did not stop to think whether the other was socially important and could be of benefit to him. More than half a century later Shri Desai relating this memory, still sounded astonished.

The concerts Inayat gave in his native town were a success. Everyone would have liked to keep him at home, but he wandered on. Not, now, because he would not have a leader's position among his uncles at the academy of music and in the musical world, but because he was a pilgrim.

The most important place of pilgrimage for a Chishti is Ajmer, a large town where the British used to have an educational institute for the sons of the hundreds of princes and potentates. But for thousands it was and is the place where the saint Khwaja Moinuddin Chishti lies buried and where each year the pilgrims flock for the anniversary of the saint's death. The mausoleum stands in the centre of the town, in its own vast grounds, with a park, mosques, houses for residents and pilgrims, stalls, rich Moghul art, motley markets and fairs. In front of the tomb, which is hidden behind beautifully carved doors and covered by a large white dome, the qawals sing, day and night. These singers have the task of creating and maintaining a sacred atmosphere. In the midst of all the hustle and bustle, surrounded by a chattering, teeming throng, they go on singing with sincere devotion. The Chishtis hold that wisdom and inner knowledge are passed on from master to master, they know their spiritual genealogy, and to visit the shrine of their greatest saint is to contact the source. Whether the pilgrim brings his own atmosphere to such a place or whether many together create an atmosphere by their devotion and mystical power makes no difference. In spite of the noise and the milling crowds around the tomb Inayat could feel serenity and peace as if he were alone. These are his own words.

During the night, far from the tomb, that feeling remained. While he was saying his midnight prayer he heard a faqir outside crying. 'Awake o man, from thy deep sleep.' The silence of the night and the solemn singing moved him. The morning dawned, the birds sang, below in the street men and women were on their way to the mosque or the temple, or simply to fetch water and be in time to earn their livelyhood somewhere. Inayat, too, went out and, lost in thought, walked out of the city. He came to a graveyard where a group of faqirs were sitting on the grass, not even on a mat. They were in rags, one wore a hat without a crown, another a shirt with only one sleeve, a third had no shoes — almost grotesque poverty.

Inayat the pilgrim stood watching. More shabby fellows arrived and he heard them call out to each other what he himself had experienced only yesterday: he who does his practices and can control his breath, he who knows what he is doing, can be alone and himself in the midst of a crowd, inwardly untouched. The two groups of ragged faqirs greeted each other with words Inayat knew very well: God is love and God is the beloved. But much of what he knew and had learnt became real for him that morning. And a few 19th-century and Indian conceptions ceased to be a matter of course.

When, as a pupil in Hyderabad, he first became acquainted with the vastness of greater worlds, even his visits to the Nizam and minister Prasad lost their interest. They faded and slipped away. But that does not mean that kings were not important to a court musician. Inayat scarcely knew another form of government than kingdoms and empires. Today these are almost forgotten, the democratic royal houses remaining cannot be compared with the inaccessible majesties of before 1914; nor with the kings of fairy tales, or the bogeymen of psychical projection, for these exist only in thought and imagination. But until half a century ago a king was a functional reality, powerful, surrounded by splendour and supposed to be good, sometimes even godly. So far Inayat had had no reason to doubt the meaning of kingship, except for the vanity of the king of Nepal. Only in this historical light can his astonishment in Ajmer be understood. To begin with, his surprise at the grim, apparently hopeless poverty of the dervishes. Then the surprise at his own response. Those men in rags began to sing, songs of his beloved Persian poets, but not at all beautifully. Twice the professional musician remarks how imperfect their singing really was. And yet it set him free as in a trance, and the surroundings were still and enchanted as the surroundings of the silent saint in the Himalayas. The funniest thing, in the eyes of the court-conscious pilgrim, came at the end. The faqirs took leave of each other with bows and princely greetings. 'O mighty emperor, your dinner is served. Salutations, o king of kings.' These men played at being kings, they had no thrones, no treasuries, no courtiers, no countries, it was all make-belief. On reflection he changed his mind. An ordinary king is dependent upon what he possesses and rules: as soon as he loses his domain, treasury and subjects, he is no longer a

73

king. At best he can preserve a dignified or regal bearing. The dervishes possessed the kingdom of God that is within us.[3]

It was essentially the same insight that had reconciled him to an unseen God when he was a boy. Now, twelve years later, he was already an advanced mystic, but the pious words, 'God is within, independent of external beauty or external dignities,' became a reality for him that day. There is no other memory he recalls so often and in such detail.

From that day on he took pleasure in recognizing illuminated souls in all kinds of disguise, even that of the so-called atheist. He mentions a wrestler, as wise and mild as he was monstrously big and brawny, and a telegraph clerk who sat behind his window happily meditating, doing his duty with his every-day consciousness and at the same time living in the greater openness.[4]

Inayat always kept an almost playful preference for holy ones disguised as poor beggars. In Bangalore, where he had given a concert for the élite, he produced a pedlar, who was actually a holy man, from behind a pillar. In Calcutta he could not rest till he had persuaded a very reluctant and rather dirty dervish to come to his house. Inayat's youngest brother, who was living with him at the time, tells this story with somewhat horrified admiration. In Moscow, in 1913, Inayat and the same youngest brother went to the third class public baths, but Maheboob and Ali Khans only frequented the marble-pillared gentleman's bathing establishment. Inayat called himself a dervish, as he went on doing during his first five years in the West.[5]

That morning outside Ajmer he considered the idea of really becoming a begging faqir, but with his usual matter-of-factness and his talent to see things from the point of view of others too, he decided not to. He did not want to be a burden to anyone. He did make up his mind, however, not to earn more with his music than he strictly needed. He would be a dervish disguised as a musician.

And so, freer than he would ever be or ever had been, he wandered on through India, among the wise and the foolish, the good and the weak, the beggars and the kings.

The worldly kings often presented greater problems to him than the dervishes. After Baroda and the pilgrimages he went south again — he always liked to go there. It was India proper, dotted with memories of the glorious past. Not only ruined forts, but also masterpieces of carving and sculpture, towering temples, looking compact from a distance, encompassing lofty pillared halls and galeries around green, dark ponds. Here Maula Bakhsh had completed his all-Indian musical studies, here Inayat himself saw a chance to realize his master's assignment: there were many groups in India that could be brought in harmony with each other if they cared to listen. He nearly always gave a lecture together with his concerts, in which he sang, played the veena and as a playful contrast to all the serious music the jaltarang, the light, porcelain percussion instrument that sounded like silver bells. His greatest satisfaction he found in being acknowledged by famous musicians and in conversation or silence with holy men. His most important patrons were the princes. Again and again he was shocked to see how their foreign education had alienated them, how court life had spoilt them, how conventionality had made them wooden and rigid. They no longer understood the art that had flourished at their courts.[6] One or two rose to a surprised appreciation, one, an exception, the maharaja of Cassimbazar, understood his music. The maharaja of Sylhet asked him to become a murshid at his court. But it was of Tanjore that Inayat cherished tender and melancholy memories. There he stayed in the sixteenth-century palace, a historical building, with a famous old library. The young maharaja and his mother, refined and courteous, lived in the midst of the old grandeur, too heavy a frame for them. 'An aristocratic house with tradition and culture, albeit worn out... Their refinement, gentleness, modesty and gracious manner proved their aristocracy more than their palaces.' With these words Inayat described this dying world.

Later, to the great disappointment of his accompanist, he declined an invitation to stay with another of his royal admirers at his palace. Not because he feared the decadence or the schizophrenic atmosphere, but because in 1909 and 1910 he thoroughly practised the simplicity of a dervish. At home, too, he slept on the floor.[7] Things had happened which made it necessary for him to experience some of the condition of the poorest of the poor. The brotherhood of man was a reality for him, but seldom for his countrymen.

Once he travelled with a conventional Pathan soldier, who took offence at Inayat's European clothes and unorthodox behaviour. Inayat tried to lead the dispute into a less controversial channel by remarking that we are all brothers. 'Brothers! how dare you!' Inayat, amused, recounts that the man was very pleased when he apologized rather ironically, 'I am sorry, I forgot. I am your servant, sir.' There was no point in any further argument with the narrow-minded military man.[8] Inayat enjoyed a discussion, but if the partner clung to his limitations, he changed the subject into vague generalities.

He was not afraid of contradiction. Nearly all his lectures were controversial sermons on renewal. The audience praised him and let it go at that. So it happened that he gave an important concert cum lecture in Kombakalum. He played northern as well as southern ragas, which was always an achievement. Everyone thought it wonderful, but none of the Brahmin gentlemen offered the Moslem barbarian accommodation for the night. Inayat realized that his own countrymen did not consider him their brother and suddenly he understood the pariah's lot. But at the same time, and this is typical of him, he tried to see the situation from the point of view of the Brahmin. He allowed himself no self-pity and went matter-of-factly to look for a place to sleep.

After a long search he was given shelter of a sort by a small merchant far outside the town. He was allowed to put up in a shed, too ramshackle to house a cow. The floor was full of holes, he could not sleep and spent the night in meditation. In the morning he was greeted with the blessing of a dervish who had been staying in this hovel for twenty years. The pilgrim-musician understood that he himself was just beginning.

Inayat was by no means a social or political reformer, that is to say he did not strive to change circumstances from the outside. But in this period of his life he went deeper into the lot of the poor than an Indian normally did. Twice he discovered holy men who concerned themselves with the fate of poor orphans or even with the living conditions in a whole town, and he made a note, later used in his biography, that this was the real service of humanity. Everything that he and his followers later formulated as the message and that, superficially read, sounds like any well-meaning abstraction, sprang from his own discoveries and experiences. In his mystical development too, he continued to grow. From an early age he had lived beside and with Hindus. Krishna and the goddess of music were part of his own mental and emotional make-up, yet his was in the first place a Moslem world where making an image of God or gods was considered idolatry. By now Inayat had already learned to reach God-realization by the methods of different Sufi schools. In the heart of South India he looked at the famous Shiva temples of Madurai and concentrated on the meaning of the images until he had evoked in himself the feelings of those who came to God-realization by first moulding their idea of God into a form. Now he could reach it by this way also.

After such close contacts with the monuments and culture of South India he found Ceylon disappointing. He may not have had the right introductions. He met Moslems so orthodox that they hardly knew there was such a thing as music and Parsis who pretended to be knowledgeable about classical music but only recognized the simplest things. He thought the scenery in Ceylon more fascinating than the people and hardly noticed it was a Buddhist country.

Burma became for him the land of Buddhism. His journey ended there and it struck a happy final chord. After the minutely discriminating Indian society with its Hindu castes, its different kinds of Moslems and a hundred other elaborate distinctions, the Buddhist and therefore caste-less Burmese world seemed to him a paradise of simplicity and brotherhood. That, in his view, was true democracy.

But Burma was no longer unimpaired either. The reason why the country seemed simple was that it had remained closed to outsiders until recently and had been under western rule only for the last few decades. As everywhere else the British government had, no doubt, brought peace and a judicial system — not always understood — but had disrupted the original economy. In addition to the small local merchants and moneylenders, not ideal characters anyway, Indian and British traders came in to set up business on a large scale. They were strangers, alienated from their own culture, and they created confusion in this country that had been closed to the world for so long. The result was more theft than ever, and bands of robbers sprang up, roaming the country for reasons of protest and poverty.[9]

The merchants themselves were even worse than those in Bombay. They were totally and single-mindedly materialistic and unable to respect either music or musicians. In a classical work it is said, 'Music is of great value and he who says differently has those people in view who want to make money with music.' These words[10] from the fifteenth century express the exact opposite of the merchants' attitude, they spring from a conception of society far removed from today's, but close to that of the court-musicians among whom Inayat was born. He took it for granted that an artist could be sure of his livelihood. Putting a market price on art was detestable. No doubt an archaic principle, but that does not mean that the subjection of art to market values is a preferable one. On the contrary, everybody concerned with art is grappling with this question. Inayat posed it, with an indignation that sprang from his cultural background; but that does not alter the reality of the problem.

In Rangoon there was a merchant who was hardly aware of his own one-sidedness. He sent a message to the musician who, according to the newspapers, was in fashion, and offered him a fabulous sum for a night's performance. The offer was contemptuously rejected. It is not recorded whether the merchant showed a healthy surprise at the refusal.

We are told more about the robber chief who had Inayat summoned by a sinister character in the middle of the night. Would he just come and play for boss Masiti? Inayat hesitated for a moment and then decided not to resist evil. Was it again a challenge to test his courage and strength?

He entered the ostentatiously savage room of the king of the underworld where his men were swaggering about, rough, armed, scarred, loud and drunk.

Inayat remained himself. Just as the clerk at the telegraph office continued his meditation during his daily routine, so the singer-mystic sat opposite the king of thieves in imperturbable concentration. The chief bragged, he was proud of this visit, but he felt he could not compel his involuntary guest to sing. Unlike the merchant, he still saw men, not objects. For Inayat it was an exercise in a thing most difficult to realize: to penetrate so deeply into the outer shell that even in a plainly bad, coarse brute the divine spirit could be found.

One wonders whether this was more difficult in the case of the robber, whose very brutality was not without some grandeur, than in that of the petty common thief, the servant who one day stole all Inayat's money. Again he made this into an exercise, for himself and for the boy. He did not go to the police, he did not borrow money from friends. He behaved as if nothing had happened, he played as usual, went out with well-fed friends, laughing, but the servant knew that for three days he could not buy any food. On the fourth day the boy returned the money.

In spite of these adventures, the memory of Burma, which in his opinion practised the ideal human equality, remained a dream.[11] He had made friends and had been happy there. But he was still searching for the highest realization and in this stage of transition his everyday experiences slipped away.

There are two pictures of Inayat taken soon after his wanderings. One shows him as the musician, in an embroidered formal Indian costume, with all his gold medals on his chest and the veena on his knee. In the other he is the pilgrim, cotton-clad, thin: it is one of the few portraits where longing and tension can be read in his face. Shortly afterwards he reached samadhi for the first time, the highest state of being, bound to the earth and at the same time liberated from all bonds in an all-pervading all-embracing vastness. This is no longer the emotional ecstasy, the first break-through, but the attainment, seeing and knowing, the mark of which is perfect peace — again an inadequate word.

In all later portraits of Inayat this ever present and ever remembered peace is the first thing that strikes one. All mystic literature testifies to the heavy tension and passionate longing which precede realization.

Inayat reached this highest state of being for the first time in Calcutta, where he had settled after his wanderings. His father wanted his eldest son, who would be the head of the family after his death, to have a permanent residence. The son would have preferred to go on wandering, he had not only learned during his journey, but he had enjoyed it. The Shiva temple in Madurai was not only edifying, but also lovely, splendidly situated by the river, weather-beaten buildings tucked away among the green. In Ceylon the scenery compensated for his disappointment in the people. And the watery land of Cochin, where all traffic between the islets went by boat, remained unforgettable: the rhythmic singing of the women encouraging the rowers rang out over the water, in the moonlight boats moved from one light-spot to another. Enormous plumed trees, their roots clawing above the water like powerful hands, stood silhouetted against the sky. Villages of ten or twenty huts squatted, fragile and trusting, among the giants.

All this had a charm, the very opposite of Calcutta's challenge. In those days Calcutta was still the capital of all India, a sophisticated city where the Bengalis, arrogant and strongly influenced by British schooling, called the tune. After the Bengalis the Punjabis began to accept the challenge of the West, and found their way to the capital. Inayat was a Punjabi on his father's side and accepting a challenge was in his nature.

The first few months were difficult. The musical world in Calcutta was not ruled by princes, but by circles and clubs of prominent citizens. The musicians had to fight for their position and the result was jealousy and mistrust, scheming and favouritism. Inayat noted that not only was he not given a chance, being a new man, but that someone even tried to check his career out of spite for his family. That may have been because Dr Pathan had a talent for making enemies. There may have been quarrels already then, either about the honour of having invented the notation system, or about the controversial issue of having notation at all. It may have been that the story of Inayat's voice, which sometimes gave out in ecstasy, had been repeated in a twisted and exaggerated form. Just as in Nepal and Hyderabad many fellow artists were annoyed that he scarcely visited their clubs and gatherings and rejected the method of becoming famous by belonging to a clique. His dervish ways were beyond their conception.

The person who broke the opposition could only be a spiritual friend. Inayat gives his name as Babu (father) Lahiri. This old man advised Inayat to perform for students, and once he did that everything went well. Soon he made his appearance under the auspices of famous Indians of the period, such as Judge Gurudas Banerjee and Rabindranath Tagore. The once reluctant Calcutta circles gave him flattering nicknames, such as 'the morning star of Indian music' and his first gramophone records bear these flowery titles.[12] From an artistic point of view his success in Calcutta was a greater achievement than praise from the Nizam, who paid special attention to the spiritual effect of the performance.

For Inayat himself music, character building and spiritual development remained inseparably linked. In Calcutta he made another Maula-Bakhshian effort to bring the culture of his country to everyone. He joined forces with a friend and they planned a new school or academy; moreover he suggested to the government that music be made a compulsory subject in the ordinary curriculum. But he was so busy that he never got round to carrying out his plans. Again and again he had to perform outside Calcutta; in the meantime his father had died and he had to act as the head of the family and guardian of his youngest brother.

During the last years of his father's life Inayat's bond with him was so strong that the son could feel when the old man was seriously ill. The first time this happened, he immediately took a train and his unexpected arrival did the old man so much good that he recovered. The second time Inayat sent a telegram before he set out on the three-day journey home.[13] When he arrived Rahemat Khan had already died. He had been a lonely man, difficult for himself and others. Though he had lived intensely, he had been overshadowed by his father-in-law and restricted by his own puritanism, so that he had never had a chance to be completely himself.

The last thing Inayat had done for his father was to arrange a marriage for his brother Maheboob Khan. He found him a wife from Calcutta. Uncle Pathan was opposed to it, because he felt it was too friendly a gesture towards Calcutta society.

The house of Maula Bakhsh was no longer what it used to be. Inayat soon had his youngest brother Musharaff Khan join him in Calcutta. Later Musharaff Khan vividly described their life there. He told stories of the elder brother who returned home from giving concerts before princes, to sleep on the floor like a poor man; of visits from dervishes and holy men, and of small details of their everyday doings.

A Westerner can hardly imagine how deeply the brothers respected 'Professor.' In the first place formally and automatically, because he was the eldest; then with wonder and admiration because he had become a mystic. But in other ways too, they had strong ties. They had memories of childhood in common: always Maula Bakhsh, living and dominating or dead and daily remembered; the quiet figure of their mother, the proud aunts and gentle cousins, the sensitiveness of their father, his outbursts of anger and his Punjabi humour. They recalled their own boyish jokes, talking Marathi pig-latin so that nobody could understand them, overturning each others beds, wandering outside the town together. Maheboob Khan was five years younger than Inayat. As a child he had often been ill and that made him somewhat withdrawn. He had a beautiful voice which was rarely heard and he was the only one who liked reading. Mohammed Ali Khan was a cousin who had only lived in the house in Baroda before he was six and after he was fifteen. He was one year older than Inayat, who looked upon him as a brother and a friend, though their characters differed widely. Ali Khan was an orthodox Moslem, brought up in a provincial town and more completely stamped by the feudal system. He was robust, strong and a sportsman, possessed natural spiritual gifts and an exceptionally beautiful voice. Both were on the staff of the academy of music in Baroda and had been under Dr Pathan's influence much longer than Inayat. That accounted for the attraction the West held for them, though one of them was reserved and the other orthodox. This far-away world was romantic and 'exotic'. They had heard about its marvels.

At the time of his last visit to Baroda Inayat met a Brahmin seer, who predicted that he would go to the West. The man made no secret of the fact that he would need courage. But he was to build up something grand, something unimaginable though not something that would make him rich. When he finished, the holy one had tears in his eyes.

Sages he met had often hinted at Inayat's greatness and exceptional task. Wherever he went there was always at least one mystic, Hindu or Moslem, and with them he spent his happiest hours. Later in the West he missed no other company so much as that of congenial minds.

The end of his life among robbers, princes and holy men was in sight. His last sage showed him the way to the West, his last maharaja said that he was more of a guru than a musician, and wanted to keep him at his court in both capacities; his last robber stole all the gold medals Inayat had received as a musican. He saw this as a sign that his years as a wandering musician were over and that he had to detach himself even from these symbols of honour.[14]

Then it happened that an American who attended one of his concerts exclaimed, with the easy enthusiasm of the extrovert, 'We ought to have this in The States.' This little encouragement settled it. One of their acquaintances was going to New York just then and the brothers knew that a teacher from Baroda was studying at Columbia University.

In Baroda Maheboob and Ali Khans received a telegram: Inayat intended to go to America. Would they go with him? Neither of them hesitated. Uncle Pathan warned them that nobody was waiting for them, but that did not deter them; the call of the West and their attachment to their brother were too strong. They packed their eastern instruments and their western clothes and took final leave of Baroda and the house of Maula Bakhsh. The only survivor of the older generation was the grandmother, a hundred years old now, Fourteen year old Musharaff Khan, who was still at school, stayed behind with the landlady in Calcutta. He was not there when the other three embarked from Bombay.

It was 13th September, 1910, the ship was Italian with a Goanese crew, sailors so poor that they had caught monkeys to kill and eat. The three Moslem musicians, used to hygienic food laws and the scruples of their Brahmin friends' eating habits, shuddered at the sight of such barbarism.

The West did not eat monkeys, it considered itself civilized. The three Khans, also, saw themselves as the bearers of a civilization. For all the following years two cultures of a different nature stood gropingly facing each other.

Chapter VI (1910-1912)
Stranger

The Statue of Liberty holds a torch above New York Harbour, tourists walk inside the head and look out; emigrants from Europe look up at it from behind the railing and recognize the symbol of what they were seeking: political freedom. Inayat watched it, a figure standing against the restless autumn sky, growing larger as they approached. He would never seek political freedom in a strange country, though he wanted it to be realized in his own. But more important for him was what he called the liberation of the soul, the release of the possibilities hidden in every human being. He would have to explain this to people who already had erected this enormous statue of liberty, a kind of out-size idol. He thought of national freedom and freedom for the whole world, and at the same time of idols, images and ideals, of the symbol of wings and of all the stone that had gone into the making of this statue — a short-circuit of emotions.

Then followed greater confusion. The world of the mythical white man was not what an Oriental, at home, dreams about it. Indian streets are crowded and busy, cows and goats stroll confidently among men and vehicles, people stop to chat, sometimes they shout, but nobody is in an hurry. Even the poorest woman, carrying a load on her head, moves quietly and gracefully. Begging children, with overlarge eyes and gruesome sores horrify the Westerner. An Oriental is bewildered by another kind of horror. In Inayat's own words: 'The great activity of the people and the rapidity of things in general, the rush of machinery

Balanced Rock, Colorado, 1911. 'Indians and Americans making a tour.'
In front, second from right, carrying his coat: Inayat. In front left: Ruth St Denis.

above, below and all around; the transitoriness of affairs; men running hither and thither for trains and cars with newspapers and parcels in their hands — all this kept me under a complete spell of silence and bewilderment.'[1]

What seemed to him most odd was the passion for newspapers. That 'even a millionaire ran to catch a train' was a relative, outward difference. But that everyone in a public vehicle must have a newspaper and gobble up the ephemeral news would make people forget how to observe with their own eyes.

Observing with one's eyes, 'studying life,' was one of his principal methods. After his description of the uproar and hurry of the West he continues: 'But being a Sufi I very soon became accustomed to this change of life by attuning myself to my surroundings.' He not only means subtly focusing his inner forces, but also using his eyes to observe, and to absorb and assimilate. He needed all the lessons he had learnt and did put them into practice.

His two companions who had lived close to Dr Pathan for years, had been inoculated to some extent, they knew a little better what to expect. But just as a western dreamer going to the East discovers that his dream does not tally with the facts, so they were disappointed too. The first months in America stuck in their memory as something terrible. To top things off it was November, and the weather was harsh. They suffered from the cold, perhaps from hunger,[2] but the worst was the confusion, and having nothing to hold onto. Nothing was familiar, they had suddenly become blind men on a merry-go-round and lost their bearings. Even the thieves were ghostly and unreal.

Amongst the many outer differences were the shops, behind large glass windows instead of being open to the street and the shopkeeper squatting, surrounded by piles of merchandise. In one of the beautiful, brightly illuminated shop windows they saw musical instruments and a notice PIANOS FOR HIRE. Maheboob Khan wanted to keep up his western music, decided to hire a piano and paid the transport and one month's charge in advance.

Whatever else came to the house of their white landlady — a white person letting out rooms or carrying loads was in itself a curiosity — there was no sign of a piano. They went back to the shop. 'Rented a piano? Paid cash in advance? News to me, boys.' The shop assistant put on his most innocent face and one can imagine him winking at his mate at the back of the shop and calling out, 'Hey, did you rent a piano to this black so-and-so? Never seen the guy, have you?' The foreigners who, in their own country, knew how and in which tone to deal with a thief and swindler, were helpless here.

There were other shops too, behind glass windows to be sure, but inside they found the familiar piled-up rolls of cotton and silk and a vague smell of tea, spices, incense and sandalwood — here the Indian merchants of New York lived and worked.

There was a small Indian community in New York and about five years earlier its leader, a rich merchant, had entertained their own Gaekwar.[3] After this trip the Gaekwar had enabled the Barodan school-teacher T. R. Pandya to study in New York.

If Pandya did not put his fellow-townsmen into the saddle he at least helped them into the stirrups. He knew the one person among the millions of New Yorkers who, indeed, was waiting for them: Edmund Russell, a very wealthy, very fair-haired western dreamer, perhaps an initiate who, for some reason was only and exclusively interested in India. He lived on practically nothing, but gave 'extraordinary and famous parties.'[3] A month after their arrival he organized a grand reception in his studio for the three musicians from Baroda.

One of the guests was Dr P. M. C. Rybner, originally a concert musician, but since 1903 head of the faculty of music at Columbia University. He invited Inayat and his group to give a concert cum lecture in the University auditorium. Presumably four of them played, the additional musician being a young Indian tabla player who had been living in New York for years and was delighted to hear from home. The tabla are percussion instruments without which an Indian orchestra is not complete. Ramaswami, a Brahmin like Pandya, joined forces with the three Moslem musicians and toured with them till the spring of 1914. Because he knew the West longer than they did, he was often a great support.

Daily they added to their own knowledge of the West. When Inayat left India to 'bring East and West together through his music,' he must have seen this as a continuation of his endeavours in India to bring northern and southern music, Moghul and Hindu culture, closer to each other. 'As all Indians do,' he writes, 'I had expected all Westerners to be Christians.' His brothers were familiar with western music, he also to a certain extent. It seemed parallel to their knowledge of southern music, though they were North-Indians. But the comparison did not work. The western religions, philosophies and ways of life turned out to be a maze, and music was used in a completely different way.

The concert at Columbia University was a success, but appreciation came mostly from scholars.[4] Indian music was looked upon as folkloristic, or simply as technically instructive. For instance Rybner himself, who became a good friend, was interested in methods of voice production. In general, eastern music was almost completely unknown at that time and it was described with an almost complete lack of understanding. 'Primitive,' 'monotonous' were the usual terms. Yet, however strange the apparent simplicity of the ragas with their endless, but more and more intensive repetitions and subtle variations, might seem to be, Maheboob and Ali Khans' unusually beautiful voices and Inayat's unusually profound rendering impressed people. In March 1911 *The Musician,* a magazine which usually sported a picture of a young lady with a handsome young man at a piano, or armed with a violin and a smile, suddenly appeared adorned with a veena player and an Indian dancer. The veena player's moustache is the handlebar moustache Inayat cultivated in those days; an article on Indian music, mostly taken from Day, is sandwiched between the problems of musical instruction and illustrations of popular operas.[5]

It was not by accident that the cover displayed an Indian dancer. When this issue appeared Inayat, his brother, cousin and Ramaswami were touring the provinces, lending colour to the programme of Ruth St Denis, who for the last five years had been making a hit with oriental dances of her own invention.

St Denis was a serious artiste, but her interest in India was not as thorough and constant as Russell's. She was one of the many who had fallen in love with things mysterious. Her discovery of the East began when she saw a poster, advertising cigarettes. This fascinated her so much that she put all her meagre savings into elaborate robes, dressed up as an Egyptian princess and had herself photographed in the same pose as the model on the poster. Then she dreamed up an Egyptian ballet, but before she found a producer, she discovered a little about India and seriously concocted some dance solos, supplementing them with her own mystical commentary. Her fancies conformed to the western image of the East to such an extent that Henry B. Harris, owner of several theatres, was prepared to promote her. She had great success, in the United States as well as during a three year tour of Europe and in 1910 Harris had agreed to her staging the ballet Egypta. It was, she says in her autobiography, a success, but not a box-office success. St Denis, a born puritan, hoped to earn the money back with a tour of the provinces.

She used to recruit her Indian performers, mostly for walk-on parts, from everywhere, from shops, from universities — once she even carried off some members of a ship's crew. For a determined and self-centred lady of her calibre it was a matter of course to buttonhole the Indian musicians after their concert at Columbia University and engage them for her tour.

Inayat now became further acquainted with the States via the artist's world and life in small hotels in the provinces, but the general atmosphere of a small town — Our Town, Main Street — remained a closed book to him. It was always the hurried and hard face of America that was turned towards him. This cold attitude of business first and no nonsense was characteristic, though. It struck even Ruth St Denis, a born American, when she returned from her three-year European tour. Some artists tried to adjust themselves to it and advised their colleagues not to call themselves musicians, or music teachers, but to say that they were in the 'music-business' — that would earn them more respect from the dominating business-men.[5]

But it was not the materialism that astonished the Royal Musicians of Hindustan most — they had expected that. It was the unconscious details, everyday customs, so natural for a Westerner that he had no notion they needed explaining. A most difficult thing to get used to was not only having to start on time, but being allotted no more than a few minutes in the programme.

The first time they performed — they filled the intervals between St Denis' dances — they unhurriedly began to tune up. When they paused for a moment and wanted to begin and even more unhurriedly warm up, the audience applauded. They did not have the remotest idea of Indian music and took the tuning for the actual raga.

Later Inayat often spoke about having to play on time, inspiration or no inspiration, and he was fond of pointing out that an Indian musician plays only when he feels disposed to, and can even refuse a king.[6] But that is rather an idealized presentation. The brothers very soon began to idealize their mother country in their memory, just as Europeans do in the tropics.

Just because being punctual and keeping appointments was difficult for them, they sometimes overdid things. One day Ali Khan was ill. Perspiring after a friendly bout of wrestling and not thinking of the climate he had gone out and caught pneumonia. He had a high temperature and could not even stand up. So Inayat and Maheboob Khan, both slender, took robust, heavy Ali Khan on their shoulders and carried him to the platform. He played.[7]

The wrestler was probably a Negro. They met Negro artists too, either in artist's circles, or because of their interest in Negro spirituals. In any case Inayat was interested in the Negroes and their lot. This is not surprising, for a brown-skinned Indian was often taken for a Negro and treated accordingly.

Once it happened that somebody advised Inayat not to admit Negroes to his performances, for then 'the right kind of people would stay away.' But Inayat practised what he preached, refused to exclude anyone and took the risk of 'the right kind' staying away. No doubt stimulated by this sort of advice he devoted a remarkable passage in his autobiography to the American Negro. He began by expressing his surprise that in America, in spite of the example of Lincoln, and in spite of the great ideals of liberty, racial prejudices existed. If he said this in any company, he was, of course, told that in India, too, the low castes and the casteless were despised. Although he knew the problems of the caste system, he also knew the justifications, and on such occasions he could not help doing what all Indians do, defending his country: there were good reasons for the caste-system and anyway the casteless were not hated. The Westerner to whom he was speaking apparently said that the Americans had good reasons too, the Negroes were 'backward.' And then Inayat warmed up. On the contrary, he had noticed that Negroes excel in all fields where they

93

are given a chance, 'not only in wrestling and boxing, but also on the stage the Negroes show their strength.' What struck him most is evident form the conclusion: 'Though conscious of all the prejudices against the Negro from all around, he does not allow his ego to be affected by it. In every position of outward humiliation he is put to, he stands upright with a marvellous spirit. Which I could only wish the man in the East has, who has become as a soil worn out by a thousand harvests. The spirit in the East seems to me be deadened, being weighted down by autocratic influences, trampled upon by foreign powers, crucified by high moral and spiritual ideas and long starved by poverty.'[8]

These are words from the unpublished *Autobiography*, and when Inayat addressed Indians he severely criticized their weak points, but to the western world he upheld the dignity of India. What he appreciated in Ruth St Denis was that by drawing attention to oriental art and culture she helped to dispel the standard ideas of lazy, uncivilized savages. He also respected her for her perseverance and concentration. But he says she 'invented Indian dances of her own... for which our music became as a colour and fragrance to an imitation flower.... For the public it was only amusement and therefore painful to us. Also it was not satisfactory to combine real and imitation.' But the tour gave them a chance to make Indian music known, and after all, they had to live.

In her own autobiography Ruth St Denis defends her imitation dances.[9] She admits that not everything is 'theologically accurate;... but at no time... have I been sufficiently the scholar or sufficiently interested (!) to imitate or try to reproduce any oriental ritual or actual dance — the mood to me is all, and inevitably manifests its own pattern.'

This rather baffling confession is not quite correct. Elsewhere she tells that she always ferreted out and studied books about her latest exotic country. And when she was travelling through Illinois, Kansas and Colorado with Inayat and his musicians, the exchange of knowledge was mutual. During the long train journeys St Denis shared with them her schoolbook knowledge of Lincoln and American ideas. On the bare stage of one provincial theatre after another, before or after rehearsals, the Indians taught her something of the genuine movements and meaning of Hindu dances. When she had practised them for some time, she asked Inayat to give her a certificate of proficiency. Anyone who has seen a Hindu dance and the subtle control of all muscles even of the neck, eyes, waist and fingers, and who knows that this requires training from a very early age, will understand the refusal. And anyone who knows America, the hurry, the self-opinion and the enthusiasm, will understand the request.

The refusal led to a split. On 19th April 1911 Inayat and his troupe left St Denis and hers. A newspaper cutting with a rather ridiculous text has been preserved: 'Caruso of India no longer with Ruth St Denis,' says the headline. A few more choice phrases: 'Inayath (sic) who claims to be an extraordinary musician, since he has played before all the Rajahs, Maharajahs, Punjaubs (a people, not a prince) Emirs and Pashas of India, will no longer extract dulcet tones from his repertoire of musical instruments in the Street Scene of the Cobra Dance.... His heart was sore towards 'the dogs of infidels,' since his name was refused a position of prominence in the electric sign in front of theatres... His defection from the ranks... was aided and abetted by Ramaswami who has an ambition to be a theatrical manager. Mahabub Khan and Mahomed Khan will... remain in San Francisco, having secured positions as caterers of 57 different varieties of curry, and posing as 'real, honest-to-goodness' Hindu potentates in hard luck.'[10]

The title Caruso is not unusual. Maula Bakhsh was called the Beethoven of India. Tagore was the Shelley or Byron of India and when the Nizam called Inayat Tansen it was a compliment and exaggeration of the same kind. For the rest this newspaper article is a model of arrogance, indifference and total ignorance. No wonder that Inayat, whenever he speaks about harmony between East and West, emphazises that first of all East and West must get to know each other.

Not only was St Denis ignorant of authentic Indian dances, but her composer Walter Meyrowitz knew nothing of Indian music either. He had made something very 'exotic,' strange chords and no melody at all — whereas Indian music consists solely of varied melody. It is questionable whether the Street Scene was indeed graced by the Royal Musicians of Hindustan; according to another review St Denis kept her 'new director of music' out of her own performance. This other critic devotes a few words to those 'strange humans from India, indulging in their silly music,' though he had sense enough to add 'silly to occidental ears.'

It would appear that St Denis herself understood remarkably little. After the departure of the brothers and Ramaswami she invented a new dance, entitled The Sufi, in which she wore brown tights, a string of beads and 'a tattered automobile veil' and alternatively 'blinked at the painted sky, proudly examined her bare toes and tied herself into a knot as the curtain descended...' The audience frankly giggled.'[10] Not the best kind of introduction to Sufism. But elsewhere in the town Inayat could now give that introduction and enlightenment himself.

The only nearly correct part of the narrow-minded newspaper item of April 19th is what it says about Ramaswami. This irreplaceable helper succeeded in organizing a tour of their own for the Indian party. Apparently he had done this before. In Chicago and Denver, on days when St Denis did not dance, Inayat had given discourses of his own which, in spite of his difficulties with the language, were well received.[4]

In San Francisco a surprise awaited the strangers. Since

the Congress of Religions in 1891 a few authentic Indian sages had settled down in iron-clad America. Now, in a town full of western traffic and high western office buildings the wanderer suddenly found himself in front of a Hindu temple in genuine Indian style. He heard a familiar language, was treated with the courtesy he was used to. The Oriental is nearly always shocked by the lack of subtlety in western manners, and even more so a saint who, in India, is immediately recognized and treated with respect. He gave a successful concert and received, as was the custom at home, a written 'address' and a gold medal.

Happy though this small Indian oasis made him, he was alive to the weak points of such a purely Indian institute in the West. Apart from the fact that the learned intellectuality of Vedanta makes it too difficult for non-scholars, he had already discovered that Westerners were too busy to follow a complete course of mystical training. Already then the awareness must have been growing in him that the American or European had to find the way to his inner self by a shorter, simplified method.

And there was a demand for it. Precisely because making money and showing off money were the sanctioned ideals, some circles showed signs of a reaction dreaming of another world, a romanticized East, full of saints and happy savages. This counter-ideal was partly a heritage of romanticism, but it was also a searching for new religious forms, because the old ones no longer satisfied.

These seekers, romantics, and people resisting excessive materialism became Inayat's public. At the University of California in Berkeley and in Los Angeles he gave concerts preceded by an introduction and he drew full halls. He was under no illusion — he already knew that his music was a curiosity, 'as if he was bringing old coins to a currency bank.' It did not occur to his listeners to use the music in the way he did.

Except one. After the concert some of the public had

come to thank him and shake hands. One of these hand-shakers was not merely in pursuit of a few moments in the greenroom and an interesting group of foreigners in marvellous costumes. She also wrote a letter, which arrived when the party had to leave for Seattle where they were engaged to play the following evening.

Being punctual was an art which cost Inayat conscious effort. And for a moment he thought that if this lady was interested she should follow him to Seattle. Then something happened which he probably experienced from time to time, but which he seldom mentions. In the days of his discipleship he once told his master, Murshid Madani, that he had seen him in a vision before he had met him in the flesh. To which Murshid Madani replied, 'I am sorry.' Inayat recalls that reply as a reminder that clairvoyance and the like are secondary phenomena, to which not too much attention should be paid.[11] But these things happened to him, because he was receptive and well attuned and the phenomenon especially occurred at important turning points in his life. As had happened before he found his master, that night he had a vision of light that filled the whole room and he understood that something important was to be done next day. 'And I observed that it was the initiation of Mrs Ada Martin, my first mureed (disciple) since our arrival and I knew that this soul would give light and enlightenment to all who came in contact with her.'

And indeed, this first disciple proved to be a good and energetic leader. In the course of 1911 and 1912 more people were initiated but it was Mrs Martin who kept the Sufi work in the States going for years. Admittedly she did it somewhat to her own intellectual and sometimes even formalized way of thinking, yet, to quote Inayat further 'devoting her life to spiritual contemplation and serving humanity.' She was of Jewish descent, had a difficult life behind her, had searched in many religions, but after meeting Inayat she did not look back.

This initiation, without a preceding probation period and without keeping the disciple near him, was the start of Inayat's simplified 'mysticism,' an abc of inner development for laymen and lay-women, which could make Westerners into more complete beings, by bringing their intellectual and materialistic skill into balance with their inner potentialities. He rarely gave a complete training in mastership. If anyone became a leader of a group, it was usually because he was a good organizer, or enthusiastic, or trustfully devoted.

From Seattle the group of Indian musicians travelled back to New York via the northern route, Nothing is known of that journey. But in New York a worthy proposition awaited them. St Denis' manager, Henry B. Harris, a man of enterprise, considered staging a grand oriental show in which Inayat and his group were to play an important part. They had even to enlarge their orchestra, and therefore Musharaff Khan was invited to join his elder brothers in America. He received their letter near the time of the Nizam's death in July 1911. As the mail took its time in those days, Harris's plans must date back to May 1911 or earlier. Maybe to the end of March. St. Denis performed in Denver from 20th to 25th March and on one of the rare holidays Mr Harris invited his American and Indian artists to make the fashionable trip to Balanced Rock together. As was the custom, the whole party was photographed, in planned positions before and beside the rock, which stands balanced on its tip. The American men are wearing wide-brimmed hats and loosely knotted ties, the diffident nonconformity of those days. Some beards are in evidence too. Harris, the host, astride a donkey, is in front, to the right. St Denis, enveloped in automobile shawls — not tattered this time — has draped herself on a boulder, to the left. Inayat is standing beside Harris, in western costume, only his head is inconspicuously covered. He stands quietly, completely at ease, at home in this company, elegant and holding himself erect. But there is something in his bearing and expression, the tranquillity for one thing, that stamps him everyone's superior. One would hardly believe that this man is the same vehement young man of 1903 who, photographed by Deen Dayal in a handsome armchair, evoked memories of warriors and horses.

The same tranquillity and strength, the air of being present yet not there, strikes one in some group photos of the musicians in oriental costume. In the Balanced Rock photo, however, it is the very naturalness with which he stands among Westerners, that manifests his strength. Only one portrait reveals something of the bewilderment that followed his first impression of the alien country and it was exactly this photo which, printed on a postcard, had to introduce Professor Inayat Khan as the bearer of the Sufi Message of Spiritual Liberty.

On this postcard he is shown in the girdled robe of the initiate and it is the only portrait in which he strikes one as young; he was not yet thirty. The serenity that had been his since 1908 is certainly evident, but the strength that radiates from every other portait is lacking. One can even perceive something of amazement and perhaps hesitation.

This photo was probably taken in the first days after arrival. Not until his second stay in New York did Inayat give more initiations. One of these earliest western disciples has recorded her memories. Unlike Mrs Martin she had never been attracted to theosophy and similar speculations. But she writes that in September 1910, the same time that Inayat left India, her life began to change, and exactly a year later she met him for the first time, in New York, and soon became a disciple. She visited the brothers now and then and stayed for meals with them. In spite of all her respect for her teacher, she was 'surprised that Maheboob and Ali Khans, two very talented gentlemen, excellent musicians, had only one thought: Hazrat.'

The brothers, who were not to receive their training till

100

their wartime sojourn in London – the complete training in their case – had the Indian respect for a sage. They were with him every night and morning, when, in some chilly hotel or plain boarding house he did his practices and said his prayers. They saw him grow. Maheboob Khan, the aristocrat, the esteemed court musician, suffered under western humiliations and Ali Khan, the faithful Moslem, struggled to obtain the ritual pure food. As most Indians in the West they prepared their own meals. Hence, probably, the remark about 57 curries in the San Francisco newspaper report, which also makes twisted reference to their pride in their distinguished past. But when Maheboob Khan received an offer to become the leading musician at an Indian court, he refused.[12] They remained faithful to their brother, though their longing for India grew with the years.

In the meantime they developed a way of life which they maintained as long as they travelled together: lessons, concerts, work on publications, visits. They made some real friends, like Russell, who used to visit them again in London in 1914, and Rybner, who came to welcome Inayat years later, when he came back to New York in 1923. There were always artists and scholars who were interested in their methods. Yet Inayat's public performances, besides those at universities, were mostly arranged through Indian or Indian-minded institutions. According to the *Autobiography* he gave some discourses at a 'Sanscrit College' in New York. This probably refers to Baba Bharati's centre. Baba Bharati was a Brahmin who, says Inayat, 'tried to teach the Americans the love of Krishna.' In any case he was one of their friends. Inayat was happy with these few congenial souls, but he knew that Baba Bharati's group as well as the larger Vedanta Society were islands in a world driven by different motives and that their aims differed from his. They were like missionaries and that was exactly what Inayat was not: he wanted people to get to know their own potentialities. Love the Americans could learn from their own Christianity, if they did what Inayat had learned to do: make God a reality and revere him in every other being.

But most of those who were attracted just romanticized, making the sacred into something special and remote, putting it on a pedestal. About 1900 a gushing book had appeared about a so-called oriental saint, flowery and unreal, and that was the standard applied to Inayat. Those who enjoyed this kind of Orient of their own creation hardly ever referred to an oriental scholar or expert for information. A typical example was, and is, the Omar Khayyam craze, based on the famous, but highly arbitrary translation of Edward Fitzgerald.

This adaptation dates back to 1858. Fitzgerald under-rated the Persians both as mystics and as poets. He prefered 'old Omar' to Rumi, and felt perfectly free to 'mash' some quatrains together, even those of different authors, until his 'translation' was 'most ingeniously tesselated into a sort of Epicurean Eclogue in a Persian garden.'[13] What he really gave was an image, not of Persia in the twelfth century, but of well-to-do western Christians in the time of Darwin. The American critic Norton wrote in 1869 that 'Omar Khayyam's mystical and sensual side in its English dress... reads like the latest and freshest expression of the perplexity and of the doubt of the generation we ourselves belong to.' No wonder that about 1900 Fitzgerald's Omar became a must for all perplexed doubters. Appreciation on a large scale did not come immediately; at first the Victorians thought the imagery a little daring, even though Fitzgerald had omitted what he found too indecent. Other readers, more Voltairian than Victorian refused to see Omar's wine and beloved ones as symbols and, reasoning from the fact that Omar Khayyam was a mathematician, they made him a cynical rationalist in their own image. They might have remembered that Pythagoras, the mathematician, was also a mystic.

Inayat was shocked at the misunderstandings and falsifications. To his surprise he found in C. H. A. Bjerregaard, librarian of New York Public Library, a man who tried to explain something of Omar Khayyam the Sufi. But Mr Bjerregaard's book, *A Sufi Interpretation of Omar Khayyam and Fitzgerald,* published in 1902, was still full of vague ideas, misty poetic language and western associations. In 1915 Bjerregaard published a new edition of his Fitzgerald critique in the first series of Inayat's Sufi publications. In this second book the information given by Inayat and his direct influence are clearly visible. In 1902 Bjerregaard began cautiously and vaguely to suggest that there was more to Omar Khayyam than the western reader usually got out of his Rubayat; then he whispered in flowery phrases that 'really speaking' it was mysticism. The 1915 edition begins with the direct and matter-of-fact statement that good examples of Sufism can be found in Omar Khayyam, but that the quatrains have been interpreted wrongly because of Fitzgerald's incorrect translation. Although, compared to Inayat's, Bjerregaard's style is always somewhat excited, the tone of this new book is firmer and less tortuous. As Bjerregaard himself says in another book, published in 1912, 'it is easy to let oneself go in high-faluting language and poetic imagery.' But what people need is a 'tangible form they can recognize in their own lives.'[14] This is not Bjerregaard's usual style, nor that of his comtemporaries, but it is very much like Inayat's. An example: in 1902, in the explanation of quatrain XI, the essence of mysticism is described in vague terms. In 1915 he says briefly, 'He knows what is behind life and death.' And again, on page 34 of the revised edition a mistake in the translation is pointed out that was not mentioned in the older volume. Fitzgerald says, 'Oh make haste.' The critic says, 'Does he perhaps call to a Wisdom-Wine conference?' The irony in itself as well as the mocking at western haste in particular would be unusual for Bjerregaard if he was working alone. In general the Bjerregaard of 1912 knows more than a European could have known at that time.[15] Now and then he quotes Inayat's ideas, and he concludes with a device in capital letters — in spite of all his efforts to remain simple it sounds a bit stilted — 'The Soul Is Free!' In 1902 the last line was 'The Bird is on the Wing.' He also made haste and wrote a few more books on the same theme, such as *Jesus, a Man of Freedom*.

Freedom, vague and beautiful, was in fashion. Wilson, candidate in the 1912 elections, made freedom into a dream and political ideal. In the East people were beginning to fight for real political freedom.

For Inayat freedom meant in the first place the liberation of the soul from outer confusion and limitation.[16] That is the ultimate goal of all mystical development, as he had so fervently argued in his conversation with the Brahmin. This freedom of the soul is not escapism, but living in the presence of God, experiencing, seeing and recognizing him in all life around us. No doubt he sometimes associated this spiritual freedom with political freedom.[16] When Inayat says, 'Everyone likes freedom,' he strikes two notes at the same time — maybe even three, for occasionally he had suffered under a too severe father. He did hope for India's freedom; though his nationalism applied especially to culture, he felt hurt when his country was not seen in its dignity. Therefore he appreciated Bjerregaard's cooperation, even though this author did not mention him as his source. There were others too, who were interested in oriental culture, but used the bearer of this culture for their own glory. That was one of the subtle thefts of the West.

He also came across coarser and rather stupid spiritual robbery. Someone pretending to be a great admirer forced his way in as a disciple because he was collecting data on all 'secret societies.' This shocked Inayat more than anything else. This kind of action revealed rank misunderstanding.

In the first place there was no secret society, secondly Inayat would like nothing better than letting everyone share his experiences; thirdly knowledge in words without experience had no value. 'It made me sad that he tried to steal something that cannot be stolen.'

And so the second winter in New York passed. The strangers began to acquire a certain reputation and if they did not feel at home, at least they began to find their feet. When the youngest brother arrived, in the coldest month of the winter, they realized to what extent they themselves had already become used to the strange western world.

Young Musharaff Khan was more bewildered than any of the older brothers, for as a boy without a mother he had always been a bit lonely and he had not been very much under Uncle Alauddin Khan's influence. The western clothes bothered him and he found odd and embarassing the western habit of looking people straight in the face instead of politely keeping one's eyes down. Ali Khan showed him the shops, but everything seemed to move, even the lights turned and twisted and twinkled. It was February and freezing and he suffered so much from the cold that Inayat had to remind him of a brave ancestor to make him hold out. Only the boarding house where they lived resembled home, for the master of the house always referred them to his wife if a decision had to be taken: 'Ask Mrs Collins.'[17]

And so the brothers waited for the return of Henry Harris, who in the winter of 1912 had gone to England on business. The rich theatre director had booked his passage home on the largest and fastest ship in the world, the Titanic. What he did and said the night the unsinkable ship sank is recorded in Walter Lord's careful reconstruction. 'Women and children first,' he was told. 'Yes, I know,' Harris replied. And these were his last words.[18]

Later, when Inayat mentioned the Titanic in his lectures, he had a personal memory — his own friend who perished in the disaster. His own lot began to be linked to the West.

Yet, in his autobiography he says that the first year and a half in America had mainly served to get to know the psychology of the West and to find out how he could carry out his task. 'If I am to mention one great achievement of that period it is to have found the soul who was destined to be my life's partner.'

This life-partner was a fair-haired, slender but determined girl, Ora Ray Baker. Later she told her children how it had been possible for two people so far apart to choose each other. Her half-brother and guardian, himself the leader of one of the many movements full of real, borrowed or imagined eastern wisdom, had her take veena lessons, but so did others. She admired the teacher and was impressed, but so was everyone. But most people took him to be older than he was; he had something ageless about him. Also, it hardly occurred to Westerners that a saintly person could marry. And an Oriental, for whom marriage is a duty, taken for granted, knows only of marriages arranged by the family. If ever visions and dreams were needed, it was then. Ora Ray Baker dreamed of two Orientals, one of whom pointed at the other. When she met her veena teacher she recognized him as the younger Oriental of her dream. Inayat himself tells how after the years in Hyderabad he twice had a vision of Murshid Madani, and one of these occurred in the West, in New York, when he met his future wife.

Choosing a bride and proposing to her himself must have been a strange sensation. An Indian is not taught how to propose to a woman. The family used to, and still does, search for a suitable spouse. Nowadays the boy and the girl often have a say in the choice, and a man could always look for a courtesan; but there was no pattern for declaring one's love to a respectable girl. When Inayat says, 'A western lover knows how to woo, an eastern lover knows how to yearn,' he is not just making a poetical remark but speaking from experience. It was not only a feat to find his future wife himself, but also to make his intentions clear.

When they had become clear, half-brother Dr Bernard took action. Enthusing about oriental wisdom was one thing, allowing one's sister to marry a brown foreigner was another matter. He forbade all meetings and correspondence and threatened him alternatively with the police and a pistol.

The Royal Musicians of Hindustan who, because of the death of Harris, had lost an important objective, sailed for England. Inayat left behind in the States small nuclei of followers which continue to exist today; and Ora Ray Baker who, naturally, rebelled against her brother's orders and defied him.

Chapter VII (1912-1914)
'Votre remarquable musicien-philosophe'

Of Inayat's first visit to London — a London of silent Sundays and outspoken suffragettes — a few reviews and recommendations remain. One by the Hampstead Conservatory of Music, one by the House of Indian Activities in London, and one by Tagore. Tagore had arrived in England for an operation during the summer of 1912 and soon started writing in English. He visited Inayat at his hotel, and it was, as always, good to see an old acquaintance from India, even though the musicians had been introduced into the best artistic circles by their American friends. An international music congress was held that June and Inayat met a great many artists whom he names in his autobiography. Again, the majority of them were lovers of folk music, or else they were interested in India, for instance Cyril Scott who composed music to Kipling's *Jungle Book;* Lord Dunsany, an Irishman seriously interested in the symbolism of Persian poetry, and Sir Henry Newbolt, poet and marine officer, whose religious philosophy was somewhat akin to Inayat's. In other respects he had very little in common with these men, but they recognized that India had a culture of its own, and that carried weight with him.

Inayat did not, however, gain much from these highly respectable connections. Tagore did introduce him to the musicologist Fox Strangways, who was at the time writing his study on Indian music.[1] Inayat provided him with a few details, especially on the religious aspects of his art. In his foreword Fox Strangways remarks that he cannot possibly mention all those who had helped him, but in the course of

Moscow, Spring 1914. 'The Royal Musicians of Hindustan.'
Top centre: Inayat; top left: Maheboob Khan; top right: Ali Khan; bottom left:
Musharaff Khan; bottom right: Ramaswami.

the work itself he constantly names his sources of information. Not Inayat. As Fox Strangways's, unlike Bjerregaard, did not publish under his own supervision, in this case Inayat regarded the omission as bad form. He and his brothers had good friends in the Royal Asiatic Society, and the Journal of this society gave a lukewarm review of Fox Strangways's book, which all the same became a standard work. One of the objections was almost Inayatish: theory about music was second-rate, one should know it directly.[2] Inayat himself had told Fox Strangways that he did not see much point in writing books about music: 'One should practise it and get a fuller insight... only this could give the true benefit.' The benefit he meant was the loosening of frozen minds. So closely were music and mysticism intertwined in his life that it took him years to separate the two, at least outwardly.

In spite of his totally different life and attitude, Fox Strangways was more of a help to Inayat than the majority of Indians in London. Inayat lectured for the Indian Club, those official representatives of India, students and rich globe-trotters who made up the anglicized top drawer that Chaudhuri[3] could still call the 'dominant minority.' These people were occupied with diligently cribbing English culture. In those days, even the great leader Gokhalé had doffed his 'rebellious turban' for a top-hat.[4] To anglicize, Inayat felt, was not the way to promote understanding between two cultures: one of the two had to give way and the ultimate unity behind the diversity on the surface was not discovered. Adopting customs does not mean unity. He concluded that there was little scope for his message, that the English met him with more sympathy in England than they did in India — a discovery awaiting almost every Asian in the West — but that his music was scarcely understood. It was Fox Strangways who pointed out to him that he might find a more congenial artistic climate in France.

Certainly the British showed sympathy, and the Indians

in London were anglicized, but this did not alter the fact that all these Indians were nationalists, and this the kind British knew perfectly well. To them Inayat, suspiciously resistant to westernization and bearing a message of (spiritual) freedom, looked like a new species of agitator. Since 1907 there had been all sorts of outrages and murders in India and the plotters had fled the country. The Royal Musicians of Hindustan moved from one centre of conspiracy to the other: San Francisco, London, Paris. The word 'freedom' was suspect and the appendage 'spiritual' was meaningless, because it would be meaningless if used by the suspicious authorities themselves. The sympathetic Britishers were not taking any chances, and so they had the five musicians shadowed on their way to Paris. Paris swarmed with political dreamers and rebels from everywhere. The claim of those foreigners that they wished to introduce the public to Indian music must have struck the professional spies as a disguise – a dangerous agent might pose as an organ grinder.

In later years the brothers loved to tell how they came by their lodgings in Paris. As they were plodding through the city with all their instruments and luggage Inayat noticed an old man following them, stopping when they stopped and continuing when they did. They sat down on a park bench, Parisian children in sailor suits and lace hats played around them and elderly gentleman with canes sauntered beneath reddening trees. Their own elderly Britisher also sat. Daring children who came nearer heard the dark, large-eyed foreigners speak a strange language and suddenly laugh. 'That poor old man must be tired too,' Inayat said. 'Let's ask him if he knows of a boarding house for us, then he won't have to follow us about all the time.' And they accosted their tail, who led them to Boulevard St Michel 143 and an English-speaking landlady with whom, as usual, they were soon the best of friends. When they left more than a year later, she was sorry to see them go: all the while, she had received such a nice extra income for reporting on all their doings.

There had been nothing to report but music: practice, rehearsals, concerts, lessons, and lectures for the in-groups of those years. In 1912 Paris was awash with orientalism or what was taken for it.[5] There had been an enormous Persian ball for the high society that spring, and someone who had been hostess to a real-life maharaja wanted to repeat the performance. Parisian grandees read nothing but the Arabian Nights, and talked of nothing but turbans and veils. Musicians composed oriental ballets, Gide wrote to England and offered to translate Tagore into French. Lucien Guitry was working on a vast oriental pageant with as many authentic details as he could muster. Mata Hari, at the height of her glory, was just back from her opera appearances in Milan. All this was thought more important than the first Balkan war or a warning speech by the socialist leader and philosopher Jaurès.[5]

Socialism did not come Inayat's way until after the war. His French audiences in 1912 rather resembled his Indian ones: artists and *fin de siècle* aristocrats. Only the holy men and dervishes were missing. In France he discovered the hollowness of many traditional religions, the formality of the churches. He came across the intellectual Frenchman who balks at the very word religion and who keeps to himself any beliefs he might have, for fear of ridicule. This is not their fault, writes Inayat, it is the spirit of their surroundings. His own inner development continued unbroken while he traversed the world from provincial American theatres to French and Russian salons. More and more he saw things from above, as an adult watches children at play, involved only because he loves the children.

But there were always some games he himself joined in with abandon, as an ordinary human being. He could rise above his own limitations and those of others, but he always remained an Indian, moulded by his youth in Baroda, and above all, a musician. The happiest moment for him and his brothers in Paris was when at last someone responded to their playing as people did at home – in tears.

That was the elderly musician Edmond Bailly, 'deprived of any commercial aptitude but gifted with a rare intellectual and esthetic keenness.'[6] About 1900 he ran *L' Art Indépendant,* a bookshop and publishing firm that was a centre of artists and also a meeting place for those mystically inclined. Bailly was one of the few Europeans who had an extensive knowledge, if only on paper, of Indian ragas. Of the performance of a raga, its development, the growing intensity of elaborations and variations, he knew nothing until he heard the Khans play.

Bailly became one of their closest friends in Paris. Together with Lady Churchill, who sailed back and forth between England and France as a self-appointed cultural ambassador, he organized the first concert the Indian group had all to themselves, on the 26th October 1912. This gained them a favorable review in *Gil Blas.*[6] At that time Lucien Guitry had already engaged them for a part in *Kismet,* an oriental show by a Westerner (the unfortunate man's name was Knoblauch); very romantic, all Arabian Nights and love, with picturesque details; and music too.[7] Preparations were under way for months, and newspaper columns went on and on about the show. The Royal Musicians of Hindustan were proudly depicted on posters in Indian costume. When they mixed with the public wearing jacket and trousers, to their amusement, no one recognized them. For the rest, there was basically no difference between the great Guitry and Ruth St Denis.

In his *Autobiography,* Inayat bestows one line on this widely discussed production: that he tried to introduce Indian music by way of *Kismet,* but that this did not work out. Even Guitry, who travelled as far as Egypt to find actors – for his silent parts – and who put a good deal of research into making his oriental sets as authentic as he could, only half used the genuine thing right under his nose. He had an European write the music, while the court musicians from India were there for the atmosphere and their actual part was quite small. But the brothers did make friends among their fellow-players, and even a few disciples. Among them was a Miss Ohanian, although she danced the usual European-made 'oriental' fancy stuff.

But nothing equalled the preposterous trash produced by Mata Hari, whom Inayat and his group accompanied at least twice. This was during the period of rehearsals for *Kismet,* the first time on the 9th of October for a private performance. Years later, Ali Khan could still do a graphic impersonation and Musharaff Khan recalls: 'First she swayed to the right, then to the left, and then she stood still for a bit. And all the bald gentlemen with white beards on little gold chairs would murmur, "Ah, c'est charmant." ' There is a programme of the second performance with this illustrious lady on 14th December in the Université des Annales.[8] The items show how the group faced the dilemma of mixing real and make-believe. They gave a Thumri, or love song; Tarana, a song of meaningless syllables but beautiful as music and very effective as dance accompaniment. Ali Khan played a solo on his instrument, the dilruba, Ramaswami did a tabla-solo and at the end Inayat sang *Chant des Prêtres du Temple de Kama.* This was a private joke. The title is in western style, and notwithstanding all the sculpture of Khajurao, there is no temple of Kama (desire). Inayat improvised just as he did as a boy, and sang of the gentlemen on the little gold chairs. He and his brothers must have barely been able to contain their mirth.

The other musical contributions to this evening were highly serious: krontjong songs by another Dutch lady calling herself Madame Sorga, who also sang oriental compositions by a Westerner. M. Paul Olivier made opening and explanatory remarks. He obviously preferred rubbish to the real thing. Words could not express his admiration of Mata Hari, and he casually added that everything was quite fit for the ladies, whereupon the audience, which consisted of ladies, burst into applause. When he got around to the Indian group he started hedging. Apparently he had had a chat with them beforehand but had not heard them play. He did mouth Inayat's words to the effect that sound is the secret of Creation, but his talk was enveloped in a haze of poetry. He could not help pushing the exotic, so uncomfortably close to him in space, back to a safe distance in time: 'He wanders through the world like a medieval troubadour... with a double purpose, to gratify our ears and to ease our hearts.' This subtle twist of meaning was rewarded with a round of applause. He then continued with great caution. 'The Indians "claim" that their instruments can produce quarter-tones, so that their scale is twice as fine as ours. But in fact,' says M. Olivier, 'western experts' — he dropped a few 19th century names —' have declared that the instruments are simply off-key. The ladies must not be surprised if the music was a bit trying on the ears.'[8]

After the love song had been performed, perfectly in tune, quartertones and all — these are known as shruti, fine, connecting notes with almost imperceptible intervals, like a glissando — he remarked what everyone now could have heard for themselves, and what he should have known all along: that the most important elements of Indian music are melody, rhythm and improvised variations. After the Tarana, he caught on a little more and noted with surprise that he and the audience had been the first to witness 'this venerable music, as old as the world.' Apparently he had not been to the concert of 26th October.

The only one who realized that this was something out of the ordinary, was Mata Hari herself. She did not usually adorn the photographs in her scrap book with the names of her accompanists, but in Inayat's case she did.

In his *Autobiography,* Inayat rarely says anything unkind, and when he does he is brief and at times ironical. There is a hint at all the giddy dancing and ludicrous imitations he had to accompany when he writes about having seen Isadora Duncan perform and adds that he found her art genuine. One can almost hear a sigh of relief. For an Indian musician, dance and drama were inseparable from his own art. In *Minqar-é Musiqar,* his main work on music, he also discusses Kathak dance, diagramming the postures and explaining what they signify. Later, in London, one of the lighter topics when at dinner with admiring disciples was his animated recollections of the Russian ballet.[9]

Eventually, the Indian music group did land in its rightful place. Through their appearances in *Kismet* and the connection with Lucien Guitry they met the true artists of the era. There followed a period of unexpected popularity with society.

French society, the 'monde', was a relatively small group of people. Some men of art and letters were the rage, others were scorned socially. A singular atmosphere of decadence, melancholy and elegance prevailed, in which foreign celebrities were especially sought-after. The most perfect specimen of this genre was Gabriele D'Annunzio[9], the Italian author. He was always up to something faintly scandalous, his amorous exploits were whispered about with relish, and one time he had the organist of the Notre Dame play a concert especially for him, in the middle of the night. It is this rascally poseur, of all people, who has described, in one page, all the affected melancholy of that era, and the striking impression Inayat's singing made. The passage is from *Notturno,* written in 1915, while D'Annunzio, wounded in a flying mission, was in hospital, temporarily blinded, both eyes bandaged. The book begins with memories of friends and beloved. Soon, images and sounds from his youth take shape, he recalls an old man's song he once heard as a child; and then:

'Another song I recall to mind.[10]

It was at the house of Ilse, one wintry, eerie Paris evening.

The room was full of smoke, driven back through the glowing chimney by the wind outside. And the gooseflesh-fairy forbade the opening of windows.

Around a gilded wooden unicorn from the music-loving land of Burma, Alastair had been dancing one of his gothic dances, dressed in a blue tunic embroidered with gold. Amidst bronze deer and antelope and other nimble animals from the East, seemingly grazing on the carpet, a rhymer, dressed in purple like a bishop, had been celebrating a rhyming mass, his hair cut round in the style of Fra Angelico's tonsured holy priests. Reclining on low cushions, the lady of the house looked like a wax-figurine with enamelled eyes, betraying life only through a gently moving, delicately sculptured ankle, as a snake quietly beats its tail in love or fury.

It was one of those artificial hours, which folly, fancy and nostalgia conspire to brew, like three witches round a suspect potion.

But amidst so much hollowness and unreality were two primeval forces: the smoke, blown back by the wind, and Inayat Khan, the singer from India.

The woodsmoke killed the decadent fumes. Inayat's voice stilled the pretty moths and night-owls.

In vain the unicorn looked for a virgin lap in which to rest its proud head and sleep in the sweetness of humiliation. But through its legendary secret it seemed to contribute to the perfect stillness.

The singer sat quietly, as if the smoke came to him from the pyres at the ancestral river and could not harm his voice. He wore a robe of reddish yellow and a large amber-coloured turban. He held his brown hands outstretched upon his knees. A short black beard completed the oval of

117

his bronze face. The white of his eyes was purer than the shell of a dove's egg. And he sang with his mouth always open, modulating the tones in his throat.

He knew more than 500 ragas.

He was a fragile man, he was a wisp of a slender man, and his singing seemed to rise from the depths of the temple, to come from beneath the rocks, from beyond the inner caverns of the earth, and it seemed to gather in its sweep the longings of all generations of men, and the labour of all beginnings.

There were no more walls, no narrow chimney; there were no more phantoms, no masquerades, no lies. There was the smoke of the wood and sweat like jewels on the brow of the holy singer.

In the interval no one dared speak or say a word.

Inayat looked at me at the beginning of every song. He wanted to let me know that he sang for me alone.

For me alone he sang the chant from before the light, the song of the time before dawn, mysterious as the message of the wind sent over the sorrow of the earth by Him "Who is destined to let the Light grow." '

Of course, Inayat did not really play for Gabriele alone, but those who listened to him often had that impression. D'Annunzio must have also heard Inayat on other occasions: in one of his books,[11] he refers to the celebrated story of the lovers Majnun and Leila which Inayat often told as a parable, but which is almost unknown in the West. D'Annunzio knew Baroness D'Eichtal, one of the leaders of Inayat's French centre.

D'Annunzio was not the only one to remember the 'sacred singer' during the war. In 1917, a woman who was not to meet Inayat until 1925 was impressed by what she heard about him. It attracted and frightened her at the same time. There were others who were afraid of him. One French listener said, 'There is something overwhelmingly powerful about that man, he frightens me. I shall never go there again.' Another experienced the power of 'this restful being with shining eyes' as 'radiating peace and love.'

Some one else was not afraid: Ora Ray Baker. Neither Inayat's exceptional person nor her brother's threats alarmed her. The latter had forbidden her to communicate with Inayat and she probably did not even know that the brothers had left England for France. But one day she was dusting her brother's desk, and with lover's luck, she came across the address of the house of Maula Bakhsh. She wrote to Inayat by way of Baroda, which means it must have been at least three months before he received the letter. Then they were in touch once more.

On the 20th of March 1913, Inayat, having crossed to England alone, and Ora Ray Baker, daughter of Erastus Warner Baker, having escaped from her guardian in the States, married in London, in the Registrar's Office of St Giles. The bridegroom is registered as Inayat Khan Rahemat Khan Pathan, musician.[12] Soon afterwards he dropped the unhistorical western-style surname. An Indian Christian priest whom the pair met on the way had directed them to the registrar's office, and so Musharaff Khan thought some kind of Christian ceremony had been performed. When they arrived in Paris, Ali Khan, whom the brothers called mullah because he was a Moslem theologist, saw to a Moslem wedding.

Regardless of all these official and religious ties, half-brother Bernard called the police: American girl kidnapped by black man. The American girl, now called Amina-Begum, opened the door one afternoon to find police on her doorstep. She must return to America. Apparently she knew enough French to reply that she was married. She was told that she had to prove it.

The next morning her husband, that slender foreigner whose eyes saw in other worlds, went to the police station with the documents. The Frenchmen begged their pardon, glanced at Mr Bernard's request with a shrug: 'Qu'est-

ce qu'il veut.' The brothers had accompanied Inayat, they were rather upset; strange men had entered their house and had spoken to a woman of the Family. Such a thing could never have happened in India.

Perhaps this incident was one of the reasons why Inayat and his wife left France. They went to England while his brothers and Ramaswami were on tour in France and Belgium. A letter from a French pupil suggests they may have considered a trip to India but this did not materialize, and so Inayat's young wife who had lost the security of her American background also had to do without the experience of her husband's Indian culture. What awaited her now was the world of the followers, admiring and demanding. Inayat had warned her not to expect an easy life. In a poem entitled Struggle between Beloved and Duty she wrote 'Thou hast warned me of my duty, Which I can't forget.... For duty's sake, hence I am bound To this world of grief, An n'er untill I go to Thee, Shall I find relief.' This was said after his death, her duty then was to live on alone; but the later years of their life together, when her husband was either away or busy almost all the time, were difficult for her too. She found this even harder to bear than the poverty they had to cope with for some years.

In 1913 poverty was still far off, though they were sometimes short of money as artists will be. They travelled together and were surrounded by famous and important people. Just before they left France Inayat met Debussy.

Walter Rummel had been the go-between. This pianist knew Debussy well, was one of the Parisian in-crowd celebrities[13] — handsome, a foreigner, Isadora Duncan's lover — and had once composed a song called 'Ecstasy,' so both sides of Inayat's work appealed to him. Debussy's expression *'votre musicien-philosophe'* hints at this in his reply to Rummel's proposal that Inayat should play for him. This letter from Debussy[14] is dated 29th April 1913 and the passage runs as follows:

'A la réflexion, je crains d'abuser de votre remarquable musicien-philosophe en le faisant venir avec sa troupe en dehors de ses habitudes. Il me semble plus simple qu'un jour à son choix — vers 5 heures, qui me paraît être son heure — il vienne avec son frère.' ('On second thought, I do not wish to impose upon your remarkable musician-philosopher by summoning him here with his group at an unaccustomed hour. It would be simplest, I feel, if he and his brother were to come here on a day of his choice, at about five o'clock, which appears to be his usual time.')

As was often the case, the word philosopher meant something different to Debussy than to Inayat. For Inayat, philosophy was not 'having read all the books in the British Museum,' nor even the wisdom passed on through tradition, it was 'studying with one's soul' and observing life in all forms. More about this later; when he appeared before Debussy, it was as a musician. Debussy was one of the few who were aware that 'a rather ugly European feeling prevents us from appreciating it (eastern music)... That saves us the trouble of understanding it.'[17] Whenever there was a demonstration of Asian or African music at one of the world fairs, he would go to hear it. In 1908 he had composed *'Et la lune descend sur le temple qui fut,'* using melody in authentic Indian style. Now he took the opportunity to hear good Indian music in private, even if he did find the combination of music and philosophy a bit odd.

As yet, a letter with Debussy's comments on this private concert has not been found. Inayat does mention the meeting in his autobiography. Apparently Debussy later referred to the evening that the ragas were played for him as 'the evening of emotions.' And when they had finished, Musharaff Khan recalls, Debussy sat down at the piano and played, calling out titles that resembled the ragas' descriptive names. Indian songs are strictly tied to a certain time of day, and mood and atmosphere are indicated. Musharaff Khan recollects the names of the pieces Debussy played

121

that May evening as 'rainy season,' 'spring,' 'autumn;' modes and moods of nature, like so many of Debussy's titles. Whether these were improvisations, existing work, or some of his last, as yet unfinished preludes, no one will ever know.

I have gone into this in some detail, because the Sufis have a legend that certain of Debussy's works were inspired by Inayat. According to Monsieur Dietschy: 'Cependant, qu'il y ait eu, vers 1912-1915, de la musique hindoue dans l'air, autour de Debussy, on ne peut en douter. J'observe en page 7 de la partition de LA BOITE A JOUJOUX ces mots: 'vieux chant hindou qui sert, de nos jours encore, à apprivoiser les éléphants.' LOCKSPEISER a d'ailleurs la copie de quelques mesures d'un 'drame indien' qui devait se rapporter à Bouddha.' ('There was certainly some Hindu music in the air around Debussy between 1912 and 1915. On page 7 of the score of LA BOITE A JOUJOUX we find the words: 'old Hindu song with which, up to the present day, one tames elephants.' Besides. Lockspeiser has a copy of a few measures for a proposed 'Indian play' about Buddha.')[15]

What Inayat felt about Debussy's music is not clear. He seldom spoke of European music, except to say that an Indian has difficulty learning to appreciate western singing. 'A man from the East went to the opera, and just as he had accustomed himself to the soprano doing her best, a tenor came and interrupted her.'[16] Until 1920 he did not feel qualified to judge western music. After that, it had become so familiar that he could understand what Indian music lacked to the European. He liked Händel, Bach less so. His brothers learned to sing the lyric tenor aria's and he greatly enjoyed Mozart operas and the old Italian schools. His favourite types of concert were singing and solo performances. Of his contemporaries he highly respected Scriabine, whom he met personally, but that respect perhaps applied to Scriabine's ideas rather than to his music.

This was mutual. Of Scriabine we know[26] that he was impressed by Inayat's grandeur and calm. One of his remarks is recorded alike by Ssabaneev and Inayat himself: 'That is just what's missing in our impoverished narrow life, a culture of that kind.' But Ssabaneev also tells us that Scriabine expressed some hesitation about Indian music. Although he sensed its ardour and 'some hidden elements eluding us,' he thought he had to go to India and meet a Hindu Yogi to find the real thing. He considered Islam too easy a religion and feared its mysticism was also too easy to accept.

In Debussy Inayat recognized above all a man greater than those around him, and therefore often misunderstood. When speaking on conformism, Inayat says that even Scriabine's teacher Taneiev did not understand Debussy's music.[17] 'It seems that we are restricted by uniformity so that there is no scope.... Painters and musicians cannot get their work recognized. They must follow the crowd, instead of following the great souls. And everything that is general is commonplace.' Debussy himself said something very similar: 'That which entertains bad taste is mediocrity.'[17]

Inayat and Debussy probably met again in June 1914 at the International Music Congress in Paris, on which occasion the idea for an Indian opera with lyrics by D'Annunzio may have been born.[15] In the year that lay between these two meetings, the remarkable musician-philosopher became a celebrity in his own right.

The summer of 1913 he spent in London. These were lively months, packed with visitors and hard work. Westerners looked to him for his music and for his 'eastern wisdom,' while Indians came for advice. Apparently, in the eyes of the anglicized Indian community, his marriage had promoted him to the status of 'one of us' and the couple were invited everywhere. Sometimes a date had to be changed, as Amina-Begum was pregnant. Among the notes preserved are two or three from Sarojini Naidu, who may have met Inayat in his Hyderabad days; this summer found her working enthusiastically for better understanding between Hindus and Moslems.[18]

These finer points of Indian politics must have escaped Amina-Begum. She did what she could to become Indian and even wore a veil when she went out, though she did not keep that up for long, as some Europeans were sharply critical of it. Indians in India, had they known, would have criticized her for accompanying her husband to tea parties and dinners. She had a very busy life and a lot to learn. There was a regular exchange of letters with the brothers on the continent: she needed advice on some matter concerning Professor's turban, they sent her slippers, enquired about a manuscript and about the work. 'Take care of Professor,' one of the brothers wrote. And they were glad the couple had so many Indian friends.

Mr and Mrs Inayat Khan were also in demand with western artists and their life was hectic. Just as when on tour in America with Ruth St Denis, Inayat crammed lectures into every spare moment. A veena pupil asked 'Professor and Mrs Khan' to tea, for there was a Finnish dancer who would come especially to meet him. 'I know Professor to go to Mrs Thomson Price's at home this afternoon, so tell him to bring his veena with him and from here you both can go to her at about 5 o'clock.'

This note from an Indian lady was directed to Amina-Begum, because Inayat was incredibly absent-minded about such ordinary things. They simply did not interest him. After a hard day's work he would still spend hours meditating at night; he practised veena in the evenings and singing in the mornings, This was not always popular with the neighbours, though his wife writes that 'his music at home is much more effective than that of outside.'

There are some reviews of his public appearances in that period,[19] for instance one with a description of Inayat as 'a young man of a striking personality, possessed of glowing and eloquent eyes, and strangely deliberate and sedate in his bearing.'

The reviewer goes on to give Inayat's definition of Sufism: freedom of the soul, with music as a means to the highest spiritual goal. Another article, probably an interview, demonstrates the general ignorance about Indian music and it becomes clear that Inayat's knowledge of the West is still defective. In the first half we find a vague and incomplete description of the veena, and in the second half a vague and improbable announcement from Inayat that he and his brothers have been summoned to appear before the royal court in St Petersburg by the Russian Czar. There was, in fact, a Russian tour arranged for them, but what awaited them was anything but a court performance. The Royal Musicians of Hindustan, however, were accustomed to being personally invited by the local sovereigns and so they unthinkingly expected something of the same sort in other countries still governed by royalty.

But there were other western things that Inayat had absorbed and started incorporating into his work. He had gained respect as a musician and as a person, but he had come across few Occidentals who understood what was meant by freedom of the soul. And so, he took a step that went against his natural mistrust of bookishness: he wrote a book.

Bjerregaard's Omar Khayyam book — actually a haphazard version of Inayat's Sufism — had not yet been released. The first edition of R. A. Nicholson's *Mystics of Islam* was published in 1914. Since no authorised initiate of Sufism had written a special work on the subject, Inayat says in the preface to his first English book, on request of many European and American friends 'I have written these few pages as an introduction... I hope this may help in establishing goodwill among mankind and friendly understanding between nations.'[20]

This book was a turning-point in his career and critical in the shaping of his message for the West. His *Autobiography* states that he had great difficulty in finding a form suitable and intelligible for western ears. Writing a book must have been a hard decision. In the past Sufi masters had sometimes put their theories and experiences in writing, but Inayat knew all too well how soon ideas could fossilize once they were printed. After all the point was not to collect ideas, but to make them into a reality. His own master had greeted pencil and notebook with silence, and many a restless, pencil-scratching and paper-rustling European audience had been gently rebuked by this anecdote. But now he knew enough of the West to realise that a book got through to many people. Besides, one cannot practise what one does not know. It was also important to eliminate misunderstandings, be they of the romantic or the rationalist kind.

In many ways this book is different from his later works, which are almost all collections of speeches. There are some elements of a lecture in *A Sufi Message of Spiritual Liberty* too, but the book is arranged in an oriental way: short chapters adorned with quotations. Amidst fragments of Rumi and Saadi a sudden line from Balzac stands out. Of course Inayat, whose French was perfunctory, had not read Balzac, but he always willingly let friends draw his attention to remarks by western authors that were consonant with his own ideas. The language of this 1913 book still has a more eastern flavour than in his later lectures, which were increasingly adapted to western ears, and increasingly adapted to the specific needs of his audience. This first book is a more comprehensive survey of the theories he himself had learned eight years previously, and it contains the essence of his later work.

Many people helped him in bringing about the book. It was written in English, translated into French, and first published in Russian in 1914.

In those days culture and travel flowed freely between Russia and Western Europe. Those reading newspapers with an eye to politics sympathised with the liberal opposition to the Czar, a wife-ridden autocratic weakling compared to whom Louis XVI was sensible and broad-minded. Communists and anarchists excited fear and in a few, romantic admiration. But culturally the links between Western Europe and the Czarist empire were strong. Those Russians who could afford it set out to see France, Italy and England. Lucien Guitry lived in Russia for years. Debussy visited there in 1913 and Scriabine held concerts in London that winter. Decadent *fin de siècle* artists abounded, as well as ardent and hungry idealists. Music and drama were almost vital necessities and hundreds flocked to the theatres and concert halls of Moscow and St Petersburg, even when the country suffered from the disasters of war. In Moscow the atmosphere was a shade freer and a bit more tolerant of criticism than in St Petersburg, which had the unhappy court on its back. The students were restless, the people full of possibilities but unformed; they cracked jokes, or resigned themselves, or went in for serious and sometimes dangerous philosophy — the secret police was never far away — or they joined peculiar religious sects. There was a small well-to-do middle class living almost like the aristocracy: frequent trips to Western Europe, daily visits to the theatre or salons; much dabbling in theosophy, Tagore and the ubiquitous Omar Khayyam; dreaming and scheming to change the world.[21]

But it was neither world-reformers, nor sects, nor even theosophists that had engaged the Royal Musicians of Hindustan. It was the nightclub Maxim.

The name Maxim was in international use for the more frivolous places of entertainment, as a child could have told the Khan brothers. But what was self-evident to a Westerner was not necessarily so to Indian-bred Indians.

127

Their employers also must have had vague delusions about some kind of primitive folk music. The Russians were not only fond of opera, concerts and ballet, but the fashionable gadabouts often had a fling at gypsies, and the tango was in vogue. Who knows what sultry oriental stuff the nightclub had in mind.

Playing his music amidst popping champagne bottles really distressed Inayat. If he had known this, he would not have come. In India artists sometimes had to enliven an evening of the nautch girls (dancers) and that was bad enough. But it was just as with the difference between eastern and western thieves: in the East he knew how to carry himself with easy condescension in the face of licentiousness, and the style, even there, was modelled on courtliness. Here in Moscow there was a deliberate debauchery that was completely foreign to him. It was a test, and scarcely an amusing one, but courageously he calls it 'interesting to observe how different people changed their every day pitch.... It showed me how the dream of life has absorbed so many of them.... But God's glory is everywhere.' Here, as in the Burmese robbers' den, it was a challenge to find the spark of God hidden deep beneath the coarsest façade. His spirit stood the test; outwardly, this was one of the most painful humiliations he had to bear in all his wanderings.

After that initial shock, the months spent in Russia were among the happiest and most successful in his pre-war career. The nightclub guests were none other than those who frequented the concerts, salons, social clubs and philosophical circles.

In later years Sergei Lwovic Tolstoi, a son of the great Leo Tolstoi, still told within the family circle that he and his friend Ivanov had discovered Inayat 'in a very common restaurant.' In spite of these surroundings they were 'very much impressed' and soon organized public lectures and concerts and helped publish Inayat's books. And so it came about that the grandson of Maula Bakhsh met the leading musicians of Moscow, right up to the haughty and unapproachable Scriabine, who, after meeting him for the first time in Ivanov's *salon,* attended one of the Indian's public concerts and afterwards invited him for a talk at his own house. The first meeting was in January, the latter two at the end of April.

In between Inayat had met many other well-known Russians. A dinner was organised so that he could hear Chaliapin. Ivanov's wife translated Inayat's lectures. The poet Ivanov, very famous in his day, was a strange character, in love with his melancholy. Many of the culture-steeped and restlessly searching Russians were just as decadent as the Indian princes and the Parisian *beau monde.* But they had some things the Parisians lacked and these appealed to Inayat: their Asian touch, the earnestness of their searching; their mystical streak, which was much stronger in the people than among the priests — a fact observed by the Indian Inayat and the French diplomat Paléologue in almost identical words.

Moscow was covered with snow, it gleamed and sparkled in the frosty air. And yet, something reminded him of his own sweltering India. In the winter, and even more in the ensuing pale green spring, there was something oriental about Moscow. There were more than 1600 churches, with blue-green domes, and guilded and silver spires, like the minarets and domes of Hyderabad. There was luxury and sophistication; rare gems glinted at festivities of almost oriental splendour. And unconcealed, stark poverty reeked from the open pubs and flop-houses.

It was a far cry from hyperintellectual Paris; the Russians were a fiercely emotional people. American commercialism was still in its infancy and had hardly gained ground in Moscow, the 'moral and political capital;' the cool reserve with which visitors from the East were treated in London was totally absent. And everywhere there were sounds and

129

music, the 1600 church-bells mingled their deep booms or tinkling tones with the jingle of sleigh- and horse-bells. Even the traffic confusion was almost like home. And the clear wintery air always carried a pungent whiff of straw and horse-dung.

But there were differences. In India, even the lowest levels of the population were clearly defined and regulated; the masses of Russia were adrift in a shapeless void. India's poor were passive, Russia seethed, and not the intelligentsia alone. To Inayat's surprise, the streets were full of priests and monks, but it soon became obvious that these were not a western equivalent of holy men and faqirs. Nowhere did he find such hypocrisy and bigotry as in Russia.[22] Still, it was here that he found a few people he really enjoyed talking to.

One of the discussions is described by Musharaff Khan[22] and Inayat's autobiography relates how a Finnish philosopher, Dr E. W. Lybeck, took him to friends whose names he did not wish to disclose. It was in the evening and 'we drove in a sleigh, a thing I always enjoyed, especially if the air was dry.' They stopped in front of a mysterious building, were hustled inside, and immediately the gates fell shut behind them. But this was no robbers' den, as he had encountered five years ago in Rangoon; he was surrounded by priests and monks who did not introduce themselves and straight away started questioning him about his ideas. He began to explain gently. 'If I transcended the limits of their religious conventionalities I found them slightly chilled, but I have never seen such comprehensive minds, only they did not understand how truth in such a perfect form could exist outside their church.' But they asked sensible questions and did not run on pointlessly about some pet idea after the answer had been given.[23]

The guarded secrecy and locked doors were not surprising in Russia where the secret police kept a watchful eye on every conceivable kind of meeting and were always ready to make arrests. Inayat was privileged with a spy of his own, who approached him after one of his lectures. He introduced himself as Henry Balakin, officer, and confessed that he had been sent to observe the goings-on. But what he had heard and felt — Inayat's presence conveyed much more than the words he spoke — had moved him so deeply that he wished to be initiated. 'If the master would forgive him.' 'You serve your government and I serve mine (God),' Inayat answered and he accepted Balakin as a disciple. It was through the latter's mediation that the book on spiritual liberty could be published, 'in a place where even for the printing of a visiting card,' Inayat wrote, 'one had to get the permission of the police.'

The newspaper announcements usually contained a programme. The police must have thought a concert ending with 'Song of the Sufis, the Soul's Search for Freedom,' worth spying on. The rest of the concert was a historical survey of Indian music. Inayat's brothers have kept a few reviews, especially those which showed appreciation of the music as an art and as a spiritual experience. But the performances were also regarded in scholarly western fashion, as interesting demonstrations. According to the *Russkya Vedomosti*[24] for instance the speaker (Inayat) was clear and to the point. This critic had preferred the songs and the ensemble playing to the solos of the 'folk instruments.' 'In the overcrowded hall the audience applauded for Mr Inayat Chan and his friends.' For the next advertisement a month later, his name was set in large type and the cheapest seats were sold out first, which means that the perennially poor students of Russia were coming too. And finally: 'Repeat Performance on Saturday, May 3rd, before leaving Russia. An evening of Hindu music by the singer-poet INAYAT CHAN.'

A Russian translation of his Hindustani poems had been published, hence perhaps the label 'singer-poet.' During those months he also spent some time on a play about Shiva, with music. For the European arrangement of the music he had the help of Sergei Lvovic Tolstoi. Shiva was the Hindu god of destruction and renewal and seems aptly chosen for a country on the verge of upheaval. Unfortunately the text has been lost.

Another feature of the advertisements is that the title 'Professor' was soon dropped. This could be due to a number of things; perhaps he had discovered that the rank given him by the Music Academy of Baroda could be misconstrued when there were so many quacks decking themselves out with a turban and the false respectability of 'Professor.' But probably it was simply because the title 'Khan' carried its full import in Russia. There was a Moslem community in Moscow, and its leader, Bey Beg, organised for Inayat a memorable musical evening. Bey Beg was a Tartar. The Tartars were respected among the Russian melange of tribes and nations. Noble families, such as the Yussupovs, were proud of their Tartar descent. In America, the four men from Baroda had been coloured people; in England, natives; in France, foreigners; here, they were Khans. Bey Beg's musical evening, ringing with the music of Turks, Tartars, Siberians, Bokharians, Persians was like a dream; 'a vision of home and yet not home.... something far from my knowledge and yet so near to it.'

The brothers had never ceased longing for home, and when the ambassador of Bokhara suggested that they go home with him and return to India by way of his country, they could hardly resist the temptation. But Henry Balakin, the secret service man, dissuaded them. Ramaswami later took the overland route home, but apparently Moslems were not allowed to travel through Russian Moslem territory. Staying in Europe was made easier on them by news that reached them in Moscow: Maheboob Khan's wife, chosen for him just before he left for the West, had died in 1913. The last tie of obligation to the family had been cut.

They detached themselves from home, and from Uncle Alauddin, whose example had left its mark so deeply on their fate. It was in Moscow that Inayat called a ceremonial meeting of his brothers and cousin to decide on his proposal that they should stop accepting money from home. They did not need it, because they were now reasonably well off, but still, the decision was not an easy one. To live off their music, selling it like merchandise, meant heavy westernization. But it was a declaration of independance from their uncles, a decision in favour of freedom, and they never went back on it, not even during the war, when they were sometimes very hard up. Once a certain relationship to certain people was established, it could only be altered by a ceremonial decision. When Maheboob and Ali Khans switched to a different teacher of western music a few years later, the same procedure was followed.

There was another, professional, reason why they could not go to India in the spring of 1914; they were to play at the international music conference in Paris in June. And lastly, in the warm reception by the Russian public − who were easily inflammable, as he later realized − Inayat saw new possibilities for carrying out his task.

He still took his mission quite literally and tried to bring people consciousness of God through music. Consciousness of God meant rediscovery of one's own dormant inner potential. It was only in the course of the war, in 1917, that he began to realize the figurative import of his murshid's words 'bring harmony to the world by the harmony in your soul.' One indication that he was still taking this literally was his extraordinary plan to approach the Czar through music.

Inayat must have noticed something of the unrest and discontent that pervaded Russia. The Moscow intelligentsia took no pains to hide their opinions and there had been his own personal encounter with the secret police. He did have a tendency to idealize the Russians because of the close similarities with home, but one of these close similarities was the activity of anarchists. In 1908 one of Inayat's former classmates had been arrested and sentenced for making bombs. 'Young people are enthusiastic and strong, they want to do things.'[25]

This he could understand. But there was one difference between the Indian and the Russian political rebels: the latter revolted against their own government and their own sovereign.

Few people saw what was coming, but everyone who did not belong to the Czarina's camarilla, and certainly the highbrows of Moscow were desperate about the Czar and the ruinous people with whom he surrounded himself. Keenly observant Inayat must have detected something of what was going on in the third class public bath he frequented and in the crowded gallery at his concerts. But what he understood were people and their fundamental feelings; he never really came to grips with other than Indian political affairs. In Russia, where there was so much to remind him of his idealized India, he could not resist seeing the Czar as a sort of Nizam or Gaekwar. It took him years to realize that western kings, even if they headed the state church, like King George and the unhappy Nicholas II, were no mystics. In the war that followed he sadly discovered that 'the King of England was not interested in India for its art, poetry, philosophy or music.' And he said of Russia that the bigotry of the Orthodox Church stood in the way of the highest spiritual awakening: 'I enjoyed everything, except the bigotry.'

And yet − he remembered how he had moved the Nizam, and how only three years ago the Maharaja of Sylhet had asked him to become murshid at his court. And liking the Russian public, 'warm people in a cold land' who seemed to grasp what he was aiming at, he imagined that he could influence the Czar through his message (of spiritual freedom!) in the guise of music.

134

Apparently others too thought it possible. The *Autobiography* states that Sergei Tolstoi intended to help and introduce the singer to the Czar, but that meant waiting for three months and 'I could not wait, for I was to represent Indian music at the musical congress in Paris in 1914.'

When he said that the meeting might be arranged in three months' time, Sergei Tolstoi was probably thinking of the Czarist family's summer stay in the Crimea. There, the chance of approaching them might be slightly better than in the air-tight St Petersburg palace.

There was no more leisurely summer in the Crimea coming. Before the three months were up, the whole world had changed and half a continent lay between Inayat and his Russian dream.

But they took one warm bit of reality with them from that strange country. When the family left for France at the end of May 1914, after a flying visit to St Petersburg – a concert or a final effort to catch a glimpse of the Czar? – their party, now minus Ramaswami, numbered as many as when they had come. On January 2nd 1914 (Christmas by the Russian Calender) a daughter was born to Inayat and Amina-begum. Noor-un-Nisa was her name, but Babuli, father's child, she was called at home, and indeed she took after him. Behind her shy exterior she concealed the same versatile giftedness, idealism, strength, and fixity of purpose. There is a biography of Noor-un-Nisa written in 1950 by Jean Overton Fuller. For this descendant of the secluded women in the house of Maula Bakhsh worked for the British as a wireless operator during World War II. For a time, between July and October 1945, hers was almost the only radio link with occupied France; then she was betrayed, taken prisoner and executed – a heroine of an exceptional kind. But when she as a six-month-old baby girl, with her fair-haired mother and dark-skinned father and uncles travelled to France by way of Germany, where she would later meet her death, World War I had not yet begun. The Parisian *monde* still lived on art and gossip, not on politics. It was summer, but the international music congress drew large audiences. The main attraction was European music; the ethnomusicological demonstrations, regarded as a side issue were organized by Debussy's friend Laloy. Possibly Debussy and D'Annunzio hatched their joint idea for a play about Buddha at this time.

It looked as though the Musicians of Hindustan would continue their travels through Europe, earning their living by music. At the congress they were invited to give a series of concerts in Germany during the next season.

That was late June 1914. Two months later German cannons were pointing at Paris. At the end of August the Khan family hastily retreated to London, leaving all the Russian and American trophies and the entire collection of Indian records behind. One of the last things Inayat saw was Sarah Bernard, reciting the Marseillaise, simply; 'that was all; but when she appeared on the stage and recited this poem, she would win every heart in the audience, for at that time she was France.'[27]

An epoch had come to an end.

This was also the end of Inayat's second period of training. He had come as a stranger and now, for all his nostalgia, he had so absorbed the West that the Marseillaise moved him when France was in distress.

His next task was to give his message a form the West could understand and apply. Finding this form, as he himself testified, was difficult indeed. In London he would have all of six years for his search, the war and the two years that followed. For the time being, his wanderings were over.

Chapter VIII (1914-1920)
From musician to Murshid

Having drawn full halls in Russia and France, back in England Inayat had to face empty rooms for a few months. 'The war had paralyzed people's minds, it was like cultivating a desert.' One English poet in those days made bold to go on writing, and when this was frowned upon he remarked, 'I am working for this culture everybody is fighting for.'

Something similar happened to Inayat when he used the word peace and was told in reply that for the time being it was a case of 'kill or be killed.' He was far from irenic and not even a pacifist; such an answer was another of the hundreds of misunderstandings resulting from the inevitable use of over-worked and worn-out phrases. His concern about humanity and what would become of it went much deeper than that of the politicians. When he spoke of peace he meant the tranquillity and resilience that are the result of meditation. He who possesses that balance will not start a fight and if attacked he has untold resources.

Nearly all through the war he had to draw on his own deep reserves. Time and again he was misunderstood, disappointed, deceived and even opposed. He suffered from it, yet maintained his inner power and grew under the very pressure. A photo of December 1914 shows him cheerful and serene, although he writes that he could not forget the time when he spoke for no more than a few persons. He lived, acted and reacted on two planes of existence.

He was not the only one in London to cultivate deserts. The town was full of spiritual societies and mini-societies. One of these groups called itself 'Higher Thought.' Inayat was amused at this pretentious name, 'which suggested that any other thought was low compared to theirs.' But he courteously co-operated with them, ignoring the high-thinking ladies' gossip and allowing them to advertise in his magazine.

In spite of everything this magazine, *Sufi*, was launched within six months. After the first shock life in London had resumed its normal course. From the beginning a Zeppelin attack had been feared, but those who had no close relations at sea or overseas, could almost forget the war.[1] Though a poet had been frowned upon for writing poetry, concerts and theatres were attended as usual and charity shows for Belgian refugees or wounded servicemen provided artists with a part in the war-effort.

In the first numbers of the magazine mention is made of a fund for orphans, and of assistance to Indian students in the West. The former bears the stamp of the western co-workers, who had Amina-Begum, too, knitting for charitable purposes; the latter was more in the spirit of the brothers and their Indian friends. But what was more important, Inayat and his brothers were asked to perform for the wounded at charity concerts; they did. The Indians, for tactical reasons, had declared themselves ready to support the British in the war, just as they had done fourteen years earlier in South Africa. In August Gandhi had successfully returned from there and, with other leaders, had recommended this attitude.

Inayat sang for Gandhi once, a song of which Musharaff Khan approximately remembered the text: 'The sigh of the poor will never be in vain. If blowing a dead animal's skin (a bellows) turns iron into ashes (can melt iron), what will be the effect of the poor man's sigh.' This is a song of Kabir, slightly altered; he sang in Gujarati, which was Gandhi's native tongue too, and Gandhi was moved to tears, which startled the organisers so much that they requested the singer not to repeat the song. The releasing

138

London, 1917. Inayat with his veena.

effect of tears was forgotten in the land of the stiff upper lip; the gentlemen were either embarassed or afraid that it would harm Gandhi's health, which was not too good at that time. He returned to India in December and as he was not, like Tagore, a personal friend, the meeting had little further consequence. Except perhaps an invitation to give some concerts for the Royal Asiatic Society. For this organisation which concerned itself chiefly with the distant past, these concerts of 'modern Indian music' were a novelty.[2]

One of the concerts was attended by a Dutch singer who later became the wife of the Javanese dancer Raden Mas Jodjana. She was so fascinated that she wondered how she could approach the musicians. She did not have to try. The next day she gave one of her weekly lessons at 100 Addison Road, just off Holland Park Avenue. Her pupil, who lived on the first floor, took her downstairs, to meet the family living there. 'They are Indians, nice people, and so interesting.'

The Indians had overheard her singing upstairs and the head of the family asked her to teach western music to the 'boys.' They were Ali and Maheboob Khans. She readily consented, and at the same time was accepted as a student of Indian music with Inayat.

The house lay quiet, just out of the rattling traffic on the main road, but the few rooms on the ground floor were crowded. Apart from housing five grown-ups and a baby they had to serve for lectures and receptions. Sometime in 1915 the family moved to a three storied house in its own grounds, 86 Ladbroke Road, now north of Holland Park Avenue.

Apart from Indian friends, mostly Moslems, Westerners too found their way to Inayat's dwelling. The future Raden Aju Jodjana — then Madame de Ravalieu — remembers the faithful of the first hour, a motley crowd. There was old Mr Linzie, the English version of a dervish, in oddly assorted clothes and with strings for shoelaces. He was so

140

poor that the family shared their own poverty with him and invited him to their meals; the same food every day, rice and dahl (lentils).

The opposite of Mr Linzie, who sometimes fell asleep during the lectures and afterwards came to say thank you because it had been so beautiful, was Edmund Russell, the same man who in America had made their first contacts possible. He was rich and restful and his eyes had the open and at the same time inward look of one who lives in and by meditation. This was true also of Lucy Goodenough, the half-Austrian devotee who became a permanent, loyal helper. Mary Williams, the first English disciple, a parson's daughter, was nervous and active, an energetic worker. Then there was a young lady who had to keep her visits to Indians and her Indian music lessons a secret from her family; her name was Rose Benton and she rather fancied herself. Finally the Raden Aju remembers a poetess, a Jewish lady who worked very hard. That was Miriam Regina Bloch,[3] who worked with Inayat on his second book and helped him with the publication of his magazine.

The first issue appeared in February 1915. The greatest difficulties were over for the time being. Inayat again gave several lectures with music for the Asiatic Society and sang for wounded Indian soldiers. Sometimes his performance coincided with that of a juggler, sometimes with a visit from the Queen. But he was noticed, encored, there were interviews. His aims were described ('Society to unite the faiths. Ambitious!') as well as his person, his rooms ('a Georgian room with eastern objects, somewhat incongruous'), his family and his contacts. What he had said to Sir Henry Newbolt at a dinner party was reported. Sir Henry had adressed him as 'my dear ally.' Inayat turned the conversation towards brotherhood and did not encourage any more questions regarding the war. The interviewer caught on gracefully; 'the handsome, serious, olive-skinned gentleman with the quiet eyes, shining black hair and beard, and the dignified bearing' had contributed to the good relations between East en West by marrying a very beautiful American girl, and concluded his portrait with 'He is completely free from affectation, he does not pose or wish to allow others to give him the pose of a master surrounded by adoring disciples.' Even for the interweaving of music and philosophy this journalist showed understanding. He signed himself F. M. A. and as far as I can gather he did not belong to the immediate Sufi circle.[4]

From his own countrymen Inayat did not always get so much understanding. The Hindus especially thought it unbecoming that, during the interval of a concert, Mary Williams and even the brothers offered the magazine for sale. Inayat in his turn remarked sadly that of many Indians one would not say they belonged to a religious people. Yet, a few of them remained loyal friends to the end. One was the leader of the London Brahmo Samaj, another the Hindu colonel who had accompanied Musharaff Khan on his voyage to the West. Good Moslem friends were Yusuf Ali, a member of the Royal Asiatic Society and especially Khwaja Ismail, a lawyer who in 1920 still wrote from Hyderabad. During the war he came to help with the cooking whenever there was a 'dervish dinner.' Ali Khan who did the shopping, was indignantly shocked one day to find that a certain brand of margarine contained lard, which was not mentioned on the label.

The further preparation for a 'dervish dinner' consisted in spreading a large, borrowed, table cloth on the floor. The guests had to sit around it, also on the floor. That took some doing for ladies in corsets and long-legged men in stiff collars, and many avoided a repetition. But a regular nucleus remained, not only of initiated disciples, but especially of interested outsiders who, unlike the King, did take an interest in India because of its culture. Some of the well-known English men and women among them also appear in other Indian biographies; they include Sir Edwin

Lutyens, the architect of New Delhi, and Lady Lutyens; Lady Lutyens was a rather original and, for that time, progressive theosophist. Lord Lamington, ex-governor of Bombay, too, generally maintained his relations with Indians and he really did have a knowledge of Indian music.

The music, apparently, was flourishing again. Artist friends from America, France and Russia were loyal too and through them Inayat was engaged for the opera *Lakmé*, in a well defined separate item on the programme. The critiques said all one could wish for: 'The interpolations decidedly add to the brilliance of the whole scene and to the vitality of the drama. The Indian music... was of remarkably interesting type as sung by Inayat Khan and his three colleagues who accompanied themselves upon native instruments, which we make no attempt to describe. But if we knew to whom fell the amazing vocal cadenzas that were reeled off as if veritable child's play, we would certainly name the highly accomplished singer.'[4]

The diligent ones among his disciples, especially Mary Williams, now saw to it that the real music should not be associated with the imitation dances which embellished this opera too. They wrote letters to the press, encouraged interviewers and took advantage of the interest by organizing lectures on Indian music. The reviews of the lectures are even more interesting than the praise of the singing. The critics were fascinated as well as sceptical. One of them discovered that we Westerners know next to nothing of Sufi philosophy and said that the lecturer ought to take into account the limitations of the audience. Another admits that the foreign philosopher may be right in what he said, but will not make many 'converts,' 'as the influence of generations cannot be counteracted by reasoning — not easily at least.' In spite of their doubts the reviewers advised their reader to make a point of attending the lectures, which were, anyhow, interesting.

It looked as though even in England, even in war time,

Inayat would become as renowned as in France and Russia. There were plans to engage him and his orchestra to play for the Indian frontline troops. Meanwhile there was the prospect of another charity performance, a matinee in the New Theatre on 8th July 1915 in aid of widows and orphans of Indians killed in action. This matinee was organized by the Islamic Society.

Here the brothers sang as Indians among Indians. They talked as Indians among Indians. They were Britain's allies, 'one of us,' as Sir Henry Newbolt had suggested, 'brothers, really, deep down' as Inayat would say. But there was also a surface existence. All around them they heard the language they usually only spoke amongst themselves. Everyone said what he thought. One could make jokes about 'the people here.' Perhaps Inayat felt that he could remind his countrymen abroad of their own culture. And perhaps he was swept away by the general mood which was naturally anti-British. He had often written songs calling on his countrymen of all faiths to understand each other. Now he took one of those and changed it in such a way that it could be taken for a rebel song.[5]

> 'Call yourself Hindu or Moslem, Christian or Parsi,
> the world calls you by one name: Hindu.
> Whether you are a king or a pauper,
> where is the old respect, where the old glory?
> Where is the old wisdom, where the knowledge?
> Should Rama worship Hanuman?
> What kind of religion would that be?'

The allusion is orientally subtle: the world is topsy-turvy, we are worthy, respect is due to us, we must co-operate (or we must unite) against those blockheads who cannot even tell us apart, who are less worthy than we are. His audience understood him very well, the improvisation was a thundering success. Rarely did he find such appreciation among his countrymen.

But it meant good-bye to the chances for a whole string of concerts. The British Government was watching its Indians. Though the leaders had pledged their loyalties, there were always some conspiracies and 'seditious pamphlets' turning up. The Moslems presented a new problem. For them Turkey had been 'the last bulwark' of Islamic power and culture, and this Turkey had become Germany's ally, Britain's enemy. Moslem loyalty to the British could only be formal. It was a time of strain on all fronts, the time of the Somme offensive, the Dardanelles, and the submarine war. The Royal Musicians of Hindustan need not count on any more employment in the service of the British.

After this incident, the result of which was years of poverty, they scrupulously stayed away from all politics and avoided giving any opinion on the subject. Naturally Inayat wanted freedom for India and with his gifts he could have become a revered leader. The much more difficult and in a sense opposite task of bringing people and nations together weighed more heavily with him. His master had told him to harmonize people and he abided by this instruction, and so did his brothers. They did not try to go back to India, not even when threatened with poverty.

Utter poverty. Musharaff Khan, now a slender young man of 19, unsuccessfully tried one whole summer to find work, even as a road-worker — nobody would employ him. To introduce himself he used the best he could think of, a photo in court costume; the prospective employers may have gasped. Maheboob Khan was blessed with a student of music who had a piano with quarter tones built and played unbearable compositions on it, in the belief that she was creating Indian music.

Material relief came, the disciples did not desert the family. But the result was an embarassing dependence on the good givers, who cheerfully began to organize and lay down the law. They pinned up lists of speakers and programmes and, in spite of all their admiration for the East and their personal saint, they demanded western behaviour. Rose Benton, very tactfully she thought, presented a beautifully bound engagement book and put it in the hall. She faithfully noted down her appointments, but it made no difference, as nobody else opened the book. The good lady could never be sure of always finding the master when she wanted to.

Later Inayat trained himself to keep appointments and became used to it, though mistakes continued to occur. This was partly a difference of cultural customs, but he was aware that his being increasingly more at home in other worlds made him too indifferent to ordinary affairs. 'Indifference, my most intimate friend, I am sorry I have always to act against thee as thy opponent.'[6] Indifference here means detachment, not being bound inwardly to everyday affairs.

The difficulty was that neither he nor his disciples had any example to go by. They were creating something new. An Indian master accepts disciples or does not and that is that. He can travel through the world and his disciples will follow him; or he can stay in one place and his fame will attract people. But Inayat's disciples did not stay with him, there was no stratum of western society that would as a matter of course proclaim the existence of a master, and Westerners in general did not know what discipleship was. Inayat himself was rooted in his eastern experience but aspired to something else: to give at least something to as many people as possible. And he understood that this could not be done without an organisation. It was one more western reform and sometimes the results were excellent, but the form of the organisation and the officiousness of some committee members always brought problems and pain.

146

'In the West there are no pupils, only teachers,' he said ironically. He felt as if he were constructing a building with incomplete and imperfect tools and unskilled labourers; he included in this his own imperfect knowledge of western customs. Yet, through seeking and trying he founded the three institutions through which he would eventually and permanently reach the West: the so-called brotherhood, the actual inner school for initiates, and the Church of All or Universal Worship. When he noticed how often he was misunderstood or misinterpreted, he — probably stimulated by his surroundings — began to draw up lists of ideas and aims. Between 1915 and 1918 the wording was frequently changed. Sometimes the 'disciples' doctored them too, which is evident from the style, the corrections and the elucidations that the tutored master added. Inayat's own style was direct, concise, natural; his English shows grammatical and spelling mistakes, but he was able to express clearly what was clear in his mind. The style of his first followers, and generally of that period, was flowery, verbose and vague. The ten Sufi thoughts and the three objects which have not been changed since 1918 bear the stamp of the period in the choice of words and abundance of capital letters. In 1915 Inayat started with seven thoughts and five objects. Style brief and direct.

The thoughts were called teachings at the time, a word Inayat substituted later because it gave rise to dogmatism. This danger he sensed in 1915 already for his second 'tenet' said 'Never be enslaved by principles.' For his daily behaviour Inayat, true son of his father, did recognize principles, 'to keep to in prosperity as well as in adversity.'[7] But he could consciously and, if necessary with a solemn announcement, deviate from them. He was not the slave of any idea and he never imposed upon anyone. A principle is a guide, not a ruler. 'All things are not good for every person, nor right at all times' he would continue to say in various keys. But the warning against rigidity in its first

147

unconcealed form was crossed off the lists, probably at the advice of the committee members. In 1916 and 1917 they thought themselves so important that at the annual festivities they did not count the years from Inayat's first work in the West but from the beginning of their London society.

There was, of course, one thing that could not be tampered with, the principal aim, God-realization. In the final version of 1918 this concept, little known in the West, is woven into and explained in all the ten thoughts and in the three objects, sometimes elucidating, sometimes obscuring. In Inayat's concise style this point is worded 'rising above belief and unbelief by self-realization.'[8]

The unbelievers sometimes interested him more than the head-in-the-clouds believers; he thought them intelligent, but ignorant. The sciences, especially physical phenomena related to vibrations and sound waves, interested him.[9] He hoped that someone one day would explain the so-called mystical activities in a western, scientific manner. The word mysticism itself, with its flavour of secrecy and mystery, always created misunderstanding and as soon as he re-worded one error, another took its place.

Sometimes he despaired of ever being understood. There are lists in which the inner work is mentioned only at the very end, or in a hidden manner, whereas his aim was 'to spread the wisdom of the Sufis which hitherto was a hidden treasure.' And that made his Moslem friends angry again, for he added that Sufism meant mysticism in general and was not the property of one race or religion, but belonged to all mankind.[10]

Even more revolutionary was what followed: mysticism should no longer be a mystery, but every human being should have the opportunity that 'redeems the disbeliever from ignorance and the believer from falling a victim to hypocrisy.'

He saw how believers and unbelievers both vexedly opposed each other and that the existing religious forms

148

had had their day. He also saw the approach of a world in which there would be no more room for morals and religion imposed from above. Therefore the experience of a religious reality — to know God, not only to believe — would have to become part of everyone's daily life. The answer was meditation, but never without what he called the study of life.

Truly acting, not just talking, that was his strength. What could not be done in one way, must be tried in another way. 'Unite East and West with the music of your soul,' his master had said. Inayat kept working toward that end.

When after July 1915 there were no more invitations to perform before large British audiences, he looked for other means to bring East and West closer together, slowly beginning to interpret his master's words in a figurative sense. Every day he found that even well-meaning Westerners understood little of the East and that he himself did not know many things Westerners took for granted. Very well, East and West could learn from each other, and above all, must get to know each other better. In his magazine he made room for articles about Indian arts and languages. Persons who had contributed to a better understanding between East and West were made honorary members of the Society. One of those honorary members was Edmund Dulac, the illustrator of the Arabian Nights. He and his wife were among the regular visitors at receptions and festivities, 'very refined and very French.' The stories of the Arabian Nights are not simply fairy tales, many have a special mystical meaning.[11] Another honorary member was an English novelist, Marmaduke Pickthall, a Moslem whose translation of the Quran is well-known and who described the Middle East in his fiction.

Inayat himself impressed a few good aspects of the West upon his countrymen, when he was invited to address the first All India Music Conference in Baroda in 1916. He resisted the temptation to go there in person, but had a paper read in which he dealt with the history and decay of his beloved music and the possibilities for restoring it; he concluded with examples from the West.[12]

Amidst the London difficulties — distrusted by his own countrymen and by the British, and half understood by his admirers — the invitation from his own country must have done him good. Another joy was the birth of his first son in June 1916. These were rays of light in a somber period. The honorary membership sometimes fell to people who kept the society and, with it, the family alive. To begin with the American Edmund Russell, who had certainly deserved it; then a few others, among whom an Indian Maharani. The most warmly appreciated honorary member was their French friend Monsieur Bailly, who died in 1916 to the great sorrow of Inayat and his brothers. He had really understood their music and as he could act in the courteous way of an Indian, they could relax with him.

Understanding of their Indian manners was next to non-existant, real understanding of their music scarce. Some disciples write in their memoirs that when he played the veena he carried them 'far away from this world' or that what radiated from him when he sang could not be described.' Others, he himself writes, 'thought that I represented a religion with my music, and wanted to make a stage into a temple and a concert hall into a church.' Indeed, there is a poster of 1916 that says: 'Music, the future world religion.' Perhaps the composer of this advertisement had concluded as much from the list of Sufi thoughts which still had it that Indian music and Persian poetry were necessary for inner development.

Inayat did give poems of Rumi and Sa'di as individual exercises during the first years. To be done properly they had to be sung too, and hardly anybody could do that. One had to be familiar with eastern thought and feeling, recognize inwardly before one could use the symbolism of the ancient Persians as a medium for inner development.

150

Explanation was of the mind; when Inayat himself talked about this poetry, the spark came across for a moment and it became 'lovely,' an aesthetic pleasure and an exotic sensation. Never a possession. One day 'to spread the knowledge of Persian poetry' as one of the objects of the Sufi work, was left out.

Then there was always music. Nothing could exalt Inayat and his brothers as much as music, 'the best medium for concentration,' 'the shortest way to God.' 'It is a dream, a meditation, it is Paradise.'[13]

It was, when for hours together he made his veena hum, or when he sang his way deep into the delicate, ever varying patterns of a dhrupad, or abandoned himself to the ever more intense praise of the divine in a Carnatic song. They brought the blue skies of India, the warmth and the fragrance with them.

As long as he played it lasted. India, an increasingly beautiful India, was his home. But he lived in chilly England, which had a different musical tradition. Even the church choirs were principally an aesthetic experience. Music was 'nice' and music was entertainment. Pious people did not approve of concerts on Sunday — this Inayat found so odd that he makes special mention of it in his *Autobiography*. Ever since America he had known that his music was considered 'strange' or 'interesting;' occasionally 'wonderful;' sometimes listeners were carried away. But who among his disciples could sit down with a veena, or sing very softly, bringing the sound from deep in his throat?

The day came when even music disappeared from the neat, printed lists. This was hard on him. For him music was the real means to reach the heart. Now he had to switch to plain talking in a foreign language. He set himself to improve his English during the evenings with those few friends who had become like members of the family. Still the first book of printed lectures was called *The Mysticism of Sound*. Still he pressed the necessity of music in edu-

151

cation. And, as a veiled form of music he created *Gayan, Vadan* and *Nirtan,* his mostly widely read books.

These are collections of aphorisms under different chapter titles, all musical terms, as are the words Gayan, Vadan and Nirtan. *Gayan* is an abbreviation of 'Notes from the unstruck music from the Gayan.' Some one like Raden Aju Jodjana, who did make oriental music her own, and who has seen Inayat act, may consider it a dry book, the wrong side of a piece of embroidery, hardly an echo. No doubt this goes for everything that is written down.[14] But just as in music the 'notes' from the *Gayan* can be played, made into a reality.

The words from the three books are partly directed to his followers and readers but often the author addresses himself, as he did in *Minqar-é-Musiqar.* Inayat knew his own complicated nature, knew that his being at home in greater worlds made him both inviolable and vulnerable when confronted with trivial problems. He knew his human qualities; the impetuous young man he had been still echoes when he exhorts himself to wisdom and patience; traces of all the contradictory influences of Maula Bakhsh the proud, of his modest mother and his father's standards of honour show up now and again. He even expresses the financial problem of the day in an elegant maxim — such is the art of an improvising Indian musician. And always he ends, as in *Minqar-é-Musiqar* with the powerful current of his confidence.

The admirers around him scarcely noticed the struggle. During the war the habit of circulating his portrait — bearded sage with calm, inward looking eyes — began. No one asked now, as an artless disciple did in 1911, 'Why do you treat him as if he is perfect?' He was not perfect but he was so exceptional and impressive that guests at the Friday receptions, in an excess of reverence, did not dare to open their mouths. He broke the ice by encouraging round games which, in those pre-television days, were

152

played even by adults. Two of the brothers joined in and when everyone had warmed up, Inayat might laugh himself to tears. There is one snapshot that shows him laughing broadly and leaning out of his chair, as if he is talking to somebody or looking at something funny. It is the most earthly photo of his last ten years.

But generally he was calm, even when he laughed — there are plenty of smiling pictures — and his dignified gait was especially striking. But while walking regally he could express his playfulness as well as his unassailability. One morning he had been sitting quietly in Regent's Park with a faithful mureed; on the way back he stepped right into the chaotic traffic at Baker Street Station, to the alarm of the pupil who relates this. It was probably one of the 'amusing tests.' Normally he said little as he walked, whereas this time he calmly continued a lesson in the midst of carts, cabs and buses, while a plunging dray-horse touched his head.[15]

This disciple was probably one of the few who received a part of the Indian training. For most of the others he decided on an extremely simplified form of inner exercises, just enough to make the disciple calmer and happier. By the end of 1915 mysticism was hardly mentioned in the aims and objects; in 1916 the solution to the dilemma was worded 'to simplify mysticism through a logical and scientific training.' In this sentence Inayat took into account the limitations of his disciples as well as what he had discovered to be his own lack of knowledge. It was also a polite bow to the western gods Science and Reason.

And so the most important institution of his work in the West came into being. An inner school of simplified mysticism, open to initiates who were given some basic practices; who, in addition, could follow one or more classes of a twelve-year course. These lessons were recorded and could be read out during his absence too.

He dictated everything from memory and inspiration. A disciple who witnessed the classes coming into being writes how astonished he was at what he at first took for an exceptional memory — which partly it was. At the beginning of the lesson Inayat would ask the one who recorded his words, 'Where were we?' Having heard the answer 'Second series of group so-and-so, number such-and-such, subject this or that,' he immediately started to speak, continuing the system of subjects. Soon this witness, a businessman, understood that it was not only a question of memory, but he rightly remarks that he could not say for certain what was direct inspiration, what was derived from books or tradition or what was based on personal experience. Anyone who knows something of Inayat's life can easily recognize the personal experiences; they are mentioned more often in the public lectures than in the private lessons. In the latter the basic method, old traditions, his view of them, his new inspiration and the result of observation are blended.

The second western institution was even more adjusted to western habits of thought. He had noted that 900 out of a thousand seekers came to argue, 99 to meditate and, at best, one 'to make God a reality.'[16] The proportion of meditators and talkers would be a little different today, but the Brotherhood activity, created for the latter, still exists: an open forum for lectures on and introductions to a variety of subjects, under auspices of Inayat's society, order or movement. In the old magazine all kinds of idealists and semi-nonconformists in reform clothes — theosophists, phrenologists, rhythmic dance enthusiasts, progressive parsons — were given the opportunity to air their pet ideas side by side with Inayat's much more varied lectures. Today an occasional meeting is devoted to a particular religion or a forum of different views of life is organized. Good European love of theories in an ecumenical mould which, during W.W. I, was not yet as popular as it is now. As cited above, a society to unite faiths was considered at that time ambitious.

The third institution, too, was totally and practically ecumenical: the Church of All, or Universal Worship. Probably this service is best known to the outside world as an introduction to the Sufi Movement. It was not founded until 1921 and will be discussed in the next chapter.

Meanwhile Inayat continued to labour in his own way. In the heart of London, where he was often pulled at and put upon in the most disagreeable way, it was not easy to maintain his depth and serenity. He had to work at it, sometimes through certain abstinences, as during the period of his first training.

One of the few recorded memories of his brother Maheboob Khan tells how one night in the middle of the war policemen who were keeping an eye on the house of 'us foreigners' suddenly rang the bell because they had seen something suspicious. Inayat was doing some difficult spiritual exercises in those days which included fasting, keeping silence and certain manipulations with a sword. His room was only lit by the flames in the fireplace, and one night it happened that the curtains were not closed as carefully as the black-out regulations demanded. A shaft of light shone through and besides his movements cast strange shadows. The police wanted to know what was going on. Musharaff Khan, answering the door, said that he could not disturb his brother. All the more reason for the policemen to insist on an inspection. Musharaff Khan, embarrassed, went upstairs, knocked and explained in Hindustani that two detectives wanted to inspect the room. Inayat only answered with a 'hm' of assent. Maheboob Khan ends his story in these words: 'Murshid was sitting there in his yellow robe, he got up. As soon as the policemen entered they stopped, thunderstruck.... The tall figure standing there, a radiant, vibrant being; his eyes, radiant with light, asked the detectives why they had come. Deeply impressed they said: 'Master, forgive us for disturbing you.' They bowed and asked his blessing, Murshid blessed

155

them and they left, walking backwards, slowly and reverently.'

The admiration with which Maheboob Khan, a reserved and unromantic man, the newspaper reader of the family, describes this incident, is more significant than that of western disciples. He was in a position to compare and knew how much hard work, self-control and self-correction was continually called for.

Inayat expected hard work from serious pupils too, not just dabbling. At the opening of the new house in Ladbroke Road he said in his speech to guests and disciples: 'These headquarters are not made for our rest or comfort, but for work and endeavour, and we must not forget the meaning of Brotherhood, which has generally been overlooked when it came to self-interest by many other Societies. If we can keep our thoughts on the word Sufi, which means purification from caste, creed, race, nation and religion, we shall leave a great impression. Our services to humanity are greatly needed at such a time as this, when man has drawn his sword against his brother.'[16]

The war began to weigh more heavily with him. In the beginning he kept himself aloof, not only because wordly affairs were like the games of a child to him, but also as an ordinary human being, because it was a European conflict that concerned him only indirectly. But though as an Indian he desired freedom for his country, as an observing sage he was shocked by the pain caused by the war, and by the disastrous influences in its wake. It gave a new impetus to his ideal of making people aware of their inner brotherhood.

From Wilson and Söderblom to numerous less famous figures, many were at that time in search of ways to establish peace among countries and churches, but the principle of 'inner unity' was little known. Mysticism meant sitting on poles and gushing exaltation to those who rejected it, cosy mysteriousness, a shiver down the spine to those who were looking for it. Supporters and opponents both confused it with occultism. During all his years as a master Inayat had to warn against the tendency to see miracles as a proof of godliness, against the hobby of looking for colour auras, or worse, contact with spirits.[17] Spiritualism he condemned strongly, both as a pseudo-religion, and because of the danger it held.

But death was so close to everyone in those sombre years that he had to help people, if only by simply talking about it and making the fact sufferable. It was not by accident that precisely during the war books about life after death were in demand. Half a century later, in a television review, a doctor pointed out the taboo surrounding death: 'Since the nineteenth century ideology prescribes that our field of experiences be limited to the earthly here and now. That is simply a dogma and all the more influential because it is not taught anywhere, but tacitly assumed as a kind of axiom. It becomes an obstacle which bars the way to the very question if, and if so, how, we can learn something about life after death.'[18]

Only in days of distress 'the taboo on this dogma' – again, the television reviewer's definition – is lifted. In 1917 the mystic who was familiar with other worlds, was addressing audiences at heart still 19th-century, who day by day read lists of those killed in the submarine war or on the western front. That the soul exists he was just as sure of as others doubted it. But he did not consider a continued individual existence of the soul, the ultimate goal being to return to the source; he discussed this later in a more contemplative way.[19] The war lectures about death are simple and direct. Immediately after death, he says, there is still an individual soul and this is often drawn to the grave or crematorium where lies the body, unless it has already realized that it has nothing more to do with this abode, 'which in fact was merely the instrument of experiment.'

It is not by accident that Inayat mentions a crematorium

157

too, though as a born Moslem he did not favour cremation. But one of his disciples, Edith Ellis, the wife of Havelock Ellis, had been cremated in 1916 and Inayat had attended the cremation. Havelock Ellis was not pleased when, during the last months of her life, his wife joined 'such a movement' and he even doubted Inayat's authenticity.[20] All the more interesting is his description of what happened at the cremation furnace, where only one friend and Inayat stood beside him. Mr Ellis had expected to be horrified, but to his astonishment his pain 'merged into joy at the glory of the vision.' He attributed this unexpected joy to the beauty of 'that seemingly liquid mass of golden intense heat,' but his description closely resembles what Inayat's disciples tell about the meetings when he was in deep meditation and each one in turn was allowed to sit with him quietly and for a moment felt that he was lifted up with the master.

Inayat did not use big words when he spoke about death and dying. He recalled memories of his youth, surprised now − 'how could I have thought that I was just my body' − and described, like an anthropologist who notes down his observations of a strange tribe, what he had found in a haunted house in Secunderabad.[21] But scarcely had he related some of his memories of ghosts in one lecture, when in the next one he hastily warned his audience against fear of ghosts and against table turning and deceivers. 'It is better to have more connection with the beings living upon earth than to be obsessed with the desire to meet with the people on the other side of life,' he says. 'It is here that we are meant to evolve, and by being absorbed in those who have passed on we are taken away from the life we are meant to have.' Later, whenever he was asked questions on this subject, he replied cautiously, knowing how easily his words could be simplified, made common and rigid. But he helped people who wrestled to come to terms with loss through death and the thought of their own death.

In the hard winter of 1917, ten years after the conclusion of his own discipleship in hot, colourful Hyderabad, he himself was a murshid in cold, grey London, which was assuming a more and more gloomy atmosphere of war. He was a master in another way than the old man, who, more or less hidden, blending with the masses of his birth-place, had been his teacher. Murshid Inayat Khan lived in an alien country, whose government kept an eye of suppressed suspicion on him. He was virtually imprisoned, his garden lay between high walls, the only open space the wanderer could find was in a London park. There were no trips on horseback if he had to lecture in another part of town, but on the underground with its stench of stale smoke and lingering damp. He could not remain unknown, he had to be advertised, even on posters in the same underground. What he missed most were the kindred souls, the wandering sages with their living eyes, who recognized and understood each other everywhere. He was alone with his admiring pupils, who only half understood him. No wandering, no quiet recognition, but the busy tidying up of a neat organisation, everything cut and dried and pigeon-holed.

There were some things the disciples were really masters of; they knew how to organize. As the following grew it was necessary to think of an outer, administrative form. The society of 1915 was registered in 1917. From various details it is evident that those who drafted the statutes were theosophists.

The theosophists have done a great deal for Inayat and for Indians in general. For them wisdom came from the East and therefore they made the cause of India's independence their own. They were often more nationalist than the nationalists. No Indian could reject them, even if he knew that they sometimes talked nonsense. It is a well-known fact that the sages in the Himalayas, from whom Madame Blavatsky claimed to have derived her secrets were a figment of her imagination. It takes the philosopher Bolland several scornful articles to reveal this.[22] Inayat says the same thing in a single phrase: 'Certain masters... hardly to be found in any sacred tradition.'

With all their admiration for the East most western admirers were western down to their fingertips, for instance in intellectual classification and recording . See the 1917 *Rules and Regulations of the Sufi Order.* Headquarters was called Khanqah, an allusion to the title Khan, considered to be the family name, and at the same time an existing term for an oriental monastery which has living-rooms, guest-accommodation and an office too. Theosophists are fond of counting in sacred numbers. The Khanqah was supposed to have seven kinds of rooms, and the committee also consisted of seven members; to complete another series of seven the accommodation 'departments' were counted in with the managing departments. Votes were taken in the meetings, but the chairman's vote counted as 7, the general secretary's as 6, and so on.

The so-called propaganda department did useful work. Now that Inayat no longer travelled as a musician, he had to reach the public in other ways. As early as 1916 a branch had been founded in Brighton; in 1917 Harrogate followed. People were tired of the war and longed for peace. Inayat's words, his attitude of inner peace were as hungrily sought after as they had been impatiently shoved aside in the beginning. The lecture tours, stretching as far as Scotland, were a success, the halls full again. Usually the theosophists acted as hosts, but the listeners came from everywhere, bringing with them their Christian ideas, problems, doubts and certainties, their deep-rooted habits of thought and of life. Inayat came to tell them that everyone could strive for inner growth in his own way, that it was not necessary to fight about right and wrong, the results would show whether the seeker was genuine or not. By preference he used the example of an orchestra in which everyone plays his own part, and he himself thought that important. 'If there is anything in my philosophy, it is the law of harmony.'[23]

But his audience asked for crutches to lean on, prescriptions, commandments. When new disciples who had followed him from a distance to Edinburgh kept insisting on rules of behaviour he finally replied that he would tell them 'how, under certain circumstances, I at least try to act:' seeing from the point of view of another as well as from one's own, taking into account human imperfection and ignorance. Though Inayat deplored nothing so much as self-pity, he advocated reasonable self-criticism; loyalty in friendship, a realistic withdrawal if someone did not respond to good-will; accepting opposition for that was to be expected if one 'raised one's head in the world.' Towards the end the address gathered momentum, he became enthusiastic, literally 'in God.' Then he came down to earth again and concluded: 'Take from these ideas what seems to you to be best, and forget the rest.' He could also be strict. Once he had made initiation for the many possible, he made it quite clear who was and who was not capable of mystical development. Those were who felt the need for knowledge other than the world can offer, those whose hearts began to be in tune with everything, those who began to see the connection between opposites and their balance. Those not capable of mystical development were people who could not subscribe to the Sufi ideas and aims, who wanted to emphasize the differences between religions, or who already belonged to an esoteric order, 'because one cannot travel in two boats at the same time with one foot in each.' Also unsuitable were those who had advanced to a certain extent and then put some unalterable principle as a wall before them, and those who came only out of curiosity. He also indicated what should be avoided after initiation: miracle working, exorcism, spiritualism, showing of one's superior knowledge, fortune telling,

161

sanctimoniousness, over-righteousness, teaching and advising others before having acquired self-knowledge. There is also a list of what *is* necessary: an attitude of respect, first towards the master and through him eventually to all others. That was essential. But it is exactly the enumeration of negatives that shows the limitations − rigidity, naive vanity, shallowness, ingnorance, haste − he had to cope with. When the movement was still small he had needed patience and confidence, now that it was growing he needed strenght, tact and even more patience.

In 1919 he fell ill for the first time: pneumonia. One or two years earlier he had cheerfully said that for at least ten years he had meditated more than he had slept at night and flourished under it. He assumed that his illness was the result of having to neglect his practices, because of too many callers, too much work and too much late travelling. The disciple who records this, a doctor and blood specialist, also describes the impression he made, the absolute concentrated silence he could command in a lecture hall. 'But the hall could only seat a hundred people.'

The war was over. In the general need for renewal Inayat's Sufism found a natural niche. Anniversaries were again attended by a variety of guests, highly placed Britishers too, including Robert Bridges . The committee thought a larger house was needed in spite of the hardly sufficient funds. A disciple whom Inayat had helped in the establishment of a small factory − not with direct financial advice, but with encouragement and the kind of unspoken guidance that makes every one find the right way for himself − was prepared to pay the lease on an enormous house, 29 Gordon Square. He did not like this too spacious mansion, but a festive affair was organized for the opening of the new Khanqah and once again they had impressive visitors. New plans were made and carried out. In the spring of 1920 Inayat crossed to France and gave his old group there new élan. The American centre had maintained itself well during the war, that had always been a consolation. Contact with Russian disciples was possible till 1921, in spite of war, revolution and famine. He was now going to Switzerland, Belgium, Germany and Holland.

But at the same time new difficulties began. A Moslem friend had made him a member of Anjuman Islam, a committee 'to bring the Muslims and the non-Muslims to a better understanding.' There was also a charity fund for Moslem orphans connected with this committee. Neither Inayat nor his friends knew that such a fund ought to be registered. When an active secretary started to collect money by sending out letters, they were in for a lot of suspicion and misunderstanding by the authorities.[24] Further, theosophists started talking about him being a world teacher, and this was resented both by Mary Williams and his Moslem friends. To top things a hysterical woman imagined he had made passes at her. This typical spinster's dream was believed by the lady mill-owner who paid the rent. She withdrew and suddenly the Sufi society and the family were facing a debt of a few hundred pounds.

Inayat answered the authorities with a dignified and clear letter, stating the purpose of his movement as 'solely to spread the Truth underlying all Faiths and Beliefs.' The dispute between Mary Williams and the theosophists caused a palace revolution, of which he only says in his autobiography: 'A difference among my loving friends threatened our movement with a breakdown.' The woman who had lent the money for the big house is mentioned in one sentence. 'She was enthusiastic for some time and did a great deal then.' If anyone came to him complaining of the wickedness of others he often replied, 'A person may have done something wrong yesterday and do better tomorrow, man can change.' When four years later the woman who had caused the catastrophe presented herself and asked for forgiveness he granted it. He lived as he preached.

Which does not mean this was easy, even for him. That there were disciples who did not put complete faith in their master he could never understand. Desertion, for whatever reason, always hurt. And for a person of integrity to be accused of things that do not even enter his mind, is always bewildering. Raden Aju Jodjana, mureed, music pupil, and friend of Amina-Begum was present when the news came and saw the astonishment, the shock, the grief. But while others were still saying 'how can they', 'they don't know him,' he was rising above it. 'This does not exist in reality, this does not exist,' he said, as in *Minqar-é-Musiqar* he had stated what did exist. In essence it was the same action, widening himself into God-realization, in which all evil dissolved. They saw him change before their very eyes.[25]

In his own letters on the same subject, the two planes on which he lived and dealt with sorrow can be recognized. The English financial problems were finally solved by a pupil in Southampton. This was Miss Dowland, owner of the Polygon Hotel, with whom he for several years conducted a frank correspondance about all developments. His letters were cordial, matter-of-fact, grateful for the understanding he so rarely enjoyed and very direct. 'My hair is turning grey with all the difficulties.' 'The rift during the difficult times has caused a lot of irritation everywhere and we cannot open our hearts to everybody and show the wounds.'[26] But he had got over, and discarded, washed away, the London misery too. When one day his correspondent mentioned again the dangerous repercussions of gossip he replied: 'I tell you, my dear mureed, the more we shall think of the critical world the more it will confuse us... They are out in the world to criticize, our work in life is to work.' And with that he passed on to the next thing to be done. No post-mortems.

But though his inner being could rise above the difficulties, and though his outer being could face everything and live through suffering, the affair had material consequences. It was a matter of a few hundred pounds, but he did not have them.

Had he again worked in vain for years? The faithful pupil in Southampton advised him to leave England. At the same time a pupil in South-Africa sent some money, he had a feeling the master could probably do with it. A third one, an English woman married to a Frenchman, knew of an empty summerhouse they might rent, in Tremblaye. Inayat authorized Miss Dowland to work in England on his behalf, packed his veena and took the whole family and a faithful maid-servant back to France.

His eldest son Vilayat, who was four at the time, remembers the crossing; a small boat in a storm, and everyone seasick. He also remembers the first house in France, small and damp, and dry bread on the table. But the children's lasting memories were to be of the large house in Suresnes, an invasion of disciples every year and a father they had to share with others — as all children of famous men have to — and who, most of the time, was away travelling.

Chapter IX (1920-1924)
En route

Tremblaye is a village south-east of Paris. It was pleasant, but not a suitable place to start international work or to give oriental concerts. Money was running out.

Following an impulse Inayat went to Geneva.[1] He travelled on a single ticket and spent the night in a small hotel near the station. That took his last francs, but, as always, he trusted his intuition and walked into the town, for the first time in years alone, for the first time in years in a new country, for the first time in years in the open: the lake of Geneva stretched before him in the autumn light.

Did he think of the lakes of Hyderabad and Ajmer in the glaring sun? In any case when he saw the Maison Royale his thoughts went back to the palaces in Baroda built in the same style. He saw a quay with the charming name Quai des Eaux Vives, living water, an image from Persian poetry. He imagined himself settled at this spot. A few years later his headquarters were lodged there.

Inayat had arrived in Geneva without a penny and without any contacts; within a month he was able to start his journeys around the world and within a few years the Sufi Movement had become known everywhere in the world. And in places as far apart as Brazil, South Africa and China he had at least one disciple who represented him and founded a centre.

It began with some old friends, American or English, who saw him wandering along the quays of Geneva. Surprised and delighted, they invited him to lunch. Afterwards, honoured by his company, they asked if he would

America, 1923.

accept a thank-offering in the form of money. Tactfully, and at the right time, as the mureed from South Africa had done a few weeks before.

They must have done more, guided him round Geneva and introduced him here and there, for he not only bought a ticket home, but a return ticket to Geneva as well. On 11th November he wrote to a Swiss friend, who had become his disciple in London, that he was to give lectures in several Swiss towns. At the end of November he wrote again, and by then a society had already been founded. 'I have made acquaintance with some interesting people here, natives and foreigners. It happens to be a good time as the League of Nations is here.... Unfortunately things have gone wrong in Paris with our Society; therefore I must go there on the first of December and be there for the whole month. Then probably I may have to go to London before I return to make things right there.'[2]

These few lines provide the *Leitmotiv* for the following years: establish new centres, pay attention to the problems of the day, keep the old centres pure, and travel, travel, travel, always on the road.

The wanderer was wandering once more, not by bullock cart, but by train or steamship, and as a rare treat riding, not on an elephant, but in an open aeroplane. Again, he stayed wherever he could find shelter, humbly on the floor at his headquarters, grandly in an ambassador's house, expensively at the Waldorf Astoria, but mostly in small hotels or in the chilly spare room of some kindly matron, on whose mantelpiece stood a Buddha figurine. He met no arrogant Brahmins, he did meet arrogant white sahibs, were they intellectuals, businessmen or servants; other intellectuals, businessmen and simple people admired him, admiration or contempt did not depend on class. If he met robbers at all, they were 'robbers of happiness.'[3] If anyone argued with him, it was hardly ever an equal or a superior, as the Hindu priest who once honoured him with a scarf had been. When someone did give him a scarf it was a warm muffler, offered as a Christmas present by an anxious mureed, and he was honoured with bunches of flowers on his birthday. Neither his birthday nor Christmas had ever been celebrated at home. Everything was different from his youth, his India. Even making music became more and more rare.

In the spring of 1920, during his short visits to France, he had still been able to give a few concerts.[4] 'In France I felt like singing again,' he writes. And his eldest son Vilayat remembers his relief when he returned home one day: 'What a country, sun and freedom.' He loved French courtesy and the artistic climate. French intellectualism, sceptical of all religious feeling, he was well acquainted with, though.

He knew many European ways of reacting and every day in the post-war world taught him more. A new era had begun, miles lay between the playful decadence of pre-1914 and the bitter seriousness of post-war idealists and post-war cynics; miles also between the almost playful confidence with which, in 1910, he expected to sing East and West together and the perseverance he needed now. Time and again he had to brace and adjust himself, tuning to another person's pitch so that he might give just as much as the other could take in.

He no longer thought only of the relations between white and coloured,[5] he now knew the tensions, the hatred and prejudice the western countries nurtured for one another, and in contrast to the cool acceptance of the caste system, he now discovered the embittered class struggle. He could see no cure in hatred and chauvinism, nor in bringing everyone down to the same level. Co-operating, uniting was good, but unity did not mean uniformity. 'The world is suffering from the wrong application of a good principle.'

He heard of the famine in Russia, he passed through

crushed and humiliated Germany; he saw Belgium wounded and embittered, and England ruling India with an iron hand, America withdrawing lest she burn her fingers and her interest. The world was in chaos, old forms were used up, new ones not yet tested.

During the war Inayat had often been asked to say something about the future. He had refused for the same reason he refused everything that bordered on occultism and miracle-working. Moreover, he knew that the inquirers had wanted to hear that the war would be over within a month, whereupon a heaven on earth would begin. The only time he relented he immediately put an end to that illusion. He expected that at first things would get worse and that only after complete demolition – 'the worst condition ends the cycle' – a new era with new concepts of personal relationship based on equality would dawn; but that was still far off, he himself would not see it.

When the war was over, many, from sheer relief, turned to an easy optimism. The League of Nations would save the world, socialism would save the world, freer living would save the world. In the spring of 1921 the freedom movement in India, too, experienced a wave of joyful hope. But Inayat, who was by no means a pessimist, said at the time, 'The world is sick.' He noted the evil effects of the war; the only good thing had been a bit of warmth and feeling of togetherness, but that soon disappeared with the danger.

Yet he did not doubt that a new civilization was in the making. The most remarkable thing in his description of the future is not that it fits today, but that he expected a world completely contrary to what, in his heart, he still preferred. 'Titles will have little importance. Signs of honour will become conspicuous... Women will become freer everyday in all aspects of life.... No work will be considered menial. No position in life will be humiliating.... Servant and master will be so only during working hours, and the feeling of superiority and inferiority among people will vanish.' Nothing like the courtliness and courtesy of the aristocratic society, the best remnants of which he had known. He also expected changes that did conform to his own hopes and aims, but the overall picture was of a life that had little privacy, where it would be more and more customary to eat out and where everybody would talk unceremoniously. That picture lacked the sheltered refinement of his youth, when a son who did not agree with his father, bowed to him and left the room. But the main thing was that human beings would be human again, with respect for themselves and each other, and religion functional, without empty formalities. 'It will have a beauty of its own,' he once said. And all the glow and splendour of Hyderabad's Arabian Nights became a dream, for ever.

But that this wonderful future was still far away and different from his dearest memories was no reason why serious workers for a better world should not be welcomed as allies. In London he had already co-operated with small pre-ecumenical groups. In Geneva and Paris he met the Bahai leaders and as soon as the work in France was settled, he returned to where the League of Nations struggled. He considered all societies that aimed at bringing people closer together as co-workers; 'a thousand of these organisations would still not be sufficient.'

Contacts with people outside his own organisation were short-lived, as he seldom remained in one place for more than a fortnight. And then he stood on some railway platform again, calm and dignified among his hurrying fellow-travellers from London to Brighton; in his pocket was a note saying '27th leave Holland, 28th arrive in England, 14th leave England for Brussels.' Even if there was anything amiss, he showed no sign of it. Once he forgot his passport, and had to go back. A passport was new, an object that underlined the distrust between nations. Another time he had left his keys somewhere. But very soon an administrator or a secretary travelled with him and he was

171

at least relieved of these external worries.

In the train he usually closed his eyes and meditated. His last secretary once asked him politely if her sitting opposite him would disturb him. He replied, 'When I close my eyes I am alone.' In a very crowded train he might look around him, help a mother with a child, or amuse himself. Once he sat among a rowdy group of youngsters, listening to their loud chattering. Suddenly he took off his hat, a so-called Turkish hat, a tall kind of fez without a tassel. This happened in England where a person in oriental dress did not draw special attention, but without his hat it was not his ethno-geographical type that became evident, but his personality. The boys and girls, surprised, began to make guesses about who he could be, from what country he could have come. He pretended that he did not understand English, he let them look and ask questions and replied in *Tarana,* the unconnected syllables of some songs. In their amazement the young people became quiet.

It might happen that a disciple travelling with him caught a glimpse of what Inayat saw when he sat with his eyes closed. Two stories are told by two vastly different characters.

A critical young man had become a mureed after years of hesitation and in the presence of Inayat he resented the very thing other pupils were enthusiastic about: that questions answered themselves, that consciousness expanded. 'I wanted to know how this came about,' the young man writes, 'I resented the blurring effect.' One day he boarded a tram to Suresnes and heard the passengers comment on the odd clothes of someone sitting at the back. It was the master. The pupil asked whether he could sit with him and with a gesture Inayat indicated the seat opposite. Not a word was spoken, but the young man noticed once again that he could not hold his thoughts. He observed himself and found that he was no longer looking at streets, vehicles, houses: all ordinary, visible things faded away.

This is what Inayat himself had discovered during his discipleship and recorded in *Minqar-é-Musiqar:* even the glory of the court faded away when he learnt to find his way in a different sphere.

The other story comes from an Englishwoman who happened to accompany Inayat on a journey through the battlefields of Belgium.[6] For the English Flanders still means poppy fields and fallen soldiers; every 11th November the dead are still remembered with paper poppy buttonholes. Inayat felt what was going on in her mind, requested a non-English disciple to leave the compartment for a few minutes and closed his eyes. The disciple closed hers too. Then she had a vision of the war, not in actual events, as a panorama, but as one horrifying whole. But she also saw, or felt, something of another world, light and glory breaking forth from the terror of fire and distress. 'Light and glory.' Havelock Ellis, confronted with death and fire in Inayat's presence used the words 'joy and glory,' not knowing that he was transported.

Another of the many train stories, a simple one. Italy between Rome and Naples, and a conversation with an Italian sea captain. 'And what is your profession?' the sailor asked. Inayat replied that he was a musician.

A musician he was and always remained. Before he had a secretary travelling with him, he did his correspondance after breakfast. He found it hard going. 'My hands were made for the veena, not for the pen.' In those days he still carried his veena with him on his journeys, later he had to leave it at home. 'I am a musician who must tune the souls of men, instead of strings.' This he meant in the broadest sense of the word, he had to touch as many countries as possible, hence his apparently restless travelling.

Switzerland was a good springboard. His first lecture was attended by many foreigners. Among the most enthusiastic was the Netherlands ambassador's family, and so it happened that the first country Inayat visited during his

173

new wanderings was Holland.

One evening he arrived in Rotterdam. In his pocket he had the address of a family, with whom Tagore had stayed the year before. These people, the Willebeek Lemaires, knew that he was coming, but they had just returned from a long journey abroad and had asked friends to 'take over' the guest. But these friends were not informed of his time of arrival, so there was nobody to meet him. Inayat calmly rode to the Willebeek Lemaire residence. The daughter — an artist — and her future husband soon became active, persevering followers, who would not dream of letting anyone else take care of the master if they could do so themselves.

Something like that happened in The Hague. 'Can you take him?' a prospective hostess, whose house happened to be full, asked. And consequently the Barodan musician became the guest of the descendants of Rycklof Volckert van Goens, who had visited Baroda in 1654. In 1924 Maheboob Khan married the daughter of the house. Later Musharaff Khan, too, married in Holland. The Headquarters always remained in Geneva, Inayat's house and summer school in Suresnes, but in Holland a comparatively strong centre came into being.

Not just because of family connections. Norway and Sweden, where Inayat went only once, produced good, constant mureeds too. In these countries, between the orthodox Christians and dogmatic agnostics there was a large group of people who were 'looking for something' and who were able to criticize religious forms without throwing away the baby with the bathwater.

Such a marginal group hardly existed among the Belgians whom Inayat visited, still thinking of their fate in the war. The Sufi centres he founded in after years had their ups and downs. When he came, he was warmly welcomed by several societies — in addition to the Theosophists, English clubs now often organized the first lecture — and

174

by a group of which, unusual for him, he said that it was too exclusively aristocratic. Unlike before the war he no longer looked upon Western aristocracy as a kind of Brahmins and raja's, whose influence could be helpful. He discovered that for the spreading of his philosophy the most apt were those citizens he called the middle classes or the intellectuals. The working classes were too busy fighting for their basic material needs, which the master understood.

What he had to give was meant for all and indeed he reached everyone. The reactions of ordinary people were often very direct. Madame van Goens remembered: 'When I went for a walk with Murshid − there was time for that during the first years − the labourers would take off their caps, not the gentry.' And there are numerous stories of porters who would not accept a tip, maid-servants and caretakers who wanted to be initiated and could consider themselves mureeds after a chat or a handshake. Inayat's second son Hidayat says that once a man came up to him and asked: 'That gentleman with the beard who used to live here, was that your father?' He was a road worker who had been digging in front of the gate one day when Inayat came out and suddenly shook hands with him: 'And I have never been able to forget that,' the man said.

Years after Inayat's death a Dutch journalist[7] was brought to a pub in Paris and among the regulars − the usual misunderstood poet and a tragic girl − he met a man who was known as the Heavenly Grape. In almost perpetual drunkenness he preached, all day long, the words of his 'great and only friend Inayat Khan.' If anybody was desperate or irritable, if he himself climbed a chair to make some sublime statement and fell off in the progress, if one of the regulars wanted to bash him on the head, or if a visitor was surprised at his sermons from the gutter, he could always quote a relevant and authentic saying of 'his incomparable master' Inayat. This drunken apostle, ac-

175

cording to his own story, had been a dock labourer in Marseilles. After an accident Inayat had found and cured him and then, supposedly, delegated him to the darkest part of Paris.

Yet, as far as is known, most of Inayat's co-workers came from that group he called intellectuals, because of their restless thinking and questioning. He found their all-round general knowledge curious. He himself was and always remained against standardized book learning, but he understood that he had to adjust himself and see to it that his own books reached the public.

Sales began to pick up after he had visited England again in March 1921. Faithful Miss Dowland was put in charge of publications, till, during his later years, an official publisher took over.

It seems that after this journey the work in the English centres got going again, and elsewhere things went smoothly. In November attendance at his lectures in Switzerland had been moderate to fair, in March there were hardly enough extra chairs, people sat on the floor, and some had to be refused admittance.[8]

In England again in May, he began to design the Service of the Universal Worship, giving it the finishing touches that summer in Wissous and Holland. In Wissous the family had found better accomodation than in Tremblaye, in a house belonging to a naval officer. It stood on the edge of the village, looking out over the fields. It was there that the first summer meeting was held, attended by few people as yet, but everyone had the feeling that the foundations were good now and the work could begin. Everything that has been written about Wissous, in the magazine then and in memoirs later, has something fresh and gay, as if it were spring instead of summer.

In the mornings the disciples saw their master sit silently in the garden. Nobody disturbed him, only the children played around him. In the afternoons everyone in turn sat with him at a small table and had some special subject dictated to him or her. Sometimes when visitors came, he played the veena or sang, in his French summer garden. Quite late in the evening they all gathered in the large living-room. The Indian musical instruments were lying on the naval officer's billiard table and the divans were arranged in oriental fashion, under a mariner's stuffed albatross on the wall. The Begum was there, the brothers — who had been travelling and giving concerts all winter, without Hazrat — two or three mureeds, and the servant-girl. These evening meetings were held in silence, which made them unforgettable. The brothers played in the background. An oil lamp provided all the light they needed.

An oil lamp was the only light, too, at the simple dinners on Sundays or birthdays — Indian food, meat curry and rice. It was peaceful. Once, after dessert, Inayat tried to make everyone sing in turn. They did, shyly. It never became a carefree feast of equals, as in the old days, or as once with the Persians and the Tartars in Russia.

For the Universal Worship the mureeds had to learn to speak in public, which was a stumbling block for many. Someone who had studied, judged and condemned quite a number of philosophers and fashionable ministers went to a Sufi Service and listening to the lay preacher he thought, 'Well, my friend, you are no theologian, your style is not always perfect, but this is certainly the new religious life I have been in search for so long.'

The cherag (officiant) who gives the address means what he says; he or she can hardly be as complete and clear as Inayat himself, but the form of the service itself provides completeness. The ceremony developed from the prayer meetings — including an address — that had already been held during the war. The ritual in use today was designed in 1921, mainly in co-operation with Sophia Saintsbury-Green, and later tried out and improved upon in Wissous and Holland.

177

Symbolically all religions are represented to express the inner unity as well as the outer differences. There are candles and flowers on the altar, which is covered with a yellow cloth. The cherags wear loose black gowns. Inayat would have preferred to see the cherags (the words means a lamp, a light) in white or yellow, but his Westerners advised against such lack of solemnity; it was not done to show light and warmth in church. Inayat let them their dark Sunday robes, but could not help remarking, now and then, that a man with a long face was not necessarily a religious man.

The black gowns, — rather like kaftans — were made by Amina-Begum. She continued to do this as long as her husband was alive. She made all the clothes for the family, his too, even to the Turkish hat. Her work was always in the background, as is the traditional role for a master's wife in the East. The last few years when Inayat was not only travelling most of the time, but also claimed by his disciples from morning till evening during the summer school, were difficult for her. Wissous may have been her last happy summer, there they still found quiet, and time, in the lingering light after the long day, to walk among the cornfields together.

The disciples describe the summer in Wissous as an idyll. But there was more. One afternoon a thunderstorm broke unexpectedly and everyone ran to the house for shelter. The last one, closing the door, looked back and saw Inayat standing on a small hill, his hair streaming in the wind, leaves whirling all around him. Great, but different from the greatness the disciples loved to see. Loneliness.

How much Inayat's view of things differed from that of his disciples is evident from the Dowland letters. At heart he was the most trusting of persons, he would never give up, he called himself an optimist with open eyes. For the first blossoming he had done the spade work. In the spring of 1921 he wrote from Brussels. 'At present my life is one

178

constant struggle and full of activity, but the order is in such an unfounded and unsettled condition that however much I work it is never enough.' Miss Dowland had advised him to rest but he did not want to think of that for another year. Writing from Wissous, in July, thanking her for a birthday present, his tone is not cheerful. Only the second letter from Wissous strikes a more satisfied note and in early September he at last happily wrote, 'I wish you were here.' That was in Katwijk on the Dutch coast, where every evening he stood by the sea — wide open space. He stayed at a disciple's summer house, Baron van Tuyll's, at the end of the promenade. The following year he conducted a sequel to the summer school there. In 1921 he travelled from Katwijk to several other Dutch towns, where his lectures attracted many listeners.

It was this very success that brought new difficulties. On 14th September he wrote from Amsterdam. 'The Message is forcing its way out, it is I who am holding it back with all my might.' There were too many candidates for executive posts and he had continually to waste time on trifles. He told himself and Miss Dowland that difficulties were part of every beginning, but it turned his hair grey. 'We are living in such dreadful times. It takes such a lot of energy to spiritualize the material souls and as soon as the thought of matter is brought to their mind they drop from spirit to matter by the law of gravitation.... There is no one to help with the outer work of the order, upon my mind there is a double strain and until God sends some one with mind, means, tact and enthusiasm, with sympathy for Murshid, and devotion to the cause, my difficulty will be incalculable.' Such things, among others, passed through his mind while everyone who met him felt the peace and clarity that radiated from him. From these days too, date some descriptions of his wonderful performance on the veena, serene, elevating. When he closed his eyes he was alone.

The struggle in itself was probably not the worst thing.

He was a fighter and saw life as a struggle. The energy and strength that were so striking in him as a young man had been transformed and refined, but the dash was still there. Not only in his strength of purpose, but even physically. On the beach near Katwijk one day an engineer and a fisherman stood talking. Suddenly a galloping horseman appeared in the distance and flew past a moment later, 'unrecognizably enveloped in a flowing mantle... Was he a priest? In any case an excellent horseman, judging by his seat in the gallop... The fisherman said, "You know, sir, they have a black man there in Katwijk. I wouldn't be surprised if that was him. They call him John the Baptist there. He is staying with the baron." ' The engineer who tells this story became a mureed and, among other things, worked on a children's class with the master. In spite of all Inayat's strength and dignity, which reminded one of Biblical figures, nothing was too trifling for him. But childish narrowness, childish ambition, were torture.

It was exactly those admirers who had executive ambitions who found it hard to disentangle their dreams of spirituality from their illusions of their own greatness. They wanted to become Sufis, not because in spite of all external differences we were all one, brothers, but because they considered themselves special and better than others. Often Inayat's teachings were only half understood. He himself had difficulty in finding a satisfactory form for the organisation. But the main problem, especially in the beginning, was the money that wasn't there. He regrets it briefly in a letter to Miss Dowland, he mentions it in a stylized form in his *Gayan* and *Vadan,* where all his different moods can be found; in the *Autobiography* he reluctantly devotes a paragraph to it. It hurt his old Maula Bakhsh pride.

As an artist and a courtier he had learnt to disdain money matters. It was not done to talk about it, even not think about it. The first time he earned a large sum of money, or

180

rather was richly rewarded, he sent the money – gold pieces of course – to his father via his brother. A prudish way round, but that was the proper way to do it.

For a Westerner it went without saying that he should be paid: he worked hard, gave lectures, wrote books, helped innumerable people – but directly accepting a fee he found difficult. He begged his last secretary never to talk about money to him. Some disciples, even one who worked with him, supposed that he hardly knew what money was. Another was shocked when he saw him pay for his tram-ticket:'his beautiful hands and that dirty small change.'Yet he not only knew what to do with small change and with his first-earned gold, but also with dollars borrowed for the nth time. 'Dear S...,' he wrote to one of his administrators, 'I am sending you today a money order of $ 500.– to give you back the money you gave me in New York for using in arranging lectures, now I think you will need it as there is the summerschool affair to arrange. I thank you for having lent me. 'The rest of the letter concerns work and the health of the adressee.

It was often the gifts of wealthy pupils that made it possible for him to travel. Since they had moved to Suresnes in 1922 his family was financially looked after by an old Dutch lady who came to live with them. He did not accept money from just anyone – he once refused a castle plus livelihood and he preferred many small contributions to one large one. Earning money with his music had been an inner *tour de force* for him, asking money for spiritual work was almost impossible. Just as for music respect was the only acceptable reward. Until 1920 he had not even asked any fees for his lectures, only his travel and hotel expenses were reimbursed. But he made the discovery all idealists make: that which can be had free is either taken wrongly or not appreciated. When Miss Dowland was reorganising the society in England she did not want to ask for subscriptions. Inayat replied that originally he had not done so either because he thought that 'it would remain private,' that is to say in the beginning he saw himself as a master with a few disciples around him. 'Scientific societies and literary societies also take subscriptions. Now that I am opening a branch here and a branch there it cannot remain free, for that will attract the inquisitive. Those who really do not have anything naturally need not pay and they will appreciate that.'

In October 1921 the worst financial worries were over, the English debt had been paid off and the struggle for power between new and old committee members had been smoothed out. For a little while he felt free from daily cares and began to work in Germany. Defeated, post war Germany, where a million mark note was worth one pound one week and ten shillings the next, nothing at all a week later. Inflation, humiliation, confusion. Shame and bitterness under the surface, feelings of guilt and idealism in the temporary rulers; one of the few German pupils keeps on repeating in her memoirs that she was a pacifist. And everyone watched with mixed feeling the foreigners who flooded the country because one could buy so cheaply with these funny a thousand-a-penny marks.

'This land of musicians and philosophers I saw at its worst,' Inayat says in the *Autobiography* and on 26th October he wrote to Miss Dowland from Berlin that he had fallen into the wrong hands. 'The one who arranged my tour happens to be a false man, an agent of an organisation which works against all that is not Catholic. Thank heaven I have got rid of him now, but still he exists and can do a lot of harm.' One professor Schermann saved him from the false impresario, but Inayat did not stay much longer after that. During the following years he made a few more trips to Germany and attracted large audiences, to the astonishment of the organizers sometimes, but he himself did not have the feeling that the work made any impact. 'I strongly felt the clouds of depression which cover the heart of Germany.' Indeed, the German centres were short-lived and under Hitler the movement was forbidden. After World War II the work finally took root. Inayat's son Vilayat as well as his grandson Fazal work there now, as in the 'old' countries. The master's most interesting meeting was probably with the philosopher R. C. Eucken in Jena, a then famous Nobel prize winner.

The false impresario had been clever. He pretended to protect his foreign lecturer. Places Inayat wished to visit were declared unsuitable — 'you are too good for them' — and the people who wanted to speak to him after the lectures were not admitted. But these private talks after lectures were essential. Addressing a large audience was only a preamble — personal contacts gave meaning to the work, even though most people did not come to find spiritual guidance, but consolation. Unhappy love affairs, marriages gone wrong, business problems, illness, worry, loss, suicide plans, even political perils were all confided to him. He listened, did not say much, sometimes something very down-to-the-earth, as, when a woman complained about her unfaithful husband: 'But you knew you were marrying an artist, didn't you?' He seldom gave advice, sometimes a stimulus. For example, when a man who was out of work asked if he should resign himself: 'Action, you know,' Inayat cried, jumping up. Mostly he made people discover their own way. If he did too much himself it would be of no help after he had gone. Someone wrote to him that her husband was very nice and good to her as long as the master was in town, after that he fell back into his old habits.

And so, among piled-up chairs and bare tables in speakers' waiting rooms he became acquainted with western homelife — its saddest aspect. His help was meaningful and welcome, but it was not what he had expected to give. He was more often seen as a consoler than as a teacher. But even consoling could only help if the sufferer co-operated instead of merely remaining passive. He noted the rather lax tendency not only to look to others for help and consolation but also to impute all faults to others — in family quarrels, in business and working life, even in politics.

He painted the western idiosyncrasies with a few swift strokes in his play *The Bogeyman*.[9] The first act begins in a railway waiting room, a setting he was well acquainted with. There a speculator and a 'modernist' politician are busy discussing the newspaper from which they draw their one-day wisdom. An unhappy lover enters, wailing; the speculator advises him to get rich quickly, then he can have all he wants. The modernist thinks he can help him by a scientific analysis of the phenomenon love, while the rejected lover goes on lamenting. A lady who quarrels with everybody and complains about everything is the fourth to appear. Finally a sage enters, the modernist immediately calls him a charlatan, the lady thinks him a bogeyman. The speculator is not averse to a little prediction, clairvoyant investment advice; he is rather baffled when he gets veiled mystical answers. On second thought the modernist wants to know whether his party will win and now a kind of conversation develops: both sage and modernist want happiness for everyone but their methods differ. 'Do you think a sense of mutual goodwill can be aroused among the people in high position without strong measures?' the politician asks. The sage replies that every attack is reciprocated by a counter-attack. The complaining woman is advised not to approach the people of her time 'who cannot be different from what they are' with thoughts of self-pity. The lover is given a similar reply: his tearful, demanding attitude is not yet love. 'Loving is living' and pain is part of it. But the wailing lover commits suicide. None of the four understands the bogeyman. The modernist comprehends intellectually what the strange man is aiming at, but does not believe that what he wants to do can be realized.

Neither did Inayat believe that the methods of the modernist could be a lasting help. Politics, in the sense of

184

struggle for power or even distribution of power, was something new to him. In the India of his childhood there were rulers, good or bad, loved or unloved. There were also the rich, often wicked or stupid, and the poor for whom a good rich man might do something. All straightforward human relationships. The division into political parties after the western example had only started in India after he left. The parliamentary game, in which two opponents could call each other the most awful names in the House and afterwards have a friendly cup of coffee together, he and his brothers found ridiculous. They always remained the sons of Rahemat Khan: if one was insulted in public – that was how they saw the parliamentary debate – one would control oneself and remain polite, no more. 'Treat a friend warmly and an enemy politely.'

Economics Inayat considered as one-sided materialism, with the emphasis on one-sided. In his disciples he often corrected one-sided spiritual interests and for his own country he thought some development along western lines necessary. But a world ruled by commercialism and technology produced humans who no longer knew they were human. His view of the world was psychological and he could not help feeling this was an eastern attainment. He was pleasantly surprised when he noticed that western physicians were beginning to take psychological causes for illness into account. More than once he compared eastern and western methods of self-knowledge and healing,[10] and in his *Autobiography* he also deals with psychology in a survey of religions and philosophies. The Coué method he found a primitive beginning about which too much fuss was made: 'In the East any child in the street knows this.' His objections to psychoanalysis was that it revealed too much too crudely: there were things that had better remain unsaid. He himself had a different method to get to the bottom of things. He, too, liberated man from outside influences and knew different levels of consciousness and the opposing tendencies in man. But his hidden last cause did not lie somewhere in a childhood memory. Being a mystic he went back as far as the moment of creation, in which a self-respecting rationalist is not supposed to believe.

About sexuality he had an open mind as he did not have the overcompensating need of the post- and contra-Victorians to push it into the foreground everywhere. He saw that unbalance was caused by the tensions of a competitive society and by a one-sided limitation of living. The psychiatrist's 'narcissism' is his 'false ego' or 'vanity' − and this he calls one of the strongest human incentives − which we can never completely get rid of as long as we live, we can only transform and refine it. But under the false ego he sees the real ego hidden, the shared divine origin which makes all men brothers. He liberated those who came to him from the straitjacket of ready-made virtues, but at the same time gave clear-cut but never rigid morals. Everyone could search for his real being and purpose in life and live towards it. 'For one person it may be good to be a nun, for another to sit in cafés.' That one who walked the mystic path needed discipline, was a different matter. His psychology, as an art of life, was both liberating and ethical, flexible, yet giving direction. Of course, in the last instance he based everything on his philosophy of 'God in all of us.' But the more he got to know the lamenters in the consulting room and realized how few people were ready for mysticism and how many had suspicious reactions to the word religion, the more he began to speak of the problems of everyday life. And so his books about daily problems came into being and he thought them important. Twice over he wrote to Miss Dowland that his book about 'the art of living' should be published first and only then another book on pure mysticism.[11]

That, too, was a matter of balance between 'floating in the clouds' and having one's feet on the ground, working for as many people as possible and working for his dis-

186

ciples. Already at the annual celebration in 1922 he said that he did not mean to make everyone a Sufi, that is a practising member of the order. If only people learned to live together. Or, as he says elsewhere, 'There is no point in thinking that people will become saints, or sages or great men; as long as they live according to the law of reciprocity, give and take, but not overvalue what they themselves give. Ask a practical man, a man with common sense, if it is possible to live in this world, and not observe this law of give and take.' Of course, critical souls often saw fit to remind him of this common sense. He possessed a good deal of it and he tried to instill it in his disciples. 'The inner life is not only uplifting, it has practical value too. Praying without living in brotherhood has no value.'

Warnings such as this were directed at efforts towards mysticism which emptied themselves in − or originated in − escape from the world and self-elevation. During one of his visits to England he was taken to a school where concentration was taught. Ten or fifteen children were seated before a blank curtain and each in turn had to say what was there. Obediently they declared that they saw a rose, or a lily, or something equally poetical. Only one said shyly, 'I don't see anything.' Inayat: 'I thought, that is better, at any rate he says what he sees... It was a lesson in hypocrisy.'

This sober denial is not contradictory to the story he liked to tell of the dervishes in Ajmer, the ragged fellows who addressed each other as Maharaja. These dervishes meant what they said and experienced something real, they were not play-acting or pretending, but each bowed to the divine in the other. They had gone through the same training as Inayat. In the beginning he, too, had to restrain himself if the poet in him started to drift away with 'something beautiful.' The danger of aimless floating was great. Occasionally he said that people need not become sages or saints or that it was not his aim to make a world full of esoteric centres.

Yet he needed a number of inner schools to produce a nucleus of workers who not only accepted the theory of his ethics, but had got to know the source. He did strive after that but for the Westerners of that period the discipline of meditation was so new that he could do very little with them as yet. As a consequence the external work, the spreading of the message, was increasingly emphasized.

His own inner evolution never stopped. A great realization was usually preceded by a passionate longing; one can feel it in many pages of *Gayan* and *Vadan,* the books of aphorisms, in which he addresses not only his fellowmen, but also himself; and God. Sometimes the disciples witnessed this tension of expectation and on one occasion they saw the fulfilment.

In September 1922 Inayat stayed in Katwijk, at the time a small fishing-village on the Dutch North Sea coast. One afternoon he took two of his followers, an Englishwoman and a Dutchman with him and, his hair streaming in the wind, he almost ran along the beach in a state of restlessness altogether new to them. At some distance from the village he went into the dunes alone and returned after half an hour, quiet and dignified again.[12] He called this spot 'the place of wish fulfilment.' Since then Katwijk has been extended almost as far as this little valley. The Sufis have bought the land and now, next to a camping ground a building has arisen with rooms for meetings, Universal Worship and meditation.

In the New Forest near Southampton Inayat liked to walk with Miss Dowland and other old pupils. Sometimes he took his veena with him, as when he was a boy in the Himalayas, and there discovered the enchanted silence of the wordless muni. The Himalayas were not essential. In the middle of a conversation with two companions the master suddenly hurried on ahead, showing a certain restlessness, as in Katwijk. But this time the disciples stayed with him and witnessed the moment of upliftment; they saw that nature responded too, as Inayat had seen when he met the muni in the Himalayas. He himself recalls this event in one of his letters: 'I cannot forget the most worshipful time in the forest.'

This he mentioned lightly in between a request for corrected proofs and an enquiry after the health of a relative. He easily moved from one level to another. One good observer describes how, as a guest in someone's house Inayat was sitting, quiet and withdrawn, left in peace by the adults. Then a child came in with a picture book and at once all his attention was focused on the little boy and the book in the foreign language.

He was indifferent to the world and full of attention for people, mild and ironical, strict and forgiving, kind to all, demanding for himself and his closest co-workers, grateful for understanding and the least little help, certainly irritated by dull ignorance. He was practical and impractical, dignified in attitude and bearing, but sometimes passionately impatient for the moment of upliftment. He suffered when he met with disappointment and opposition, and rose above it. He worked almost without stopping. Occasionally he allowed himself some recreation; he admired a sunrise in America seen from a train window, enjoyed skaters on a canal in Amsterdam. He revived under the blue skies of France and Italy, comforted himself with the mountains and forests in Germany. With luck there might be time for a concert, or a Russian ballet, or a ride on horseback. He loved wide open spaces: the Swiss lakes, the sea in California and Holland, a trip in a sailing-boat and a ride in an aeroplane. And in spite of all this need for nature and space, he was able to ignore even the most beautiful landscape, and continue to work. 'Are we here to do the work or to look at nature?' This to his startled secretary who wished to walk into a flowering field of rare Alpine lilies.

A sculptress writes that it was impossible to get a good likeness in a portrait – one moment he looked serious and old, then again young and radiant. Not even all the photos put together can give a complete picture. True, compared to earlier photos, he has matured and changed in later ones. Little was left of the elegant gentleman of 1911 in Denver; something of the passionate strength of the young Indian in Hyderabad still shows, but now completely sublimated. In most photos he looks old, not only because his hair was graying; his eyes hold a memory of too many things seen. But in spite of his hard daily life and in spite of the fact that too little exercise and too much hotel food made him put on weight, an increasingly refined and illuminated face looks at you — or inwards.

Mario Montessori, who was present when Inayat visited Madame Montessori in the spring of 1924, was surprised when I showed him a portrait of that period. 'But he looks much older than I remember. My impression was of a man in the prime of his life. Had he been ill? If one looks at those eyes... The impression I had in Rome was of a kind of inner peace, in this photo he is sad and veiled. What struck me during the conversation was the inner calm while his eyes were radiant.'

The photo was taken before Inayat's most serious illness in 1925; before that he sometimes had pneumonia and one time he travelled while he was still ill. The difference between photo and living memory may relate to Inayat's own remark that the expression of a mystic can change twenty times a day. In the spring of 1924 he was not yet forty-two years old; Ali Khan, the lively one, who was a year older, was once taken for his son. The visit to Maria Montessori in the warmth of Italy was one of the rare contacts with a person of any stature who understood him. Independant of each other they had worked out a 'game of silence' for children.

An even rarer meeting was with an abbé in Paris, a hidden western mystic who understood completely what Inayat meant and lived. The master recorded it with surprised delight. Another joy was the arrival of the Gaekwar

190

in London, in 1920. It was the Gaekwar who advised him to write his biography and autobiography. This flesh-and-blood bit of home — the ruler too — did him good, all the more so because during his wanderings he hardly saw any of his fellow countrymen, and for a few years did not even have his brothers with him. He was lonely.

Yet, in spite of his unceasing longing for India, he felt more and more at home in the West. With surprise he discovered that he even began to feel the lack of counterpoint in Indian music, because he was getting accustomed to western harmony. European music and a European musician provided another of the congenial meetings he loved to recall. In Geneva he was a guest at one of the official dinner parties Paderewski used to give. After the other guests had left, the maestro played for the master.[13] Inayat recalls, 'Once I was privileged to hear Paderewski in his own house. He began to play softly. Every note led him deeper and deeper into the ocean of music. Any meditative person could see that he was absorbed.... that he did not know where he was.' Paderewski was also impressed with his guest and the next day he came to Inayat's lecture.

As far as I know this contact did not lead to anything further; a travelling life offers little oppertunity for the development of steady friendships. And that, too, made him lonely.

Wandering, though, suited him. *Who's Who* of 1916-1928 lists Inayat's recreations as travelling and music. That sounds as if painting is the painter's recreation. Travelling was necessary and he loved it, music was his profession and the need of his soul. Giving up playing and even regular practice was a sacrifice. The last concert he took part in was in 1923 in Paris, and the last printed review is an admiring article by a Dutch author, in 1924. Even the short invocation which used to precede his lectures was omitted during the last years. That moment of soft chanting always made a deep impression; it was common practice, Tagore did it too and it was always considered wonderful. But people 'whose work in life was criticizing' said that Inayat used his strange singing to hypnotize his audience. This was sufficient reason for him to stop it, for even the slightest trace of miracle-working had to be avoided. Doing this, he made life difficult for himself, but cheap success was dangerous and undesirable. He sought to make an un-obtrusive but lasting effect. Apart from cheap success, which he could avoid, he found superficial success, and, as a contrast, a real understanding of his message. From the packed halls in Berlin he did not expect much, but those in America in 1923, sometimes packed, sometimes not, were 'perhaps not a success in the American way, but they were in mine.'

After two, three years of struggling and building, the American tour of 1923 was, on the whole, good. He had already thought of going early in 1922, but at that time his touring plans were not yet always successful: he wanted to go to Prague, but this never occurred, and to Denmark, where he did go later. In America his first pupil Mrs Martin was working. She invited him and, especially in California, prepared his tour very well.

There were difficulties at first. He had left the European centres behind under a new organisation, which had had a painful birth. He sailed on a small ship, in bad weather, and was seasick until a sailor told him, 'There is no medicine for it, but you must fix your eyes on the horizon.' He thought this a beautiful symbol, 'fix your eyes as far as you can see.'[14] Towards the end of the journey he had made friends with all the passengers. He worked on board, gave lectures to a casual audience who had not gone out to buy tickets to hear him and he contentedly remarked that 'the message was felt by people from different countries, who all had different opinions.' It was not what he said that impressed people most, it was the natural way he said it, and the depth it came from. His combined simplicity, kindness, and impressiveness charmed almost any company he stayed with; not only his fellow-passengers on this journey, not only his hosts and their families, including the servants – but even officials. In a letter from Cleveland he wrote: 'The people here did not let me in at first, and now they don't wish me to leave. What do you think of that? Don't you think it funny?'

This refers to his entry, which was not all that funny. The New York *Times* of Wednesday 28th February 1923, page 23, reports, sandwiched between 'Fight in Tokyo Parliament' and 'Klan candidates win': 'ADMITS HINDU MYSTIC – Board of Inquiry decides Inaya Khan may lecture here. Inaya Khan, Hindu mystic and poet, who was taken to Ellis Island after his arrival here Monday because the quota of Hindus had been filled, was ordered admitted yesterday following a hearing before a special board of enquiry. The Khan, it was brought out, had been in the United States in 1912 on a lecture tour. He also played the buena, a native string instrument.' (Follows name of his hotel and of one of his rescuers).

To the list of questions put before him Inayat had deliberately given nonsense answers, as a dervish does who wants to show the absurdity of certain customs by playing the fool himself. He records the event in his *Autobiography*. 'I was brought before a tribunal and my answers interested them, though they did not comply with the demands of the law. They wanted to know my place of birth, I replied: the world. After religion I filled in: all religions, and as my profession I gave: searching for Truth and serving God and man. At first the officials were suspicious, but finally showed some interest and exempted me of the law of geographical compulsion.' Yet it needed the factual information supplied by some of his old friends to liberate him from what he called 'this house of welcome.'

The unsolicited interest the newspapers took immediately made him known. The lectures in New York went well.

193

There was also a pleasant feeling of homecoming, at least of recognizing and being recognized. Not only the small number of old mureeds came, but also his first western sponsor, Professor Rybner. Again he travelled westwards across the continent, just as he had done twelve years ago; and again he found the best opportunities in San Francisco where faithful, sturdy Mrs Martin awaited him with her disciples, her organisation and a well-prepared series of lectures at various universities on his favourite subjects: Persian poets and Indian music. According to American custom he was taken to meet all kinds of celebrities of the day, for instance the horticulturist Luther Burbank, who was always in the news. Mrs Martin also invited a Japanese Zen Buddhist to meet him, Nyogen Senzaki, who has left an amusing record of the meeting. 'Murshid, I see a Zen in you.' 'Mr Senzaki, I see a Sufi in you.'[15] And that, according to Mr Senzaki, was the end of the interview. Whereupon Mrs Martin and another of her guests present carried on an animated discussion about reincarnation; of course reincarnation. There was a person who, after one of his 1923 lectures asked Inayat the same question about reincarnation she had asked him in 1911. She was to ask it again in 1926.

There were others too. In California, between 24th March and 8th May he initiated hundreds of disciples, from all levels of society. Not many according to American standards but sufficient by his own. Among them was a young man Samuel Lewis who would later continue Mrs Martin's work. Another one — according to one source of information an ex-commercial traveller, according to another an ex-cowboy — first went to Europe with Inayat and later travelled all over the United States to spread the message. In the new world there were even more sects and movements than in London, some very odd personal obsessions, led by men and women with a fine sense of publicity.

194

It was the beginning of the Gay Twenties, the time of corruption under President Harding, of prohibition and bootlegging, crime kings and Ku Klux Klan, preachers and jazz.

All this was nothing new to Inayat. He had been the victim and the guest of robbers. The surfeit of sects he called 'sectionalism' and mentioned it in the same breath as nationalism: all of them one-sided groups, emphasizing difference. Light-hearted frivolity he had seen plenty of too.

The music interested him. Jazz was new, many considered it a craze and only critisized it. Though Inayat only came across the dance music and never had an opportunity to hear concert jazz, he recognized its attraction.[16] 'The syncopation is the secret of its charm, the rhythm arouses a kind of life among performers and audience alike, and it is the love of this life that has given such popularity to jazz.... It does not make the brain think much; it does not trouble the soul to think of spiritual things, it does not trouble the heart to feel deeply... it touches the physical body... and gives a renewed strength by the continuation of a particular rhythm.' He saw it was there to stay: 'Restaurants and factories need it as background music.' But misuse shocked him. Once he witnessed a maddening all-night dance in a New York hotel. 'Everyone was ill the next day, they were mad, really mad, because they misused the rhythm.'

In spite of excesses and in spite of all the emphasis on toughness Inayat Khan liked America: a young country, enthusiastic about one thing after another. Totally in the grip of commercialism, of course. 'The world...needs all the spirituality that can be put into it,' noted one of the journalists who came to interview him.[17] In general, the interviews, even if they gave a more or less correct resumé of what he had said, sketched but a clumsy image. They touched only the fringe. However, it was useful that the press, albeit in its inevitable superficial way, was interested in him.

195

This happy journey did not go off altogether without some friction with his own helpers. The centre leaders thought his books too expensive, at the same time they wished to make a profit on them. Nobody was making a profit on the books. Mrs Martin soon understood this, but the leader in New York continued to grumble. This was the kind of practical detail Inayat had to cope with, apart from his proper work, the lectures followed by discussions and private talks, the Universal Worship, classes and initiations, interviews, visitors and correspondance. The most spiritually inclined disciples were not keen on executive posts. Paul Reps, for instance, who has now become well-known through his books on Zen but still considers himself a disciple of Inayat, wrote to me that he had been drawn into the American organisation temporarily, but had withdrawn from it as soon as possible.

And so Inayat was plagued with administrative worries to the very end, though many devotees put their heart and soul into the work. The total commitment of some followers is impressive. If he wrote on 29 June, 'I need you on 1 July for the summer school,' the disciple would be there. That a man, well-to-do or not – the young American, Fatha Engle, who travelled with him was not rich – could do this was one thing. But it happened that a father who was not a mureed, not even religious, but who held Inayat in high regard, gave his daughter the fare to America, so that she could go and help – a married daughter whose husband agreed to her helping the master.

This Dutch woman accompanied Inayat on the second part of his journey. She arrived just in time to find lodgings in new places. Inayat had given her two addresses to try in Chicago, one of an old man who did not respond, the second of a Kabbala master who at first kept her at bay. But she, as a good Sufi, came seriously to attend lessons on this kind of mysticism with the result that the Kabbalist put a hall at Inayat's disposal when he arrived and a centre could be founded in Chicago.

This helper was an exceptionally large, fair-haired woman, physically a kind of Germania. In the train to New York a guard in the corridor scowled at them, because a coloured man was travelling with a woman so white. Inayat gave him one look, not the kind, calm glance described by so many, but reproving. The man dropped his tray and fled.

Such pinpricks were bound to occur. It was summer and sweltering, when he returned to New York. There he had to stay in a small, hot room in the house of the centre leader — the same who wanted to make a profit on the books — instead of in an hotel. He accepted the discomfort with his usual composure. It was after all not a ramshackle stable, as sometimes in India. To relax between engagements he took his new American travelling companion to some café terrace, to eat ice-cream and watch the people.

On the whole he was satisfied with his journey. What with the publicity given to the most trifling subjects and the flood of ephemeral ideas brought out in a grand manner he felt 'as though he were blowing a whistle in the noise of a thousand drums,' but he was not disappointed. 'Thinking souls responded and I felt encouraged and happy.' On the way back he sang. That did not happen in days of worry and struggle. He knew now that the work had taken root. He was aware of the limitations he had to take into account, and he recognized the possibilities he could make use of. As he had adjusted his mysticism to what people around him could digest, so he had adjusted his artistry. No more Persian poets for his disciples, but plays in which they could recognize themselves, and him. One of these plays he dictated on the return journey from America. In a few sentences he sketches several personages at a fancy dress ball, dressed up as, and gushing over, their past incarnations, and one too unimaginative, character. In the main character he shows the passionate search for God-realization. Among his pupils he had professional actors and gifted amateurs for the principal parts and the many smaller parts suited the many lesser talents. He sometimes had to laugh — in his beard and behind his hand — at some of the amateur performances at the summer school in Suresnes. The new mureeds, and they were in the majority, were blissfully unaware that he was a professional artist, as innocently and painstakingly they performed at the weekly concert.

Suresnes, where the family had settled for good in June 1922, never became the idyll Wissous had been. It was not a beauty spot, as it had been some thirty years before but Inayat liked it there. In Moscow and London there had been two linguists of the old school among his friends.[18] Nineteenth century linguists held the, now obsolete, view that all languages are derived from Sanscrit. Being an Indian, he liked the idea. Also he liked to play with words and sounds. Donizetti's *Una furtiva lagrima* he called 'phur-tiwala' (the energetic one) and he knew the meaning of 'a secret tear' very well. As a musician sound came first with him. The name Suresnes reminded him of Surindra, the lord Indra. Moreover, some of the earliest French saints had lived in the neighbourhood; that, too, counted.

Fazal Manzil, the abode of blessing, he called the house. It stands on high ground, overlooking the lights of Paris on one side and in front, from the tall steps, he could see as far as the Mont Valerien. There is a tiny public park now, and blocks and blocks of flats, but then there were bare fields and only a few, mostly poor, cottages.

At the top of the steps, during the first summer, he used to say good night to his pupils with a handshake, as they went to their hotels and boarding houses. In 1922 and 1923 close personal contact was still possible. In the afternoons he used to sit under one of the old trees in the heart of the garden and everyone in turn sat with him for five minutes. Babuli, his 8-year old daughter, helped with the tea. It no longer had the intimacy of Wissous, when there were few and each could have a whole hour with him, but not yet the tense rush of the last years when for three months there was hardly time for every visitor to have a five or ten minute conversation, and then it had to be previously arranged. The number of followers increased rapidly.

After the summer school followed the assembly meetings in Geneva where the Headquarters had been incorporated. The external organization remained a source of difficulties and pain. After this annual struggle he had to go travelling again, to answer questions, to avoid misunderstandings, to attune himself to the public. In essence his message remained the same, though he extended the practical application on a large scale and tried as much as he could to say things in a more and more European way. That was very difficult. As a western theologist quotes St Augustine or Luther, so he automatically turned to Quran or Vedanta, which was a broad step, really, Islam *and* Hinduism. During his years in England he accustomed himself to quoting directly from the New Testament; the stories of the Old Testament remained part of the Islamic tradition for him. He knew scores of stories, especially about Moses, that the Bible does not give, though the Jewish rabbinic tradition does. And in his public lectures he used fewer and fewer eastern terms and quotations.

According to Raden Aju Jodjana and Mahmood Khan he tried to avoid the word God. Indeed Inayat says more than once that the word God leads to misunderstanding, but he is also ironical about those who feel compelled to say 'gods' or 'the higher powers' instead of plain, old-fashioned God.[19] He tried to prevent associations with a tyrannical God, with the malpractices of established organizations and with cruelties committed in the name of God. But above all, experiencing God in the sense he meant, could not be caught in words. Notwithstanding all these difficulties he could now draw on hundreds of meetings with

Westerners and their problems, so that the audience recognized themselves in the examples he gave. More superficial, yet effective, were the references to local environment or topical events. He himself did not read newspapers, but where everyone talked about excavations in Egypt or oil-drilling in America he also knew about it, and casually wove Tutankhamon, oil wells or gold mines into his lectures.

Being a mystic he concentrated on his subject and especially on his audience, selecting from his experiences and knowledge that which harmonised with a certain situation. Therefore he used the same motive in different ways. This is also the method of the musician, who varies the given melody. If he announced that his subject could be approached in three ways and each way could be divided into two aspects, he would not omit one of these six points. To the astonishment of his companions he used to speak without a scrap of paper. He often asked for the subject of the evening when on his way to the hall. If his audience expected something occult and mysterious, or some popular fancy theory, he would mould their pet ideas to his own philosophy, lightly varying the theme. Or he gave what he intended to say a name that suited the circumstances. In Amsterdam he was to speak for the Free Church on 'The Coming World Religion.' He was already standing on the platform when he changed the title. He said practically everything he had meant to say, but he had seen three clergymen in the audience and he did not want to offend them.

In spite of all his tact he was often heckled during a discussion, and sometimes met with plain rudeness. Two men, who became mureeds later, describe the same evening at a students' club in Rotterdam. At the back of the room students were drinking beer and making silly remarks about the speaker and what he said. One of the two who tell the story thought that the man on the platform did not notice this, but at the end Inayat thanked 'those who were kind enough to listen to me.' The other one, himself a student, was also sitting at the back and could not see the platform. He had not seen the speaker enter either, but he writes that he felt, 'as if a current was passing through him.' These completely opposite reactions were not rare.

Straight opposition occurred less frequently. In Amsterdam, in the Industrial Club, two members were whispering to each other and in the interval were the first to hand in a question. The pupil who observed this, himself an Amsterdam businessman, anxiously waited for the end of the evening. The note at the bottom came up last. The question was, 'Is socialism good?' If the speaker said yes, simplified reasoning would make him out to be a revolutionary and an atheist. If he said it was not good he would disappoint idealists and the socially conscious. His answer came easily. 'Socialism is good, if it brings you nearer to God.'

He had been thinking about this already. In the *Autobiography* he deals with socialism, as with psychology, under the heading 'Religions,' meaning spiritual and philosophical trends. As far as socialism concerned itself with working out of consideration for others he saw it akin to his own aims. 'To create happiness for oneself and others is the whole philosophy of religion.' But he rejected every element of self-pity, always and everywhere. And, of course, one-sided materialism, whether it was found in capitalism, socialism, technology, psychology or anything else, was something he automatically complemented with 'one cannot put enough spirituality in.' As, on the other hand, he complemented 'drifting away in the clouds' with common sense.

This is one of the reasons his sayings sometimes appear to be contradictory: he counteracted any sort of one-sidedness. It would be easy to show that he defended socialism as well as capitalism, as the case might be — with some remark quoted out of context. There is, for instance, one passage in which he points out that a factory cannot be kept going without the workers and their co-operation; and several in which he condemns the soul-destroying senselessness of working on a production line. But elsewhere he expresses respect for a businessman whose lifelong toil to achieve something he compares to the exertion and inner discipline of a mystic. Naturally either's way of living was different from his and, as he saw them, more like each other than they thought: 'Socialism and capitalism have the same god.' But everyone has to go the way that suits him. If all people lived alike and acted alike 'the world would become uninteresting. It would be like tuning all the keys of the piano to the same note.' Every society model could be good, on one condition: that there was love in the relationships, whether between equals or unequals; that someone who was different would be respected as a higher or lower note forming part of the symphony.

Love. People had heard it so often, it was a signal, such a stereotyped notion — a word and no more — that the clever boys in the back row could laugh and drink their beer: this black man is saying nothing new, and that, too, in English with an Indian accent.

Those who did feel a current and were not afraid of what radiated from Inayat were not afraid of the old word love either; and many came because they needed to receive his love and consolation. Some were attracted by his very power and unusualness. In many followers admiration came first and was not always accompanied by application of his teachings.

He knew all those contrary responses, all those forms of misinterpretation and rejection, of half-listening and wrong understanding. He had to defend himself as much from underestimation as from adoration. 'Some did say that I knew nothing, some still held that I knew all.'

Chapter X (1924-1926)
'Some did say that I knew nothing'

Once upon a time there was a madzub, that is a mystic in the guise of an idiot, who stood in the middle of the street and laughed. The foolishness of his fellow men and the things they made a fuss about amused him. Inayat told that story often and with relish, but he could not follow the example of his colleagues back home, not between the high, square automobiles in the western streets thronged with western faces. For him, something else was called for: a mystic sees so much foolishness that he simply holds his tongue.[1]

On September 17th, 1921, he wrote to Miss Dowland from Etretat in Normandy, saying that he was still working on the papers she had sent; he would have liked to come to England 'but I had something to do with friends with whom I am staying.' On the same day he wrote to his Dutch assistent, Van Stolk: 'There is not much to be expected from social meetings like this for our cause.'

Between the writing of these two letters, there must have occurred one of the absurd scenes that the well-meaning host at Le Chateau du Grand Val was wont to inflict upon his guests. That host was André Germain, a small and weak man, whose father had founded the Crédit Lyonnais. He himself was unfit for business or any other kind of bold pursuit, but thanks to his family and large fortune, he knew his way around in the *monde* and could afford to travel and collect celebrities. He saw himself as a poet and a historian. Sometimes he would try to arrange meetings between the great who crossed his path, for instance between Rilke and a French poetess. These usually failed to come off, as he admits frankly enough in his best work, his memoirs. About September 1924 he is frank only in part. On one page he informs us that he had rented an attractive small eighteenth century castle and that an Indian sage, noble ladies, a Dutch poet and some others visited him there; in a different place, he mentions an unsuccessful visit to André Gide and makes it appear that only his most distinguished guest, the Duchess de Clermont-Tonnerre, was with him.[2] However, the Dutch witness who was present, the prince and dean of poets Adriaan Roland Holst, told me about the whole extraordinary expedition.

Germain piled all his guests into a number of automobiles. Among them was another well-known oriental, Kahlil Gibran and his American secretary; also a German officer-poet, a young couple and a friend of the Duchess's. This curious company arrived unannounced on Gide's doorstep. The great man was playing tennis. From the first automobile alighted Mme Clermont-Tonnerre, whom he knew rather well, and so he interrupted his game and unwillingly showed her inside. The second car discharged the small and delicate Germain, the Duchess's tall and stately friend, and silent, observing Inayat. Gide was painstakingly discourteous, did not offer them tea, dropped numerous broad hints: 'Germain, your voiture is sounding its horn,' 'Which road did you take on the way up, you had better go back by such-and-such a route.' The embarrassed party stole glances at each other around a large table, until the Duchess finally gave the signal to depart.

Probably Germain had wanted not only to introduce both poets to each other, but also, or especially, the Orientals to the Frenchman, because Gide had gone to some trouble in 1913 for his translation of Tagore, and had put two more of the latter's plays into French in 1922.[3]

That was something Roland Holst had not known about and could hardly believe. It was his honest opinion that neither Tagore nor Inayat Khan had come into contact

En route, about 1925.

with Europeans of top rank. Now Roland Holst is a great poet and also the most western Westerner imaginable. He created his own paradise, 'far off, in the west, and past the sea;' and, like many who still remember the hypocrisy of the nineteenth century, he is allergic to anything faintly reminiscent of moralism. Therefore, he could only paint a mocking portrait: 'A handsome brown man with a fine bronze voice, with which he brought out, in very slow and Indian English, the greatest platitudes: 'we must see dze good in everydzing, we must see dze good in everydzing.' And the slower and bronzer, the more all those women melted with awe.'

Inayat did not have a secretary with him at Etretat and the ladies who were present did not show any signs of being swept off their feet. On the contrary. Germain's guests must have been somewhat nettled about his effort to unite East and West. First Roland Holst laid the Germain guest a wager that he could imitate Gibran's style. Indeed he could, Gibran's secretary took the parody seriously and offered the poet translation rights, which he managed to escape with some difficulty. The Duchess in turn tried to have a go at Inayat, but she was also forced to cover her retreat.

Exactly what happened is difficult to make out from Roland Holst's story, told more than forty years later. He thought the western lady had asked the eastern sage whether he had anything else to wear than always the same black robe. 'Certainly.' 'Will you show it?' The story has it that Inayat did in fact come in wearing another robe and asked whether she wished to see yet a third. Roland Holst could not remember the colours, 'Purple, let's say,' he said, 'or mauve.' It can only have been yellow, perhaps with a jewel — his emblem — added as a variation. That he complied with the silly request is not impossible. 'From the point of view of the wise human nature is childish.'[4] But the wise man does not fight or call himself superior. Better join in the game 'and throw light upon it.' He may have expected the tableau that followed. Roland Holst, conjuring up the scene with amusement and describing it as a real poet, ended the story on a note of astonishment and surprise: 'She stood gazing at him through her lorgnettes and calling out "Oh, how lovely, Oh, how beautiful." But she was the one who looked ridiculous. He stood there with dignity.'

Poor Duchess. Her nursery — she has written delightful memoirs — was graced by a bearded portrait of someone they called Our Lord, and all she knew about him was that he would punish her if she were naughty.[5] Such things can trigger a grudge against someone whose appearance and nature reminded Katwijk fishermen and London cockneys of John the Baptist and even Christ.[6] To her, Eastern meant indolent and passive; she would not hear of church or confession since the miracles that had been promised to her after communion as a child never materialized.

Roland Holst's associations also reveal defences against Roman Catholic customs. Not only did his memory give Inayat's clothing the colour of a priest's robe, but other bits and pieces of conversation that he could not recall literally were also filled in with Western stereotypes. 'He wanted to explain the meaning of Omar Khayyam, wine is the blood of Christ, or something of the sort,' — so he knew it was actually different — 'but I don't care for rational explications of poems I like.'

If Roland Holst had made this clear, Inayat would have appreciated it; he resorted to explanations only because most intellectuals needed them, but he held intuitive understanding in much more esteem. He thought highly of poets because they, like mystics, must trust to inspiration. Though there were friends of his disciples among Germain's guests, he took walks with Roland Holst the poet. But the latter turned his intellectual side towards the man from the East and started provoking discussions, not for the sake of the subject, but to draw the other out. Whenever a conversation took that turn, Inayat limited himself to general remarks and he also warned those in charge at his centres not to commit themselves in certain cases.

He knew the disappointment a child feels when her communion wonders do not come true, he knew Roland Holst's need for dispute and many other ways of holding off anything rightly or wrongly called religion. He knew how people mistook the abuses of an institutionalized church for true worship. How they lumped together faith and superstition as comforters for the gullible, how they lost their faith through despair over injustice in the world or because of their own sufferings. He knew materialists afraid to perceive 'in any other way than with their senses,' the intellectuals for whom it was bad form to talk seriously about religion. He knew silent indifference, rebellion against dogma without love, the assumption that a mystic must be someone with his head in the clouds or a pious person someone with a long face. The jokers appear in the play quoted earlier, when one of the characters in the waiting room approaches the silent sage saying, 'Now I'll have some fun.' It did not surprise the master that he could not get through to people who were very wrapped-up in their own circle and ideas. He had grown accustomed to being 'a freethinker among the religious and considered religous among the intellectual philosophers.'[7]

If only his pupils could see him as he was. In his first days as a pupil in Hyderabad, he had gone on and on about his murshid and would tell anyone and everyone what a marvellous man he was. And when he would finally mention his name, chances were someone would say: 'But I have known this Syed Madani for years and have never noticed anything out of the ordinary about him.' Now this old master in Hyderabad wished to remain unknown to the world at large. For Inayat, working publicly was imperative. When a stranger smiled at a pupil's enthusiastic tales about Inayat, the pupil minded more than he. But some of his western disciples had a very western bias in their thinking. They admired their murshid, but still thought they knew best.

This was borne out once again at the meetings in Geneva following the relative calm in Etretat. In 1923, he had established the International Headquarters of the Sufi Movement, incorporated in Switzerland. Inayat had high hopes for it, and expected that now he could leave administration and co-ordination of the work to others. In fact, the Board started with a vigorous and expert handling of publishing and publicity.

But some could not resist playing at government and turned the organisation, meant to be a means to take care of publicity, administration and co-ordination, into an object in itself. At the meeting of 1st October 1924 there was already a proposal, in all seriousness, to have a general assembly of members in Geneva 'to increase in the members a sense of brotherhood and give them a true concept of the significance of International Headquarters.'[8] It seems that, for them, three months of summer school were not enough to encourage brotherhood. In the international organisation each country had its national representative, and Inayat − always 'Murshid' to his disciples − received the administrative 'rank' of 'general representative.' The meeting at Geneva agreed to create a special travel fund fot their 'general representative,' but this official − their murshid Inayat Khan − would always have to tell the committee where he was going. In other words, he worked for their organization and not the other way round. No wonder the master often preferred to borrow money privately and repay the loan. Once, when being given a series of photographs of himself to inspect, he discovered one showing him less as a sage than as a rather authoritative gentleman. 'O yes, the general representative,' he said, amused.

But there were things he could not take as a joke. West-

209

ern lack of consideration and style shocked and amazed him. 'In India, no one in his right mind would dream of judging a sage.' The Westerner was at it day and night. Advice was heaped on him as if he were a child. 'In spite of knowing that I had already worked and had some experience, people used to say, "The character of our people is different from that of every other people."' He thought this remark particularly dense, because he was not only well aware of the outward differences − in his autobiography he gives a brief outline of each country − but especially because it showed that his chief principle had not been understood: people are outwardly different, but a Sufi acts on his knowledge of everyone's unity in God. This he meant by brotherhood. But that term was noddingly accepted without a second thought. Brotherhood had been a familiar slogan in Europe since the eighteenth century, blindly accepted as a password for meaning well.

After Geneva, a disappointment because he had hoped for more wisdom and less display of ego in his own people, he made another trip to Germany, which turned out better than expected. The atmosphere in Berlin had already changed since his last visit, but the people were still hypersensitive. Later, during the radio talk in Chicago on the 24th April 1926, he was to sound a warning against the thirst for revenge felt in Germany. If this did not abate, the result would be catastrophic. Getting his lectures translated was always more difficult in Germany than elsewhere, but nevertheless he managed to start centres in several places.

After that came Scandinavia, which delighted him. He was enchanted by the lakes and fjords, even though he only saw them through the old, dancing telegraph wires along his train route. He soon noticed how much calmer the population was here than in the rest of Europe. Even the difference between the Norwegians and the Swedish struck him. His autobiography describes the Norwegians as 'being of a democratic spirit and responding readily to the Message,' and Copenhagen he found 'more open than any other place in the North.' In Sweden he initiated one of the few disciples capable of the entire training. When he left, he had started centres in all three countries; they were probably the steadiest and least troublesome he had anywhere.

He also paid a short visit to Archbishop Söderblom in Siguna, who, after years of laying the groundwork, was in the midst of organizing his first large ecumenical assembly. This was one of the few occasions on which Inayat did not have to use child's talk. It may be that there was no one anywhere in the world, not even in India, whose work and aspirations had so much affinity to his own. Söderblom, too, had known doubt in his youth and, unlike most Protestants, he was alive to mysticism.[9] A conviction that the ultimate and only reality for all was in God had guided his ecumenical inspiration. Like Inayat, by this he did not mean syncretism (throwing everything in one heap and calling it universal), but unity beneath diversity. He was well-informed about eastern religions and regarded Buddhism and Islam with unromantic respect. But lest we fall into syncretism ourselves: there were also important differences. Söderblom's way was that of the scholar and he always kept a preference for Christianity, especially its Lutheran form; there was a time that he even sent out missionaries. Still, he parted from Inayat with the words that bringing together all Christian faiths was only the first step.

'I was glad to hear him say that,' Inayat notes in his journal, 'that showed that he believed in the second step also.' He himself was paving the way for that second step, and not only for churches, but for hundreds and thousands of other wrangling groups as well. He knew from experience how much weight was sometimes attached to sectarian differences within one religion, they had entered into one of his Indian marriages. In 1915, he had still named the antagonism of Shia's and Sunnites as one of the conflicts to be outgrown. But since then his field of vision had become much broader. He knew that in spite of prevailing nationalism — he sometimes called nationalism 'the religion of the age' — the world was heading for more and more communication and that mutual respect was indispensable, even though almost no one was ready for it. He sketched the main outlines. Throughout his work one can always recognize the Indian musician, who develops and elaborates the theme of his raga in the singing. Whereas Söderblom, the scholar, slowly pieced together his great organization of organizations by painstaking and diplomatic negotiation, Inayat, the inspired mystic and improvising artist, started with individuals and left them the theme for a great raga. Söderblom had a whole life in which to build and work in a world that he knew like the back of his hand. Inayat was a stranger who rapidly sized up the outward characteristics of each setting and then concentrated on the common base, the divine origin. And his time was running out.

Did he know this? On he travelled. Germany, Holland, Belgium, a brief rest at the end of the year, and on again.

In February 1925 he made his third trip to Italy. Though he enjoyed the sun and the blue skies, he found it a difficult ground for his work. No wonder, fascism had already gained hold there. Abroad, Mussolini was still looked on favourably because he had the trains running on schedule, but Mario Montessori told me it had taken a certain amount of courage for his mother to receive the nonconformist stranger. Most of the Italian Sufi centres were directed by foreigners. Still, one of the most highly thought-of disciples, Zanetti, was an Italian by origin. When Inayat had been in Italy for the first time, in 1923, he had been amazed to see the priests, some fifteen, some twenty, some hundred indeed 'moving hither and thither through the streets, a new sight, as nowhere in the West.' But he found the services he attended disappointing. 'A preparation for what a service should be, a perfectly organised drill by which to learn to respect man but done in a narrow way.' In that same year he was even introduced at the Vatican. He happened to see Monsignor Cascia and through him Cardinal Gaspari, who had asked him, among other things, what he meant by wisdom. His explanation was greeted hesitantly, 'with consent and half consent.' The consenting part of them must have been weak and the hesitance strong, for eventually the Vatican placed Inayat Khan's work on the index, banned to the highest degree.

It could hardly have been otherwise. All those who claimed exclusive rights to the truth, most of all the established churches, rejected his notion of unity beneath diversity. The Catholic church could do this by means of the index; individual Roman-Catholics, if they dared, responded to him as far as they knew anything of their own mysticism.

Protestantism was a different story. Inayat himself was doubtful about doctrine founded on a book. 'A book is a dead teacher.' This he said, firstly, because he was a mystic whose experiences of the transcendental could never really be captured in a sensory image.[10] And secondly, because he was an Indian musician, whose song can never be adequately put down in notation and who keeps his best songs for his pupils instead of publishing them. Hence, for him a printed book is synonymous with a second-rate selection. He also felt that Protestantism lacked the 'unity of illuminated souls,' the passing down of mystical reality from master to disciple. In the exercises for the complete training we find the names of the whole chain of masters. Holy men and sages, those who helped mankind, resemble one another, because the same spirit, or degree of evolution, is active in them all. A murshid purposely lets his pupils partake of his atmosphere; if they are open enough to him, they can go on growing on their own. Protestants are usually individualists, consciously confined to themselves.

This is their strength as well as their limitation. If he came across a Protestant who was content and strong in his faith, Inayat would never dream of trying to dissuade him. Everyone has the beliefs, or even the non-beliefs, that suit him best. If only he does not spend his life rigidly in one spot. Inayat's definition of religion is movement, developing, 'the unswerving progress to the purpose of every soul.' which means rediscovering and experiencing the divine source. Not just faith, but knowledge of God. He understood perfectly well why the agnostics rejected religion: how could they love someone they did not know? As an adolescent he himself had felt this protest, on the roof of his father's house.

Consideration for another and this other's point of view were not mutual. If members of an established church became impressed by Inayat, they often wanted to annex him; two English old ladies urged him to become a Christian on the spot. They could see the proper place of such a godly man only in the Church of England.

Serious Protestant theologians reacted more or less like the great man in the Vatican; with an initial assent that quickly turned to rejection. Some set out to weigh him in the balance, convinced from the outset that he would be found wanting. They chiefly deplored his lack of reverence for books; and of course the absence of the concept of sin. A more cautious and differentiated judgment is given by the Dutch theologian Professor van Mourik Broekman.[11] He also looked in vain for conceptions of sin, mercy, and redemption in Inayat's discussion of Christianity, but appreciates that the Sufis strive to help a person understand his own religion better instead of trying to convert him. In this way, the theologian and scholar hopes, those on the fringe may return to the Christian faith; however, he is also alive to the possibility that some may outgrow their historical tradition, and he does not veto this, 'as long as it is not done rashly.' That is quite a different thing than bans and the index. Accordingly, more Protestants than Catholics have become Sufis without discarding their religion. There were several clergymen among Inayat's disciples, and an English mureed, a university engineer who had fought in both world wars, took up theology in 1945 in order to put more people in touch with certain aspects of Sufism as a minister. Of course, the religion that is experienced more deeply by the disciple does not necessarily have to be Christianity. Paul Reps, know in his own right for his books, chose Zen Buddhism. One of Mrs Martin's successors, Samuel Lewis, went to receive a complete training from the Sufis in Ajmer and in Pakistan after Inayat's death.[12] This has given his group a somewhat Islamic accent, but its members still regard themselves as followers of Inayat and work together with other groups.

Apart from the dogmatic theologians, there were also dogmatic atheists. Then as well as now some brisk minds proclaimed that God was dead, usually meaning the authoritarian God of an old religion. Of this, Inayat writes in his biography: 'an old religion that has served its term is as dead bloodcells in the body, but... a creed which holds a divine message freshly given works like the heart that circulates the blood throughout the body... One... need not compare the heart with the dead blood-cells.'

The origin of this unexpected metaphor is not difficult to trace. An English mureed who used to help Inayat with his books in 1919 and 1920 was a physician who specialized in blood diseases. In that period, Inayat had his first attack of pneumonia, and after his recovery he asked a great many questions about the functions of the blood and circulatory system and had a look through the microscope.

Fifty years later this Doctor Gruner recalls: 'He had a very peculiar blood, His red cells were in 'spikes' instead of being round. This was seen without a reagent which was very unusual. The fresh blood was probably very watery.' A doctor whom I asked for explanation told me that unusually shaped blood cells are quite common in non-European peoples and that 'watery' blood could be a sign of anaemia. I go into this in some detail, because in the later years of his life Inayat suffered from a chronic disease which could never be satisfactorily treated. His death certificate states heart valve deficiency as the cause of his decease. He never showed outward signs of illness, not even on his deathbed, though he did appear somewhat fatter than he really was, because his digestion had been disturbed by constant travelling. The attacks of pneumonia were recurrent too. Pupils admiringly recall how once he travelled to Geneva from Berlin while in a fever, which they only noticed when they pressed his burning hand. Their murshid masked pain with the same self-control he used to meet mental blows. Still, he could not completely ignore his physical health and had to keep to his bed for some time during the winter of 1922 and the spring of 1924.

Touring England in April 1925 the master again fell ill. A doctor who had never treated him before gave him a medicine that did not agree with him, but caused serious poisoning. For several days he lay in his hotelroom unattended; the prudish English ladies thought it improper to visit him in a bedroom. Maybe some of his pupils thought he had shut himself in for meditation, which he sometimes did. Not until several days had passed was he taken to Suresnes, in great pain. His brothers were just then on a concert tour of Germany. Though he was cared for devotedly at home, he missed them. He sent word to Musharaff Khan asking him to come to him as soon as the concerts were over. He did not ask Maheboob Khan, because his first child was expected to arrive at the end of April. But the prospective father came along to Suresnes first, and great was Inayat's joy to have his companions, his own people with him again. They were a fragment of India, moving, speaking and reacting in ways so natural to him.

No one in the West, not even his wife, could understand

the longing he felt for India, his old, familiar and idealised world. There, no one would behave so rudely to his guests, even uninvited ones, as Gide had done. There, no harsh grey winters. There, a master had disciples who would be masters themselves some day. There, a holy man was recognized and treated with respect. There, so he thought, his illness would be cured.

For he had a certain mistrust of western skills. Some might say that he knew nothing or had said nothing that was new, but he, in turn, was convinced that the West knew little and had discovered nothing that was new. Not only was psychology child's play compared to psychological knowledge and practice in the East, he also regarded the discoveries of biology and physics as ancient history. Centuries ahead of Darwin, Rumi had expressed the theory of evolution in his poems. Whatever western science had revealed about sound vibrations, light rays, electricity and radio waves, the eastern mystic had known it all along. And the most complete knowledge had been possessed by Avicenna, an Arabian-Persian doctor and mystic. Avicenna[13] – the name is a latinization of Ibn Sina – did in fact explain and outline the entire field of medical science in an unequalled compendium used for hundreds of years, influencing western philosophical and medical thinking right into the Renaissance. Avicenna died in 1037. But Inayat thought there would still be doctors in India who commanded the old knowledge as well as the new, and could cure him. He would go home.

His wife was upset when he mentioned a journey to India. The children were still very young, she could not accompany him and she intuitively felt that, if he really went, she would not see him again. She herself did not dare nor wish to argue and keep him back, but she told the brothers about his plans. Maheboob Khan managed to persuade him not to go to India as yet, but to have another trip to America first.

217

Yet his brothers understood why he wished to go. They knew that though being misconstrued and attacked amused him as a wise man, he was affected by these things as a person — that is, as an Indian. He had brought his message; a school and a movement could be kept going by others. The West would not breed many holy men. The summer school, a great event in the lives of most disciples, was a strain on him and not half what a gathering of master and disciples in the East would be. And the quarrelling attitude at Headquarters was almost inconceivable to an Indian.

Even his autobiography notes that the council in Geneva in 1925 was 'more lively than previous years, the present spirit of the people and nations knocking at our door also.' In a letter to the administrator at Suresnes he wrote with the same terse irony 'The council meetings have gone smoothly... hot discussions in soft words... cold eyes with warm smiles.' How anyone could call himself spiritual and at the same time aspire to power astonished him time and again. Once he was asked whether he was the head of the Sufi Movement. He answered, 'No, God is.' 'Then what are you?' 'Its feet.' To such a question the committee members could have replied that they were its hands, but they obviously felt like the heads. This phenomenon is not uncommon: originally the word minister meant servant, but most people of our time take jobs in governing bodies mainly for the status involved or to show their mettle, not from a desire to serve a cause or help people. Söderblom could have told Inayat about all the touchiness, priority shuffling, and personal ambitions he, too, had to cope with. Working in a large administrative body with paper instead of people tends to isolate the government from the governed. In Inayat's local centres the leaders knew each member personally. Especially if they had initiated someone themselves, a strong bond was formed. A number of those local leaders were unforgettable and true passers-on of Inayat's inspiring spirit.

He did not do much travelling in the autumn of 1925. After summer school and the Geneva assembly he probably had to regain strength for the American tour. An administrator and a secretary were to go with him; the latter had some nursing experience, so that she could give the master the intramuscular injections he needed since his illness.

They embarked for America in late November. On board, seasick or not, they prepared press releases, with good results. A rush of reporters awaited him, from the moment he set foot on land, and difficulties with the immigration officers were unheard-of. Not that the press was overly understanding. Even if a journalist had grasped the idea, he was only allowed to vent this in certain ways: dry, funny or sensational. Some turned his words around to a contrary meaning. 'In the place of a horse it was a donkey, in the place of a man it was a monkey,' the biography states. The newspapers, which were read by so many, could not put across what the master really meant. More than once he discussed this problem with his interviewers. An Italian reporter had replied that this could not be helped, because the press must work quickly. An American, who had listened attentively to what was said and really understood some of it, finally sighed, 'How can I get this through to the man in the street?' A third was prevented by his editor from putting it down as he had heard it.

Hence the diversity of what the journalists turned out. A long article in a Boston newspaper started with sceptical scorn for the benefit of publishers and colleagues, but reported Inayat's words with reasonable accuracy; however, derisive pictures of a Moslem extolling the holy war against Europeans were added and, even more caustically, a photograph showing the faithful praying for victory against the British, provided with a caption that the Moslem country Turkey was England's enemy. Next to this there was a good portrait of Inayat, looking the reader straight in the eye and under his moustache his mouth shows the trace of a smile, a touch of irritation, a certain reserve, but above all strength. He knew where he was going and did not look back.

This ambiguous article was of some use, but another showed the unerring journalistic instinct to describe Inayat not as a mystic, but as and Indian, shaped by his own cultural background, and critical of certain western customs. A third indulged in a cheap joke: 'the master was welcome to see if he could 'turn the thoughts of all America toward the spiritual life', but he will need to have some regard for material things while negotiating street crossings.'[14]

Some restricted themselves to a formal announcement of his lectures. Only one dared to say that this murshid differs from the 'many yogis, swamis, sufis and what-nots who come out of the Orient from year to year to proclaim the superiority of particular doctrines or creeds' and he actually concludes his article, courageously, with a serious description of the mystical oneness. And yet, an announcement like this, which stands on its own in a newspaper, is still left hanging. The most sensible journalist left the floor to Inayat himself, quoting a few pages from the *Gayan;* an American selection, a passage with many maxims about success, power and achievement. That did not matter, 'take from these ideas what seem to you to be best, and forget the rest.' But the paper omitted one quotation of its series of sixteen, the one about love. They must have been afraid that love was a weak thing. Or too emotional, not enough of the brain. For the only information added to the quotations was that Inayat had been lecturing at the Sorbonne. They meant three lectures given in March 1925. Many other brief announcements also referred to this appearance at the illustrious French University, 'where a large number of intellectuals heard his spiritual philosophy.' They might also have mentioned that he had addressed their own Columbia University fourteen years ago, and had lectured at several Californian universities in 1911 and 1923. But apparently the fact that the rational French had approved of the mystic was the best recommendation they could offer. That religion was only for the gullible was a deep-seated notion indeed. 'The ignorant believer, by his claim of belief, causes a revolt in an intelligent person, thereby turning him into an unbeliever.' These are words from Inayat's *Gayan*.[15]

He himself did respect science and logic. Sometimes, in certain periods or for certain audiences, he would remark what a logical and scientific occupation mysticism was, and he repeatedly asked an intelligent or scholarly mureed to write a book about mysticism for western readers. Though he countered western presumption 'we have discovered everything' with a just as presumptuous 'we knew it all along,' he did believe to some extent in the progress of physics and chemistry, perhaps to a great extent. He expected that someday science would be able to explain mysticism. A book like *The Origin of Metaphysics in Science* (1965) by the American philosopher E. E. Harris, is a step in this direction. Its author and his co-workers have knowledge both of philosophy and science and technology. On the whole, the endeavours of Inayat's pupils lost themselves in cosmic speculations. Two pupils with a bent for physics never went beyond simple examples; one of them did not risk writing a book but often addressed students.

Inayat himself went to see laboratories wherever he could. After the war, in France, he had visited institutes for treating poison gas victims by means of breathing techniques.[16] This work was related to his own, so he was able to appreciate its merits. His approach to investigations of vibrations, rays and sound waves was a bit more cautious, but he did see parallels to his own knowledge. There was a doctor in California who maintaned that illness was caused by a disequilibrium in (electrical) vibrations; Inayat said

221

he was on the right track. He was not so enthusiastic about a number of investigators in New York. Not because of their work, which was quite worthwhile, but because of their attitude to his work. One professor, no different from the most immature of listeners, would have him do occult tricks. Another proudly confided that he had at last discovered the soul. That was just like someone going up to the baker, beaming: 'Baker, I have just discovered flour.' From a child he could take this, but from an educated man he found it downright embarrassing.

It may well be that Inayat's respect for science still reflects his Indian veneration for the caste of wise men, scholars and musicians, the Brahmins. But this can be only part of the story, since he was particularly attentive to science and medicine, much less so to law and humanities. Perhaps this was because the former are active, observing and exploring disciplines, while the latter rely more heavily on books. That his knowledge of western history and literature was scanty did not disturb him. He honoured it as part of the culture. However, he had no wish to adopt it, the less so when many Indians, doing just that, lost what was most valuable in their own culture. His work between 1920 and 1925 sounds 'western' because he had woven into it his extensive experience with all sorts of western people; western-style displays of literary and historical traditions are scarce. Some of the pupils, editing his manuscripts after his death, found this regrettable. In their forewords, they apologize that Inayat seems 'so simple' and take pains to flash some western names. They were forgetting that to learn and apply his many-sided teachings was not simple in the least, and above all they forgot that, besides being an accomplished mystic and an accomplished musician, he was an erudite Indian with a command of that culture's classics and semi-classics in Sanskrit, Arabian and Persian and with fluency in the living languages Hindustani, Urdu, Marathi and Gujerati. His lectures contain hundreds of different quotations from poets in all of these tongues, off-handedly translated into English as he goes along. Who of those who mocked his English could quote in Urdu from seven western languages, preferably without an accent?

Tagore, and also Gibran who is still read avidly in some circles, both had help with their English. To them, a book was an end in itself; but for Inayat printing was almost a necessary evil. 'Have you studied the books?' he once asked a new disciple. 'Yes Murshid,' the young man answered. 'Of course it is not in the books.' The paradox was understood by the pupil, who noted this down. Time and again does the Sufi master remind us in his lectures that we should study life, ourselves and those around us, and learn more from these than from a thousand books. Or he told the story of Rumi, whose master threw out all his books saying, from now on you must study life.[17]

Studying life, constant observance − for him this was the true method to functional knowledge. This method called for an objective approach: being a spectator of life as at a play, crying or lauging at what one sees, is not the same thing as being 'a student of life', observing everything from above 'as from an aeroplane.' i.e. from a broad vantage point, seeing the world in its true perspective. Whenever he was out, on a visit or in a new environment, he was always looking, observing. The Japanese Zen Buddhist whom he spoke to in San Francisco recognized the method immediately.

There was one difficulty: he had to practise his method of observation against a strange cultural background. Sometimes he noticed things that others overlooked, but it was possible that he might mistake the meaning of a casual fact. Of this he was aware and from the very beginning it was his custom to see as much as he could of the countless different faces of western society: insane asylum, sanatorium, laboratory, building exhibition, ballroom, casino, school, church, factory, cinema, theatre − he even learned to drive a car.

But of course the main purpose of the method is to gain understanding of people, their conduct toward others and their attitude towards themselves. Inayat had an eye for boys playing football in the streets as well as for golfing gentlemen, for a begging lupus patient without a nose as well as for the hothouse nerves of a baroness. And he discovered every variety of believer and unbeliever.[18] The unthinking ones, whose 'belief reminds one of sheep: where one goes, all the others follow;... if a person stays in the middle of the street looking at the sky, in ten minutes' time a hundred people are also looking at the sky.' The more or less intelligent ones who explain their faith, or explain it away. He was not surprised by non-believers whose youth had been burdened by empty conventions, nor by those whose only belief was in their material possessions.

A young Italian once challenged him: 'I believe in eternal matter.' He expected a sermon on the loftiness of spirit and the inferiority of matter, as he was used to hear from his priests. But Inayat answered, 'Then both of us believe in something eternal' and thus captured the young man's attention.

Among non-believers, too, the old idea held sway that spirit was opposed to matter and that those who chose the 'spiritual' must give up material things. This dualistic approach, in which good and bad, spirit and matter, and above all God and man are regarded as totally separate, is characteristic of our culture and any culture influenced by the western religions, i.e. Judaism, Christianity and Islam. In Europe, we often forget that the Quran is closely related to the Old and New Testaments. Abraham, Moses and Jesus are traditional Moslem heroes and saints. But in the course of a few hundred years the Moslem mystics developed a distinct tendency to monism, a philosophy more typical of 'oriental' religions such as Hinduism and Buddhism. By this philosophy, all things — spirit, soul, body, matter, good and bad — spring from one eternal essence to which all will again return. The object of creation is to learn and experience, good and bad alike, and then go back to the source where all is one. A mystic is capable of fulfilling this process of unification, entirely or in part, in his lifetime. The state of complete return is best known under the name Nirvana, better interpreted as 'being all things' than as 'being nothing.' The Roman Catholic theologian Zaehner emphasizes the dualism in Christian mysticism — the encounter between man and God — as against eastern monism, in which man becomes conscious of God in himself.

Inayat knew and described both ways.[19] Encountering God as the other, the beloved, is a stage, an ecstasy, that precedes the peace of complete oneness. In some passages he passionately searches for God — as a beloved, as a king, as a saint — and always the end is 'I found thee in myself.' At this point, he recognizes God in each shape, each sound, in everything he touches and tastes, in all places and in all men. Sometimes this is lucidly expressed in two lines. 'First believe in the God who is all-exclusive and then realise the God who is all-inclusive.' In other words: if there is no initial ideal, then there is no purpose or direction; but in the end, the ideal, too, must be broken, because it is a limiting form. Some present-day psychologists and philosophers regard meditation as a highly valuable achievement, but find the notion of a temporary image of God difficult to accept, because to them almost every kind of faith is bound up with an undesirable father role, authority and dependence. They keep their meditation as abstract as possible. 'The intellectual student of philosophy says, "I do not believe in God, although I believe in the abstract.".... He may have got hold of some truth, but it is a flower without fragrance.' One cannot love the abstract. Inayat's advice was to start with an image of God, to learn love. There is no loving without an ideal. To love one must see, with eyes, heart and

225

soul. There is no oneness without love. 'The mystic does not think of God as abstract, although he knows God to be so.[20]

Such things the master could say to those who had already started thinking and searching. But he was also asked to say a few words when he was a guest of honour at parties and social gatherings, like all well-known foreigners on tour in America. He stood there in his long robe and distant calm, in front of the clean-shaven men of that time and the women with their sleek shingled hair and knee-length evening gowns, all of them children of their own society with deep, pompous or high, tittering voices. He would say just a few sentences, for instance that it was not necessary always to carry on blindly, that a person could give direction to his life.

That was all, and always as simple as possible. In his lectures, too, when discussing the transition from dualistic to monistic experience, he always spoke in the plainest of terms but vividly. Not everyone appreciated this simplicity. At one of the lectures in New York a few people got up and left, because they thought he had nothing new to say. 'Some had the patience to stay there five minutes,' the *Autobiography* states. Naturally, they had hoped to see dancing tables or someone climbing a standing rope.

Yet, the beginning was unusual enough. 'Probably the most prolonged silence in any room in New York where a few hundred persons are assembled takes place for several minutes every Sunday night in the Astor Gallery of the Waldorf-Astoria hotel,' an astonished reporter wrote.[21] Inayat had stopped singing the invocation prayer, which affected people so deeply that someone had called it 'hypnotic;' reason enough for him to omit it. Now, he kept a few minutes' silence before speaking, that is, he attuned himself both to his inspiration and to his audience. Of course it was much more difficult than singing – the audiences were not accustomed to this kind of thing and there were always one or two nervous creatures who would start to giggle. But most of his listeners understood, perhaps even relaxed. In any case, his lectures made an impression – though he found addressing a large gathering through a microphone unnatural and trying. He was invited to give a Christmas speech on the radio. America had already millions of private receivers for this new means of communication.

And so the grandson of Maula Bakhsh, who had wandered through India on camels, living in tents, found himself in a recording studio gleaming with steel and technical controls, before an invisible audience. Long ago, in a smoke-filled hall in Bombay, he had tried to forget his indifferent listeners by imagining that he was playing for himself alone. Now, he was alone with a microphone and had to imagine the manifold individuals all over this foreign country. His first radio talk begins strongly, but then follows a somewhat over-crowded part. In a few sentences all manner of things are compressed, from the highest ecstasy down to correction of the silliest misconceptions. Towards the end Inayat's usual balanced manner returns, as when he speaks of youth and the future.

I have not found any reactions to this radio talk, not even from his secretary, but at Easter he was asked again and was allotted twice as much time. His beautiful voice and genuine delivery must have taken effect. In his own opinion, a voice over a telephone could convey something about a person. Still, seeing him was always most effective. His secretary was sometimes stopped in the street by people wanting to know who he was.

In January, there was a new wave of newspaper articles about him. 'His words were not of advice or warning, but his message was provocative in its simplicity and depth of vision. He preached no particular religion, but recognized as a fundamantal characteristic man's wish to believe in immortality. No matter how gloomy one's prospect may be,... he will cling desperately to his right to live.'

Some saw only that he was unusual, and made haste to introduce him to others who looked like deviants from the current religious path. One of these was an ex-bishop, Brown, who was fond of making the front pages with the announcement that he did not take everything in the Bible literally. Inayat did not like the association. He left, or gave, everyone the beliefs that suited him and thought such public announcements lacking in respect for simple souls who needed the security of a book to lean on.

He preferred citing his talk with Henry Ford, though the detailed newspaper report on the sage's meeting with the automobile tycoon shows that Inayat did notice Mr Ford's weak points. Ford was a byword, a symbol, in those years. For the West, an example of efficiency and 'how far hard work can get you.' In the East he was a bearer of boons, because he made agricultural machines; there is a special Indian biography about him and an Indian talking to Ruth St Denis rated Ford higher than saints and poets.

Henry Ford worked at his image. In 1917 he concerned himself with peace negotiations and he generally tried to associate himself with anything that was news. Besides new production methods he also developed new philosophies, though how and when he did this is a mystery. For he did invite Inayat, but could not find time to attend the mystic's lectures — he had a stenographer take them down. Thereupon he gave his visitor the opportunity to have a quick look at his own ideas by having him wait in the library and giving him an article about religion by Henry the Great himself to read. The reporter writes that there was a query in the dark eyes of 'the elderly prophet.... That sketchy article did not go far into the subject.' Then with rapid strides Ford breezes into the room, waving the typed-out lectures that he had not had time to read. Nevertheless he immediately announces that according to him there is something good in every religion. Lightly he skimmed over many noble concepts and concluded that one can find no

228

better renewal of strength than in the thought of being a part of God. 'Except,' said his visitor, 'The full realising of that idea, the full self-forgetting in unity with the One.' Eventually, Ford put forward the objection one could expect from him. 'If one meditates too much there is not likely to be much work done.' 'But if one meditates somewhat,' replied Inayat, 'there will really be much more work done, and better done, and with it will be happiness and peace. I do not preach the denial of things of the world, nor do I condemn worldly accomplishment. I preach only that with the things we must do here in the material world there must also be real attainment in the world of the spirit.'

After this discussion, the 'old' mystic — Inayat was 43 — was shown around the factory, starting at the first sheet of steel on the assembly line right up to the finished car. In one of his lectures he remarks that the division of labour makes people helpless; therefore it is 'necessary to introduce in education the spirit of providing for oneself all that one needs,' to make a real sense of living and growing possible. 'Imagine a person spending from morning till evening in a factory and only making needles.... What does he know of life?'

He did respect Ford's capacity for concentration. Working to reach a goal was for him a valuable thing, akin to the striving of the mystic. Conversely, Ford had said to him that he would have made a good businessman if he had wished to. This he would scarcely have taken as a compliment twenty years ago in India, but now he gaily wrote about it to his relatives and co-workers in amused letters laced with teasing jokes.

Perhaps these letters were meant to be reassuring, for one wonders whether he felt as cheerful as all that. He had always been cheerful by nature, but when writing to his assistant van Stolk about the organization of the summer school, he sounds weary and not too happy. And during this trip he did not sing, not even once. It was, however, a

229

very rewarding trip for his work, and his person commanded respect and admiration. No one would dream of
barring the impressive 'black man' from a bus, as had happened in the past. A young waiter in San Francisco grew red
in the face from bashful reverence each time he neared
Inayat's table. Well-known clubs asked the eastern master
to lunch, leading figures of society invited him to their
homes. He was taken sight-seeing; he rode through the
Grand Canyon on a pony, Paul Reps drove him all over
California in his car, Mrs Martin treated him to a flight in
an open aeroplane, circling above the blooming spring
country-side. The secretary who accompanied him on this
flight still remembers the fragrance that rose up from the
blossoms beneath. And then they landed again and went to
work. He dictated, listened to complaints and requests,
held conferences, lectured, and initiated hundreds of
mureeds. 'Some will stay, some will leave.'

For seven months, he crossed through America, sleeping in 159 different beds. On 27th June he discussed the
problems the American centre leaders encountered in
their work, especially the taking on and guiding of disciples. An individual master could refuse a candidate, Inayat's
movement, with its aim of offering a philosophy of life and
opportunity for spiritual attainment to as many people as
possible, could not. If someone only wanted to join out of
curiosity, sensationalism, muddle-headedness or vanity,
there were ways of postponing his initiation. 'Waiting is the
greatest test.' And if such a one still succeeded in getting in,
he should not be given too many exercises at once. The
initiator must turn a pebble into a diamond, slowly and in
time,.... But to maintain a hope and to persevere with a
person is one thing, to trust a person who is still unripe with
practices is another. The first attitude is strength, the
second is weakness.... We must persevere sincerely without
being annoyed with an unsuitable person. Our duty to that
person is greater that to those who are fitting.'

230

Besides the actually undesirable pupils, there were many who came only for personal affairs, for solace and support. They were admiring and sometimes dedicated, they might grow into real workers and helpers. For the true pupil, he who came to discover and experience God, also came to help others. 'If you do not see God in man, you will not see Him anywhere.'[22]

Some were like that, which was something. Some non-members understood, that was something again. But most of the time he felt he 'had to sell his pearls at the value of pebbles.' Time and again he was seen through eyes veiled and blinkered by environment, education, prejudice, wishes or fears.

Inayat suffered under the lack of understanding and cramped interpretations of his work, but always he kept to the trust his master had instilled in him. 'I am what I am, you make me what you will make me, but I become what I wish to become.'

Chapter XI (1924-1926)
'Some still held that I knew all'

In one of his last letters from America, 25th May 1926, Inayat asked his pupil van Stolk, who managed Suresnes, 'Can you not cover the front part of our ground with straw or reed? I would like it so much to speak some times in the open.' The land he referred to, an orchard opposite Fazal Manzil, had been purchased in 1923. At the end was a small hall where the meetings and lectures were held, but in the centre grew an old spreading apricot tree, ideal to sit under. Inayat's small sons climbed the younger trees, they were not yet ten, and loudly announced to each other how high they dared to go. One day Inayat passed by with a disciple who remarked, 'It is hard to imagine that these are your sons.' 'Why, I was worse,' replied their father, the sage. He remembered the pear tree he used to climb, the puddles he used to run through, the walls he jumped up and down from; his happy childhood in Baroda.

He once told his secretary that everything he had wished for in his life had come to him. One of these things was to found a school, as Maula Bakhsh had done. He had accomplished that, but under such strange circumstances that he was often misunderstood, even by his disciples. There were hardly any who knew the real India, and few who made real progress in their mystical development. Many seekers took the start for the goal, their conception of religion was static. They worshipped a word or an idea, and what they thought was reverence for a sage took the form of idolization. In all Inayat's contacts with his Westerners, differences of evolution and culture were almost inextricably entangled.

Suresnes, 1926.

'In the West people have the idea that a sage must be kind, retiring and renouncing, and perhaps even a wonder-worker.'[1] Indeed, even outsiders always begin their description with his kindness. Some disciples and journalists look for miracles and asceticism. And all memoirs of mureeds are full of his sympathy and openness to their problems, the way he gave them his whole attention, 'his deep warm glance,' 'his all understanding glance,' his eyes that saw everything and lovingly enveloped you – that was unforgettable.'[2]

The disciples were men and women from many countries, of all ages, from all kinds of environment and with very different intellectual and emotional needs. Inayat dealt with them according to their nature. One might understand him immediately, without words, with another he held an ordinary conversation. Often he greeted a person who came to see him for the first time as if he were an old friend, and indeed during a lecture, or at an earlier meeting, even in a tram, even years ago he might have recognized the responsiveness. Sometimes it was years before a prospective disciple was accepted – the candidate himself might hesitate, or the master might postpone the initiation. It also happened that someone who had only just been accepted as a disciple was requested to do some active work in the movement. To their own astonishment they proved to be capable. These workers were genuinely aiming at spiritual development and they were open to others. 'If anything can be called religion, it is a true human relation with others.'[3] They were by no means always people who had already searched in other religions, let alone given a thought to mysticism. Inayat and all he stood for was a discovery in their lives, a revelation.

True, many were influenced by established churches and habits of thinking. One man considered himself too sinful to be initiated. 'Do you love Murshid?' asked Inayat. 'Yes.' 'And do you believe that Murshid loves you?' 'Oh,

234

yes.' 'That is all that matters.' Another pupil-to-be came and airily told that he had done wrong sometimes, but he did not think that would stand in the way of his initiation. In his case Inayat asked what wrong he had done, the man had to tell him every detail until, ashamed, he said, 'Now I suppose you don't want me as your disciple.' 'Now I do.'

It was often necessary to restore the balance like that. One who was firmly determined to do everything himself and on his own was told, 'Let Murshid help you.' That was an exception, though; more often Inayat had to ignore self-pity, teach weak ones to stand on their own two feet and keep off seekers after sensation. But there were no set rules. Once or twice even the invitation to become a mureed came from him. One of those invited by the master himself was M. E. de Cruzat Zanetti, an international lawyer in Geneva, who composed the constitution of the movement. Zanetti was quite self-assured, almost vain; very intellectual, and almost pompous, but he had grandeur and style. Inayat valued him greatly.

Especially those candidates who already had an idea of spiritual life often had difficulties in the beginning. One serious, very ascetic girl was not immediately initiated but allowed to return for at least half an hour's conversation. She was looking forward to hearing words of wisdom, but as soon as she arrived tea and cake were served. The master began to eat with obvious relish and kept on offering her more. She could not refuse. Nothing profound was cut into, the cake was. Since that day, she says, she saw life in a different light.

Inayat himself seldom fasted and he was not a veg-etarian. At the end of his training in Hyderabad, during an ecstasy, his master had given him wine to drink to liberate him from outward signs and symbols. 'Be the disciple of love and give up the things that create differences.'[4] Paul Reps thoughtfully wanted to turn Inayat's bed in an American hotel to the East, but the master stopped him with a smile.

But just as he himself in the beginning wanted to practise self-denial by staying awake all night — 'Whom do you torture?' Murshid Madani had asked — so many of his disciples imposed fasts and abstinences upon themselves. 'Life today is enough of a trial,' Inayat said. Only those who received part of the complete training needed it during special periods. For others he did not even prescribe vegetarianism. He thought that for most Westerners learning from life plus about twenty minutes meditation a day was sufficient.[4]

Inayat knew that many did not keep up the meditation. 'If the mureed has good feeling, a desire for progress, respect for his teachter, sympathy with the others, wish for spreading the Message or Cause,... one day he will be awakened to it,' he said in the American instruction-interview.

Meditation was practically unknown in the West half a century ago. Some pupils hardly had an opportunity at home to sit quietly and alone. Today young people in sandals can walk down Oxford Street, repeating a mantram, without causing much comment. Inayat's disciples, who were not given that kind of spectacular thing to do, were often considered crazy by those around them, until some member of the family happened to meet the master. 'That Murshid of yours is a nice chap; really,' said one father who had at first come in a red hot fury to give the master a piece of his mind about mystical nonsense. He had expected something very odd. After all, for most Westerners a faqir is a kind of magician, someone who performs seemingly impossible tricks. Actually the word faqir means a poor man, a devotee who has chosen poverty to be free from all worldly bonds. There are, of course, esoteric schools where training is aimed at controlling pain and blood circulation; beds of nails originated there. Romanticists in the West had thought up easier miracles. If one presses one's eyeballs, or keeps staring through tightly narrowed eyes, one can soon see haloes of coloured light and double contours – say auras and ethereal doubles, and one feels a pleasurable shiver down the spine. Inayat often warned against this kind of occultism, and against looking for miracles.

But his pupils had the feeling that he did perform miracles, for the simple reason that he immediately reacted to what they thought and felt. Something they thought was only possible in dreams, really existed. A mureed who went to India years later and met another advanced mystic there discovered with surprise that he radiated the same sort of atmosphere as the lonely murshid in the West. 'A godly man is recognized not by what he says and not by what he seems to be, but by the atmosphere that his presence creates.' These words of his own master Inayat quoted on more than one occasion.[5]

Some people were afraid of this radiance. A Frenchman who translated some of Inayat's lectures at the Musée Guimet wrote, 'The remarkable thing was that I... spoke with a certainty that surprised me. But after the lecture I was exhausted and I could not remember one word of what had been said... In any case I had the impression of somehow being under the spell of a powerful personality who was no doubt sympathetic, but did not allow me to be completely myself. So I decided to withdraw from the Pir-o-Murshid.'

In stories told by disciples we often read that someone was suddenly able to speak or translate, found himself enveloped by the master's being, and did not know what words had been spoken. But words did not matter, his presence was everything.

A pianist who had by chance attended one lecture but had never become a pupil told me, 'What he said I can't remember, but if I have ever seen a saint it was he. When I came home my husband was reading his newspaper as if nothing had happened.' Forty years later she still wondered at the contrast between the narrow scope of daily life and her experience of being raised above it all.

Inayat used to say that there were more Sufis outside the movement than in it. Sometimes non-members had the same feeling. A woman lawyer at the League of Nations had several conversations with him about spirituality in daily life; her impression was that he enjoyed talking to her because she understood that she had to find her own answer. A woman in Rotterdam, poor and not very well-educated, but somewhat clairvoyant and a pillar of strength to those around her could not come to terms with something terrible: a crime done to children. Someone offered to take her to Inayat after one of his lectures and to translate her questions. She sat in the audience and did not understand a word, but when the lecture was over, she no longer needed the interview. 'I know now why it happened,' she said, but could not explain it in words. All the same the pupil who had taken her mentioned her problem to Inayat. 'She already has her answer,' he said.

This kind of wordless contact was not accidental, but essential. During his own training Inayat once took a friend, who 'had twenty thousand questions to ask' to see his murshid Syed Madani. 'The moment he reached my murshid's presence he forgot every question and did not know what to ask.' This 'breathing the atmosphere of the master's presence' happened to Inayat's best mureeds too. One man describes how after his first meeting he paused at the door, and looking back saw Murshid standing in the middle of the room, his head bent, and suddenly this pupil saw his whole life before him. Inayat apologized. The mystic had learned to empty himself and then he naturally reflected others.

When people were able to understand 'the voice of his silence' he was happy, words were too limited to explain the inner experience and led to misunderstanding. But they had to take a conversation without words as naturally as he

238

did. How many disciples could do this? For most it was a miracle and one more reason to put him on a pedestal and call him perfect. In all sort of ways he tried to get this idea out of their minds. A mystic is human too and has human limitations and faults. He said that in his lectures, in his plays, in jokes. 'Murshid, someone told me something bad about you.' 'Has anyone ever told you something good about me?' 'Oh yes.' 'Then you have the complete picture.'

He was so averse to the preoccupation with so-called occult phenomena and the sentimental nonsense about miracles that his brothers might tease him about it. When Inayat had learned to drive a car — not without some difficulty — he took Musharaff Khan, himself a driver, out in the family Ford to demonstrate his newly acquired skill in the Bois de Boulogne. He drove almost as slowly as he used to walk — at a dignified pace. 'How am I doing?' 'It is a miracle,' Musharaff Khan said mischievously. The slow-driving saint looked curiously at his brother from the corner of his eye. There was no flattery meant. 'It is a miracle how you turn a motorcar into an ox-cart.'

Inayat hardly used his driving license. One of the disciples thought that he learned to drive to keep in touch with worldly things. That is possible, but he always had a kind of playful enthusiasm for something new and out of the ordinary. In Paris, in broken French, he used to buy oriental antiques for his house, a lamp that gave no light, 'but it is beautiful,' or a carpet with a hole in it, 'but it comes from the palace of the Sultan of Morocco.' Others he could give practical advice, but he writes in his *Autobiography* that by nature he took little interest in worldly activities, and, as time passed, grew further and further away from them so that he had trouble with 'ordinary things.' Indeed there is an element of surprise in his wording when he speaks of other people's subjects of dispute: 'What do they get so excited about?' He knew this aloofness could become too one-sided and wrote in *Vadan*, 'In order to arrive at spiritual attainment two gulfs must be crossed, the sea of attachment and the ocean of detachment.' As long as he was alive he must not be so detached that there was no longer a bridge between him and others.[6]

At home he noticed it. He loved his children, followed their lessons, especially the music-lessons – when they were older they played together on all sorts of instruments – he sang lullabies to them, and they tried to stay awake to hear more; but it was difficult for him to punish. If one of the four had been naughty he took the child apart and explained what he had done wrong, but when it came to punishing a meeting was held with Uncle Musharaff Khan as the judge who had to suggest punishments. The child could choose the one that best fitted his offence.

In his book *Education* Inayat advises to teach a child religion simply in the beginning – 'broadness comes later' – but if his children asked him something the answer came from his own broadness. They were quarrelling about some toy for instance, with fierce 'This is mine,' 'no mine.' 'It belongs to God,' said their father. Noor-un-Nisa's biographer mentions similar incidents.[7]

Inayat's second son Hidayat remembers that his father sometimes took him shopping in Paris. In the Galeries Lafayette he saw him choose the yellow curtains – 'yellow is the colour of the Sufis' – for the lecture hall. This hall was close to Inayat's heart. After the American tour of 1923 when he knew that his words had taken root for good, it was his great desire to establish a permanent centre.

In Paris a mosque was being built at that time and Inayat would have liked to make use of the oriental artists and workmen who were there, to erect on his piece of land an authentic oriental building, a Sufi temple. He discussed it with his friends who gave it the name Universel. Everyone thought it an excellent idea but, he says in the *Autobiography*,' plans remained scattered, owing to diversity of opinion.' It was at least something that within a year they

240

could boast of a small wooden hall with a platform.

His real conception was a work of art, grand and light as St Peter's in Rome, but it would not only serve as a temple or church. His Universel was intended to accomodate all forms of spiritual life — it would be a radiating centre, not only for worship and meditation, but also for music, dance and drama. And apart from being an 'ecumenical' meeting place for all religions, he probably saw it also as a symbol of world unity. When the foundation stone was laid, coins from all countries where there were Sufi centres were put under it.[8]

Laying the foundation stone was the last act in Suresnes and the only thing he ever saw of his Sufi temple. At the last moment he created a new motif, one more 'raga' to elaborate on, the Confraternity of the Message, which was to bring about the Universel in all its aspects.

There is a film of that last day, 13th September 1926. The pupils walk in procession past the spot where the stone will be placed and each puts down a coin; Inayat hangs a ribbon round the neck of his eldest son Vilayat, a boy of ten in a sailor suit, and ordains him as the head of the new activity. And we see the master move, lay the foundation stone and walk slowly down the long path across the land. For a moment he stops, looks at you and lifts his hand, in farewell, or blessing, or both. In spite of his rather sturdy figure he seems transparent at that moment. His glance comes from far away, but from his remoteness he yet observes those who pass in front of him.

Many have described this transparency of the last year. Apart from those closest to him, who knew, only one of all those writers of memoirs noticed that he was tired and ill.

In their eyes the perfect master could not be ill. Like many people who have had a mystical training he had healing power. Ali Khan was known to be a healer, even outside the Sufi circle. Neither he nor Inayat rejected western medical science — if they heard of a medicine that

241

had good results they bought large quantities of it. The disciples prefer to tell about miracle cures, but there is also a conscientious description of someone who was advised to 'go to the best surgeon.' Though Inayat thought he might have a better chance to be cured in India, where the doctors knew both ancient and modern methods, he also consulted western physicians. Many years after his death Musharaff Khan went to see a specialist in The Hague. During the second visit the doctor showed him an old engagement book that had Inayat's name in it. He said nothing and completed the examination of the brother in a kind of reverent remembrance.

The cases of healing related by the mureeds were not only psychosomatic, but concerned organic diseases as well. The most accurately described is the case of a baby who had pneumonia. The child was a week old and the doctors had given him up. The mother tells the story. 'He stroked my hands with his hands, from the fingers up towards my shoulder, and blessed me with a repeated 'God bless you, be calm, he will be cured.' I conveyed his blessing to the child by putting my hands on him and I thought, 'I see his being so great at this moment that it is almost too much to bear.' Hardly had I thought this when Murshid slowly retreated to the door and I thought, 'Oh, stay with me.' ... And Murshid understood my wish and came closer again, laid both his hands on my head and murmured, 'God bless you and your child.'... Downstairs Murshid met the doctor and said, 'Are you the doctor? I wish you good success, sir." Upstairs the doctor saw the child sleeping soundly... 'It can't be true. Don't put too much hope on it, he may just appear to be better.' But the next morning the baby made little sounds and drank... The specialist had telephoned the family doctor... From experience he knew the exact moment death should have occurred. When he heard the opposite had happened he thought the doctor was joking and said, 'You should not make fun of such things.' But when the doctor replied it was true and that the very next morning the child had taken its mother's milk, the specialist said, 'I cannot believe it. If it is true a miracle must have happened and I don't believe in miracles.' 'Indeed,' the doctor said, 'a kind of saint went to see the baby.' The specialist never took the trouble to find out if the miracle had really happened. He was a professor.'

Official medical science in those days was even more averse to alternative methods than it is now — though it was talked about in hospital. An assistant doctor who took life very seriously and was going through a hard time was advised by her colleagues 'to go and see that Indian who cured Mrs Kramer's child.' She did and became one of those quiet mureeds who, also as a doctor, was a support to many.

There were cases of illness that Inayat knew he could do nothing about. Then he restricted himself to silently preparing the patient and his family. Sometimes healing was also given silently and without any contact, at a distance even. Himself he would or could not always cure. In the spring of 1925 his valued disciple Zanetti, the stolid lawyer, came to Suresnes, hoping to be cured of a slight indisposition. He was healed, but noticed with dismay that the master himself was in great pain and had to lie down again immediately. How could that be? The same alarmed question Inayat had asked at the sickbed of his own master. He gave the same answer he had received twenty years ago: it was necessary for the sake of experience. The advanced mystic has to learn everything about life, 'soar higher than the highest heaven and dive deeper than the depth of the ocean.' Nothing is further from the rosy conception of an always perfect saint then this saying from *Vadan*.

It was not easy to live close to someone who carried with him so much of other worlds and so much of the extremes of ours. The mother of the child who was healed wrote that at a certain point it became too much for her. Others have recorded similar things. Van Stolk writes in his book that the master sometimes let him do his meditation practices in his presence. 'At those moments he attuned and raised my consciousness to such a high level that I could hardly stand it... and I longed to return to the limited security of my own little personality, where I could go on living at my own rythm.'[9]

It also often happened that a person, to his own absolute astonishment, suddenly burst into tears in Inayat's presence. An American girl writes that she 'was not a weepy sort of person' but that at the first meeting she uttered sobs instead of words. She had expected to 'meet a God, someone very remote from human difficulties, trials and every day experience.... Instead I met the most understanding, humble, witty, patient, in short the most human being I have ever met.' But at the same time 'his presence was so powerful and overwhelming that I could not speak.' Another one came to Suresnes full of longing, enjoyed the first week and then could not take any more. Even the most guileless soul felt a kind of thrill. The Van Tuyll family's servant-girl told me − she was seventy now, but her bearing and eyes became those of a twenty-year old again − 'It was so wonderful, I just could not help hopping and dancing in the street. And then I suddenly saw that at the top of the street Murshid was watching me. What must he have thought. There I was, dancing in the street.'

For Inayat's wife everything was even more difficult than for the disciples. After his death she was able to express herself in a poem. 'It is not easy to be married to a saint,' she wrote. She had known from the beginning that she would have to make sacrifices, but she, too, had involuntary wishes, determined by her American upbringing. She seemed almost a guest in her large French house that was always full of pupils. And India, where she would have liked to adjust herself, she came to know only partly: from the homesick stories Inayat and his brothers told her, from his personality − exceptional even for an Indian − and from the unreal India of the disciples who could not quite see the master's wife as an ordinary human being either and put her, too, on a pedestal.

The quiet mureeds, who continued to develop and who later kept the work going, understood how wrong one-sided adoration and glorification of a person really were. One woman, leader of a Dutch centre, writes, 'I have strongly felt that the personal tie was a hindrance to a certain extent, the person became so important to us that we obscured his real greatness.' And an Englishwoman notes, 'Many felt the enchantment, but not the reality.'

The reality was man *and* saint; the Indian who was homesick for his own country and the mystic whose attention was in other worlds; a man who could be irritated, ironical, even angry, and a master, tactful, patient, understanding, forgiving, correcting with a smile, supporting, guiding, liberating; a stranger, sick, tried and tormented, and the advanced soul who with one glance could raise a disciple into greater worlds.

He was vexed, and hampered in his work; hardly by deliberate mockery, as in Etretat, but to a certain extent by journalists who twisted his words; more so by dogmatists who reduced all religion to one common denominator and did not listen any more; and most of all by the admirers who only listened with one ear. With all their inclination to adore, some disciples, especially beginners and candidates were possessed of a pedantry an eastern master could not understand. In one of his plays Inayat puts them on the stage and in a few sentences sketches their restlessness and lack of faith.[10]

The excited one hurries in: 'Has the class begun? Has the class begun? Has the guru come?' The doubtful one doubts, the intellectual 'has read thousands of books on the occult sciences,' the clever one wants to put mysticism in a new coat, 'so that no one can find any ground for criticizing it.' The occultist gushes about a 'wonderful vision of you, Guru! You were all clad in blue, and then you turned red. Then your whole appearance became scarlet, and in the end it was a gold light; then your face disappeared...' The guru answers, 'You may have seen someone else, not me.' The individualists think everything marvellous, but they do not want to join a society and cannot bear discipline. These are beautiful scenes. Only one or two of the disciples in the play have trust and accept the master in his humanity and greatness.

In his *Autobiogaphy* Inayat also devotes one passage to the threshold figures who made things difficult for him. Waverers, trouble-makers and those who only wanted to be important somewhere − if not in the Sufi Movement then in another society − were bound to drop out. But even those who had taken the first step across the threshold sometimes made no further progress, through lack of self-confidence, or insufficient broadness, tact and perseverance; they caused trouble through all kinds of self-centredness, rudeness to others and even discourtesy to the master. They found his ideas nice, but too religious, or not religious enough. They would be willing to join, if things were more personal, or more impersonal; or more Christian; or more theosophical; it was too oriental , or not oriental enough. 'In some perhaps, without their realizing it, there remained a grain of nationalism or a spark of bigotry; in the hearts of some a shadow of racism.' 'If someone in the West considers someone as his ideal, he usually expects that ideal to conform to an image he has made. If someone in the East sees another as his spiritual ideal he takes him as he is, and before judging, tries to understand him.'

Not only Inayat, any Easterner in the West is painfully shocked by the lack of reverence and manners. The disciples were astonished to see with how much courtesy Inayat and the Arab mystic, Shaikh al Alawi from Algeria[11], who attended a lecture in Suresnes, treated each other. Actually

Europeans are often inclined to look upon oriental courtesy as dishonest. We admire directness and openness as virtues. A polite yes which should have been no we consider hypocrisy. On the other hand it was inconceivable to Inayat 'to see to what extent some people in the West could be outspoken. I often wondered if it was to be called honesty. If it was honesty I could not think for a moment that it was wisdom.'

Uncontrolled behaviour, especially of an adult in a responsible position, he thought such bad form that he punished the person concerned by not speaking to him or her. For the victim it was unbearable and partly incomprehensible, because our civilization does not look for self-control in formal behaviour, but, much more dangerously, expects the suppression of emotions. A man must not weep, and sex was sin. It was not said aloud, but whispered: it was not really right that the master was married. For an Indian marriage is a duty that is taken for granted. Most saints were given in marriage in their youth, like everybody else, and usually the marriage was consummated. Only Ramakrishna was an exception[12] and it is well-known that Gandhi cherished feelings of guilt about the first years of his married life. But these two were Hindus and even in the Hindu world fertility cults exist as well as passion and puritanism. The Moslem acceptance of sexual life is more natural. Because Inayat had grown up as a Moslem among Hindus he took both the natural acceptance and the self-control for granted. Moreover, as a sage he was convinced that a natural life was best. 'All that is natural, healthy and loving is good.' As a student of life he had come to know the inhibitions of the contemporary West.

The magazine *Sufi* of January 1920 carried the announcement of a book *Sex* by Inayat Khan. But the book did not appear. First the title was modified to *Rasa Shastra, the Science of Life's Creative Forces*. As *Rasa Shastra* it is mentioned in the correspondence with Miss Dowland. But Miss

Dowland did not publish it. Shortly after Inayat's death an Englishman wrote that Murshid had entrusted to him a manuscript to be published; trembling he by-passes the word sex, cautiously he prints a few pages. Only about 1938 did the entire book come out. Amused, one of the older mureeds said, 'They did not dare publish it before, because Murshid had said all these things.'

'All these things' were very innocent. The book belongs to Inayat's earlier work, with many Indian words and the Indian method of classifying people in categories from fine to coarse. A similar classification can be found in his later books, but adjusted to western conditions. *Rasa Shastra* gives the traditional Indian classification from fine to coarse in sexual life. Abstinence is not the point at issue, but the way in which mutual attraction is experienced. Inayat not only describes the lotus girl, the finest soul, to whom in his youth he had dedicated his most beautiful – and therefore never published – song but also the coarsest man who yields to all his lusts. He does not call it sin, merely states that such people exist. The subjects of prostitution and homosexuality he does not evade either. He did not say that divorce was forbidden. And when two young people loved each other, they should marry as soon as possible.

Unlike the *Kama Sutra* it is not a book of instruction. It is certainly not Inayat's most important work, but it is important that he found it necessary to dictate it. In these years after the war he once walked with a disciple through a street where a couple stood kissing in a doorway. His companion, an Englishwoman, apologized that he had to see something like that. 'Why?' he asked, 'it is wonderful, it is love.'

In books such as *Rasa Shastra* and the ones about education and modern art, it is difficult to decide how much comes from him as a human being and an Indian, and how much from the inspired sage. Especially in the last year when his longing for India made him idealize the world of his youth, he was sometimes inclined to call Indian con-

248

ditions exemplary. Whereas before he had been cautious about this; if his audience wanted to hear about eastern sages he used to begin by saying that wisdom could exist in the West as well as in the East. His message was not to be called a message from the East either. God was not of the East or the West but belonged to all. As a murshid he had grown above East and West, as a man he was an Indian in exile.

Sometimes his wisdom and his homesickness came into conflict. He was a reformer who worked for a religion that could be lived and for ethics suited to a new society of equals. He knew that equality for men and women was part of it and in his *Autobiography,* which is of 1922 and 1923, he remarks that in the East men and women rarely achieve social co-operation and that eastern society suffers from this. But there are innumerable sayings and anecdotes in which he portrays the position of the Indian woman, as he had known it at home, as ideal.

Now, in the West, he ran into demonstrative exaggerations: the suffragettes of about 1910 and the garçonnes of about 1925. We don't give them a thought any longer but then the papers were full of them. They were much talked about, it was an event when a girl or woman decided to wear short hair and skirts and to smoke cigarettes. Many a European man condemned this more strongly than Inayat. He had an oriental respect for women. He knew them as mothers, grandmothers, aunts, wives, all important figures in the house. In his India of before 1910 he had hardly seen them play any part outside the home. Though he knew that this would be a normal thing in the future, and recognized it as progress for the country, he could not help saying that a woman who took a job outside the home lost her safety and delicacy and was no longer treated with respect.

And indeed, among his disciples he met with quite a few men who had a low opinion of women — for instance his committee members in Geneva, who could hardly tolerate

249

a woman as a colleague. The person in question was Miss Goodenough, the old faithful mureed of the English days; one, moreover, who had gone through a large part of real training, who knew Persian and was able to hold twenty-three lectures in two months.[13] The master would not dream of considering her inferior to the gentlemen and to exclude her from the committee. Whatever cultural influences were working in him, his most important standard was inner evolution.

The most painful confusion of spiritual and cultural standards originated round the word democracy.[14] For Inayat democracy was not a political but a spiritual concept. A democrat for him was one who acknowledged and recognized God in everyone, and lived accordingly. As he himself did. Some disciples asked whether particular methods were meant for all kind of children and all kind of adults. 'Yes,' he replied simply. And in the instruction-interview in America he said emphatically that the grossest person could become finer if he would do a certain exercise well for six weeks. That is to say, anyone can awaken the Divine essence that is hidden deep in his heart, if he wants to. No one must be compelled. But he who wants to has to begin at the beginning, be a disciple before he can become a master. He had taken that much trouble himself. And a disciple begins by trusting his master, that means by obeying him.

The western diciples found this hard. Partly through lack of self-confidence, but also because democracy, for them, had different associations: politics, freedom, do as you like, don't take orders, have a say in all matters.

'Everyone loves freedom,' said Inayat, and he meant worldly as well as spiritual freedom, but only inner liberation could lead to outward freedom. To achieve inner freedom mystical training was necessary and the one who ventured into this should put 'do what you want' out of his mind for the time being, that would be 'starting at the end.'

Freedom, including taking a strong stand against the abuse of power, comes after training in self-control.

For Inayat it was incomprehensible that an ignorant person should have a say in things. The teacher was a leader whose ability and experience the disciple naturally trusted. If anyone said that leadership was not democratic he remarked that every group has a leader, by whatever name he may be called. Nobody was more against sheep-like obedience than he was, but also nobody found leveling as dangerous as he did. 'True democracy is to grow, bring yourself to a higher level.' But 'All people submit to power unwillingly, and to love willingly.'

For the disciples the opposite of democracy was tyranny or unrelenting authority. That was partly a difference in evolution; for them good and bad, fine and coarse, were static. Partly it was a difference in culture. Democracy in the West originated as a protest against power and abuse of power. The only thing that changes is the group in power. For Inayat the opposite of democracy was not power but aristocracy. The world he had grown up in was aristocratic. For him the true aristocrat was at the same time a true democrat: a king or a dervish who considered nobody inferior to himself and who respected everyone. But if a person could not acknowledge another as his superior he found this a great lack of moral evolution.

His own inner evolution and study of life involved observing the political democracy of the West. His attitude towards it, as a foreigner and as a mystic, was sceptical. He smiled at the weak points of right and left, both of whom cried out that they represented true democracy. But when one of them invited him to put his teachings at their disposal he refused. He knew very well that a religious movement supported by a temporal power can go far, but his Sufism must not become a political instrument.

He helped people, not groups, and he gave a counterpoise to the exclusively materialistic and commercially

251

minded attitude of most people. That was not a cliché when he said it, he was deeply concerned, for he saw the approach of what we are now beginning to recognize. But his listeners, of course, immediately filed the words materialism and spirituality in a familiar pigeon-hole, with a nod of agreement or a superior sneer. And when he mentioned aristocracy or democracy, they either thought, 'Oh, lovely, just like the days when there weren't any socialists yet,' or, 'For shame, tyranny.'

What Inayat appreciated in Zanetti was his understanding of the nuances, while working in Geneva among purely political institutions. Zanetti's first draft of the articles of incorporation for Headquarters comprised a kind of League of Nations meeting with votes for all. The idea that a spiritually not very advanced majority would govern his movement with rigidity or hair-splitting distinctions, or that a pupil should lay down the law, Inayat rejected. His organization was neither political nor economic, there was no need for disputes. Zanetti then created a constitution, not very different from that of other similar institutions, where the administration is in the hands of a committee and a society of members maintains the school. The local branches and national societies were autonomous organizations chartered by the Executive Committee. In the International Council held yearly in Geneva national representatives only had an advisory role. The actual governing was in the hands of the Committee and the 'Representative General.' Just as in 1917, the most important members of the board had two or three votes, Inayat himself four and the right of veto. In 1921 already he had written to Miss Dowland that the mureeds must do the 'arranging of things but in my way, or my difficulties would be incalculable.'

They were. 'Murshid, that is not democratic,' said a diligent, ambitious and narrow-minded man, whose own democracy meant rights for him and his equals. He was a great admirer, though, of the master as the saint-who-can-do-everything. How he hurt the master's feelings the simpleton did not understand. He spoke to a Sufi mystic who is always democratic in a spiritual sense, a master to whom trust and respect were due; and to an Easterner who felt this kind of raw, undisguised criticism as a coarse offence. It was a tragic clash between two worlds.[15]

For Inayat it was second nature to take everybody's feelings into consideration; some co-workers could not do this and at times 'this made me so sensitive that I felt as if the skin had been peeled off my heart.'

Of other pupils he says that they were nearer to him than his own friends and relations in the East, souls that were truly devoted and open, real disciples who were able to trust and receive his trust. It was the outer organization that was always presenting difficulties. He could not do without it, if he had aroused interest somewhere the people concerned had to know where they could make further enquiries. But he writes that, 'For me who was born with a tendency to be away from all worldly activities and who grew every day more apart from all worldly things, to have an organization to make, to control and to carry out has been a great trial.'

'Who grew every day more apart from all worldly things.' In his *Gayan*, written in the London days, he could still say, 'Life in the world is most interesting to me, but solitude away from the world is the longing of my soul.' The sage in one of his plays is called to worldly fame and happiness after many trials, but goes away in the end. 'Wilderness, why did I leave you?.... you were always in my heart — the memory of having meditated in the woods, of having talked with the trees of long tradition whose every leaf is a tongue of flame. Venerated trees, have I not taken refuge in your shadow from the hot sun, when tired of roaming about in the wilderness, bare-footed? Little pools of water, I drank nectar from you. Joyful I felt under the vast canopy of the blue sky. Gentle streams of water, running from hills and rocks: I bathed in you and was purified of all infirmities. High mountains with a background of white clouds. No palace in the world could be compared whith your beauty. Morning-sun, you are most glorious in the wilderness....'[16]

At the end of his *Autobiography* he delineates his ideal of India — sun, open spaces, true culture, true respect. For years it was only a dream. But in the summer of 1926 it was decided: he would go home. Passionately he wrote:

'India, India, the land of my birth,
To compare with you there is no place on the earth....
In my deepest despair I heard your call.
Your sacred rivers, your holy shrines,
Your sublime nature, your spirit divine,
Your moonlight night and your glorious dawn....
They draw me so much that I wish I could fly.'

His departure was kept secret for a long time, but it could be sensed. During the summerschool the most oriental of his plays was performed, the one that ends with a farewell: 'I am going in search of another kingdom.'[17] The ceremony of the foundation stone and the introduction of the Confraternity of the Message were acts of farewell too. Some felt they were seeing him for the last time. Many did not.

At Christmas 1926 Inayat's co-workers received his Christmas greetings from India.

The text was later printed in *Nirtan*:

'Before you judge my actions,
Lord, I pray, you will forgive.
Before my heart has broken,
Will you help my soul to live?
Before my eyes are covered,
Will you let me see your face?
Before my feet are tired,
May I reach your dwelling-place?

Before I wake from slumber,
You will watch me, Lord, I hold.
Before I throw my mantle,
Will you take me in your fold?
Before my work is over,
You, my Lord, will right the wrong.
Before you play your music,
Will you let me sing my song?'

This poem has been a comfort at the end to people who had lived their lives without religion. Anyone who thinks of his own death can say it. It is not difficult, as many other poems of Inayat's, in which the mystic is passionately searching for God and finds Him in himself, in nature, in another being. The images are reminiscent of his earlier writings, in *Minqar-é-Musiqar* he already says, 'Let me see your face' and in *Nirtan* 'I reach Thee before my feet can reach Thy dwelling place,' and 'I see Thee before mine eyes can reach Thy spheres.' The tone and form of the farewell poem are simpler.

'If you do not see God in man, you will not see Him anywhere.[18] The man who speaks in this poem is expecting death and he turns not only to a God-ideal outside himself — addressed as Thou; it is also an appeal to God in man, to you. 'God in my fellow-men, disciple, before you judge' — and they had judged — 'forgive me.' 'Before my heart has broken — that heart of which the skin seemed to be peeled off — 'will you help my soul to live?' But does not the soul of a mystic live deeply and fully? Though his soul is their soul is every soul is God. 'Will you let me see your face?' God in my disciples, in my fellow-creatures, reveal yourself. Let me see your dwelling place, see where you are, see that you are. 'Before I wake' — life is a dream for him — 'you will watch me.' 'I hold,' that is believe, but also 'I will not let go.' 'Before I lay down my life, take me in your life.' And then the musician repeats the beginning, a powerful variation. He does not ask to be forgiven, but that his mistakes may be put right. He does not request, but trusts. 'You will right the wrong.' And finally, as a signature, the personal note, words that only the singer could say: 'Let me sing my song.' Does the mystic whose whole life was God's music — 'go and unite East and West with the music of your soul' — does he ask God in his disciples — who always knew better, 'in the West there are no disciples, only masters' — to listen to his note before they go on in their own way?

It is both and more. It is also the artist who has sacrificed his music for his mission. It is also the child from the house of Maula Bakhsh, who had adjusted himself for so long, and now at last, after sixteen years of wandering in the West that seemed so wonderful at one time, joyfully returns home.

'Angels would humbly bow low, if they saw my land.' Never forgotten house in Baroda, where at night in bed the child listened to the chanting of the Quran and early in the morning his grandfather came and took him to learn his song.

Chapter XII (1926-1927)
The House of Maula Bakhsh

'In India I heard Murshid sing for the first time, a powerful voice, too big for the small house. This I had never heard in America. Now Murshid sang every day. At least in the beginning, later he didn't.'

This is a memory of the secretary, Kismet Stam, who accompanied Inayat on his last journey.[1] The work went on, until the end he dictated lessons and poems, and the correspondence was extensive. Letters to co-workers spoke of the work and their health, about his own he did not say much, but in every town in India his first visit was to a doctor.

In Venice he bought a leather and gold writing case, a present for Hakim Ajmal Khan, Gandhi's and the Gaekwar's old doctor. It was the 28th September, he wrote to Miss Dowland, who had not been to Suresnes, who had in fact never set foot outside England. He thanked her for her letter and entrusted to her and her co-workers the movement in England. 'I am leaving today on a big voyage.'

At sea he watched the mountain ranges of Italy recede in the golden sunset. The silhouette of the Apennines had been his first view of the West sixteen years before. Now he knew what lived behind those peaks and domes.

He was returning to his own world. In mid-October he arrived in Karachi and travelled via Lahore to Delhi. That was the long way round but in Lahore was the tomb of Al Hujwiri, 'the head of the saints.' For all sages and dervishes, even for conquerers this sacred spot is the gateway to the sub-continent.[2] Inayat stayed in Lahore for a few days.

257

Kismet Stam does not remember visits to a tomb. 'We walked through several mosques, one with many lamps, quite different from other mosques.' The tomb of Ali al Hujwiri lies in a mosque with many lamps.

At the station in Lahore a Hindu student, who saw Inayat standing by the window of his compartment, asked radiantly, 'Are you Tagore?' Inayat smiled. 'All helpers of man resemble each other.'[3] He was dressed in white now, wore a white turban and white shoes with yellow embroidery. People used to come up to him, ask who he was, give him their visiting card, or just stare. They took him for an ambassador, or a rich merchant; some understood what he was, certainly the mystics, faqirs and dervishes, who greeted him or called out to him, made some veiled remark, something apparently incomprehensible. For the secretary this was new, even though she had taken hundreds of dictations with dervish stories.

Everything was new for her. The first evening when Inayat went out alone, she innocently installed herself in the verandah with a book and a reading lamp. Inayat had to explain to her how this could be misinterpreted and from then on he took her with him whenever possible. Whom he visited she hardly knew, as she would stay in the tonga (two-wheeled carriage) with the trustworthy regular driver. This driver sometimes came early, sometimes late, sometimes he drove dreamily, sometimes fast. Inayat could not help writing to western friends about this man to whom time meant so little. The servant who travelled with them was like that too. He had a long rosary and if it was time to tell his beads dinner had to wait. This servant stammered and stole, but he had such a large family that Inayat let him get away with it. His secretary would just have to get used to not finding enough food on the table. The mixed attitude of reserve and respect to servants and the poor was strange to her, she did not know India and Indian relationships.

Suresnes, 13 September 1926

259

For Inayat, too, much was new. The country had changed. The days of great music had gone and tension between Hindus and Moslems was growing.[4] In his letters he always said that he had only come to India to rest and observe. It was not altogether a rest, he paid many visits. And, of course, he went to holy places.

South of sprawling New Delhi lay a small, medieval village, within high, crumbling walls. Some Hindu families have been living there for six hundred years, in peace with their Moslems neighbours. The Moslems are in the majority, naturally, as the sacred tombs of the mystic Hazrat Nizamuddin Aulia and the poet Amir Khusro lie within the walls, in their own grounds with mosques, dwellings, a market, everything that in the course of time develops around a place of pilgrimage. Today new suburbs surround the now overcrowded village. In 1926 it was still a long journey from Delhi, through lonely country, littered everywhere with the remains of medieval forts, palaces and mosques; straight red walls, marble terraces, ruined domes shining in the evening sun. One of the leading Pirs at the shrine of Hazrat Nizamuddin Aulia showed Inayat round and later told how he had taken him to a small watchtower on the roof of his house. From this small, square tower on the south-east corner Inayat looked out over the roofs, courtyards and alley-ways of the village at his feet, the domes and majestic ruins in the north and far across open fields to the south. 'Here I would like to stay,' he said.[5]

The house he finally found was far away in the north, on the edge of Old Delhi, west of Bela Road, and not very far from the Jamuna, the twin river of the Ganges. It was a simple Indian house, with a wide corridor in the centre, and a verandah, sitting-room, bedroom and bathroom on either side. In the courtyard hennah grew and large, white daturas, on the surrounding waste land poinsettias, oleander and thorny acacias. A few goats and cows grazed there. At night the jackals howled and on the opposite bank a caste

260

of professional robbers lived. In the evenings, before the short sunset, Inayat used to walk to the Jamuna, or he took a carriage from Bela Road to the old town. Below, by the river, was a Shiva temple. On the townside along a quiet road with large banyan trees lay Qudsia Gardens with its old, overgrown mosque. In the mornings he walked up and down on the north side of the house, where he found some shade. The courtyard was used as a short-cut to the road, there was a hole in the hedge and the neighbours used to spread out their meters-long turbans to dry. He talked with the passers-by. There was an old, red-cheeked Nepalese who often came; a wandering mystic who greeted him reverently and was greeted reverently; a Harijan-child who stared at him shyly when he gave it something. A poor man in the neighbourhood was given some clothes and came to show how nice he looked in them. Sometimes sick people were brought to him to be healed.

The house was called Tilak Lodge, after the freedom fighter Lokmanya Tilak. It belonged to a merchant who, when Inayat did not immediately decide to take it, doubled the rent. 'You should have taken it the first time, sir.' No Hindu friend of Maula Bakhsh would have said that nor Inayat's old friends in Hyderabad.

Slowly the disappointment grew. A letter written on 2nd November to Ronald Armstrong in England, was still cheerful. Really speaking he had come to rest, Inayat wrote, but he had been discovered already and was invited to lecture at the Universities of Delhi and Aligarh. A letter to Van Stolk, dated 23d November, sounded more hesitant: 'I am trying to accustom myself to the quiet life, and yet I hardly think that one can ever be quiet except in the caves of Himalaya. I cannot tell you my impressions here as they are so many and varied, only what I wish to say is that when you find me you will find me charged with the Indian atmosphere.'

This letter was written from Amroha, a place of pilgrimage not far from Lucknow. He had started to wander again, which had not been possible before because his companion had fallen ill with typhus in the beginning of November. Travelling did him good. A triumphant 'en route' heads a letter dated 30th November, to the family in The Hague, in which he makes amused enquiries about Maheboob Khan's small daughter and asks his sister-in-law 'how she would like to be in this part of the world where I am.' But his letters to Madame van Goens are always cheerful and sometimes hide the painful things.

The secretary did notice something of the sadness, especially when there was evidence of the decline of music, or a shopkeeper showed his worst side, or a cabman made an unnecessary detour to make the trip more expensive. 'Often Murshid said he would like to write a book about India, about the psychology of the people, the philosophical bent of their minds, their recklessness, their sense of humour, their indifference in both the good and the bad sense of the word. On several occasions Murshid said. 'In India one finds the best and the worst." '

But in the end he no longer sang and in a letter to his youngest brother, dated 15th December, he expressed his disappointment. Musharaff Khan had wanted to return too. 'Don't,' Inayat wrote. 'The country we knew has died without beauty. Only money is respected, there is no more culture and no more ideal, the poor are despised, even the freedom movement has lost its élan.'

That same fifteenth December Inayat lectured at the University of New Delhi. On the subjects of the time, the harijans (casteless), the thousands of beggars, the woman-labourers at road-and-house-constructions who, unprotected, carried heavy loads on their heads. When he was still in the West he had answered criticism of the poverty in India with 'And what about the slums in Liverpool and London and New York?' Every Indian said that. But Inayat had always been the preacher of penitence to his own people. And he had always impressed upon Indians the ideal of their common heritage and worked for understanding between all creeds and communities. He did this innocently when he was eighteen, in Madras, and now, knowing bitterly that Hindus and Moslems were growing away from each other. 'The first thing one sees at any station is a waterpipe with two taps and two notices: Hindu water, Moslem water. It is the same water.'

After the two lectures in Delhi only one person became a mureed, Mrs. Shastri, the American wife of a Hindu doctor. There already was one Moslem disciple. Hasan al Haq. Inayat did not have the feeling that what he said was very much appreciated. 'But they could not deny it.' In a letter to Musharaff Khan he had already said, 'They allow me to speak because I am famous in the West and I don't charge anything.' Yet a letter to Armstrong of the same date spoke of some expectations: now his work in India would begin.

But his own country did not know him any more. Only with the mystics he felt at home. One of those he visited was Swami Shraddhanand, an orator of the Arya Samaj.[6] The followers of the Arya Samaj based their beliefs on the excellence of the Vedas above all other scriptures, but were not anti-Moslem. The saint Shraddhanand also preached Gandhian nationalism. It is a pity that the contents of his conversation with Inayat are not known.

In a lean-to on the banks of the Jamuna lived a different kind of sage, in absolute poverty and solitude. His glance was like Inayat's, peaceful and deep, but he bore no marks of life in the world. Inayat's task had been to live among the crowds.[7] The secretary noted a difference between the two, and in the quiet forecourt of the mosque in Qudsia Gardens Inayat himself said, 'If I were to leave the world and sit here in silence, thousands would come.'

'If.' He could have been one of the last great veena players, a legend. He could have been a freedom fighter in his own country or an instrument in the politics of a western country. He could have been a miracle worker or a silent sage under a tree. Or rich. Once he was offered a castle and once a fortune. But he had sacrificed his musical fame and had not availed himself of the other opportunities. He continued to teach people what they needed and what they could do but did not.

On 22nd December he lectured at Lucknow and, according to one of his letters, found more appreciation there than in Delhi. Lucknow is a town full of Moghul memories. Inayat went round the old Dilkusha Palace. 'If that could be restored and become a Sufi centre.'

From Lucknow to Benares. On arrival he was restless and made the tonga driver go back to the station several times. On 25th December Swami Shraddhanand, whom he had so recently visited, was shot in Delhi by a Moslem fanatic, because someone else, who had also been shot meanwhile, had written a book against the Quran. Everywhere in the country Hindu shops were closed. 'Now they have a new martyr,' Inayat said. His country was still far from unity.

But he was in Benares, the sacred city where, as a boy of fourteen he had been happy. On the roads the water-carriers went to and fro with brass vessels full of holy Ganges water suspended from a bending pole on their shoulders. Inayat told the Dutch girl for whom everything was new, that some princes took barrels full of Ganges water with them when they travelled to the West. And he pointed to her, on a ghat (sandy beach) of the quiet river the hut of Harish Chandra, the Job and Abraham of India. King Harish Chandra was tested by the rishis, who wanted to see if there was such a thing as a perfectly loyal human being. Just like Job he had lost everything, kingdom, wife and child, and just like Abraham he had to be inhuman to those nearest to him for the sake of obedience; just like Job and Abraham, he had everything given back to him after the test. That was as it should be in an ancient story.

From Benares he went to Agra and Sikandra. In Sikandra another ideal example lies buried: Akbar, the founder of the Moghul greatness, the man who allowed all religions to exist side by side in peace, a Moslem with a Hindu wife; the king at whose court Tansen sang, who worked and played on a large scale, who had monuments erected even for a brave opponent. His tomb is five storeys high, a monument of art and architecture. Inayat paused by an open work marble screen with its continuously variegated carving 'like music in stone.' From the top gallery one has a view of the lotus dome and the towers of the Taj Mahal in the distance among green foliage, of the wide riverbed, of a few small houses, of someone walking below, just as people had walked there in the day of the great Moghuls. But the age of Akbar is gone. People come from far to look at the empty glory of his monuments. The most visited place is the Taj Mahal, a mausoleum, white against the blue sky, strong and elegant and proudly reflected in its pools. Inayat went there and stood still for a while at the door; just as he went in, someone demonstrated the long echo, sang a few notes that slowly faded away.

He strolled back past the long pools, looked round, started to say, 'It makes me sad that...,' but did not finsih the sentence. 'Those people knew grandeur,' he said finally.

'Where is the old wisdom, where the glory?' He also went to see Agra Fort, opposite the Taj Mahal, compact and strong outside, but deserted within. Of the five hundred buildings only a few still stand, of the gardens only the story remains, the Pearl mosque is still there, gates, galleries and space, lace work in stone, water for ablutions; but hardly anyone looked at all this.

Yet some things remained. Akbar used to travel to Ajmer every year, to visit the shrine of Khwaja Moinuddin Chishti and even now thousands of pilgrims go there every year in crowded, special trains, Moslems and Hindus.

On 29th December Inayat wrote one of his concise notes to Miss Dowland. He thanked her for Christmas cards, telegrams and books, told her of the lecture in Lucknow, repeated, as he did in all letters to disciples, that he was not in Inda to work, but to observe the situation, and that above all he needed rest. That evening he was to leave for Ajmer to pay his respects at the tomb of Khwaja Moinuddin Chishti. And after that he would go to Baroda.

These were to be highlights in his pilgrimage. Baroda, for him, meant the house that rang with music, the house of Maula Bakhsh, his last attachment to this earth. In Ajmer was the most living centre of the old Chishtia Sufi Order. There, in his youth, he had discovered the kingly dervishes and a Chishti dervish had shown Maula Bakhsh his vocation.

Externally the spectacle around the tomb and the mosque gets worse every year. The grounds are swarming with the descendants of the first caretakers who wipe imaginery dust of the marble walls, point out imaginery places and points of interest, and hold out their hands. Inayat warned his secretary, 'Many people are so disgusted with the commotion and the money making that they never come again. But that is something one can overlook, what matters is what is really there, the living example.' For mystics a visit to a holy place means the unity of illuminated souls, the continuity of and the lasting contact with all those who have learnt to detach themselves from the limitation of their senses.[8] In the midst of all the hustle and bustle was one quiet spot, near the tomb, where the qawals sat and sang for hours. The spectacle did not exist for them, it faded away, as the streets of Paris faded away for the young man who sat beside Inayat in the tram.

Inayat, though absorbed in greater worlds, was not unaware of the needs of this one. He never forgot to take a parcel of food with him for the beggars and kept it till someone asked for it. And so, for several days, he continued to visit this place of inspiration in the midst of all the noise and sat on the marble floor among the qawals — until he fell ill. It was influenza, with a lung complication, as he had had so often in the cold of Europe. The nights were cold in Northern India, eighteen or twenty degrees less than the summery temperature in the middle of the day. The secretary lit a fire in the evenings.

It looked as if all would be well. After a week's serious illness he got up again, and even answered some letters. In a note dated 13th January he seems to have been making plans for the future. But his handwriting was different, unsteady, almost groping. The downward loops became more open, grew bigger and spread searching across the page.

The journey was continued. To Jaipur, the town with the seven gates. There is not one holy tomb. It is a tourist city and a city of industry and commerce. And a town of art and music. Inayat's second marriage had been celebrated there, the family from Baroda had accompanied him and he had listened and spoken to the most famous musicians of that time. Here the maharaja had told him that during the Viceroy's celebration Maula Bakhsh sat, 'while we — the princes — were standing.' About the wedding he did not tell the secretary. He did tell her hundreds of other stories. About musicians who practised all night and tied their hair to a beam in the ceiling so that they would be jerked awake if they began to dose off. He told her of the former glory, and also of the abuses and weird excesses of the maharajas. The princes still ruled in 1926, but in a vague, estranged way. In a courtyard in Jaipur Palace stood an open treasure chest. A decorated elephant walked about, shimmering with gold and jewels. Long ago an elephant had come to the gate of the house of Maula Bakhsh to take Inayat and his brothers for a ride.

In the summer of 1926 a letter had been written to uncle Pathan, who was director of music at the Court of Nepal.

Until September no answer had been received, but that did not mean anything. Correspondence could be postponed and forgotten, as he remembered from his youth, from home.[9]

About 20th January he undertook the journey to Baroda.

It is a long way from the station to Yakudpura, past parks, palaces and the prison, the outside of which also looks like a palace in a park. At the end of the road is the gate that once marked the town boundary.

In a new, narrow side street he found the house. He was not mistaken, the name Maula Bakhsh was carved above the gate. But the double doors were closed. Behind the walls, blind to the street, there was no sound, no music, not a sign of life. The house of Maula Bakhsh was empty, deserted, it was already falling into decay.

Then Inayat went to the tomb of his grandfather. That, too, was neglected and delapidated, the roof hung crooked above it.

That same evening he took a train back to Delhi. Another twenty four hours of heat and dust. In Delhi he fell ill again, so seriously that a nurse had to be engaged. Outwardly he showed no sign of illness. He longed for music and made a sad joke; he had no 'singer' but the stammering Gaffar, the servant. But he still helped the few people around him, giving indirect advice, as usual.

During the last days he asked for passages from *Vadan* to be read to him. 'Waves, why does the wind come and then go from you?' 'It comes to wake us, and leaves us to solve the problem among ourselves.'

That was what Inayat had done.

In the night of fourth to fifth February he lost consciousness. The girl who had come with him from Europe would not believe he was dying. 'It is samadhi,' she told the English doctor, the one with whom she could speak. He looked at her, said nothing and let her find out for herself. In the

268

morning the breathing became irregular, at twenty minutes past eight Inayat died.

The nurse was in the front room, the secretary knelt by the bed for hours. The two doctors came, and mrs Shastri. That same day a piece of land was bought, opposite the little watch-tower, from which Inayat had looked out over village and wilderness. The same Pir who had once shown him round, made all the necessary arrangements. A year later the family came.

Inayat was not yet forty-five years old when he died. Today so many people from Europe and America go to visit his tomb that his countrymen are beginning to discover him. The tomb lies modestly within four walls, open to the sky. The entrance faces the small grey watch-tower, the branches of a tree growing in a compound next door overhang the wall and provide shade. And outside the village walls, not far away, stretches the open country, his beloved India, where he experienced all the joys of his youth and the last, unavoidable, liberating sorrow of his human life.

Sources and Notes

A. *Unpublished*

1. *Biography* of Hazrat Inayat Khan in India, 1882-1910, by his brother-in-law Mehr Baksh; *Autobiography* and *Journal* of the years in the West, 1910-1927. *Appendices*: genealogy, notes on music, on East and West, on organisation and western philosophies of life, a contribution of Inayat's wife and a collection of anecdotes. Manuscripts are kept by the family, in the international headquarters, in the collection-Furnée and by some of the older local leaders.

2. Letters, pictures and photographs, articles of incorporation, constitution and rules, instructions interview, *Monthly Record Headquarters*. Kept as above. Instructions interview also in the Garden of Inayat, Novato, California. Letters with addressees or their heirs.

3. Information by people who met Inayat and by members of his family; see acknowledgement.

4. Written memoirs, collected by Mrs S. J. Smit-Kerbert. Copies of this collection kept by local leaders.

These sources can be recognized by the wording in the text. In case of two versions or a necessary elucidation there is a reference to a note. Quotations from Inayat without a reference to a printed source, are from the *Autobiography* or its Appendices. Pages from his collected works mentioned in the notes are chosen at random and not exhaustive.

B. *Published*

Copies of old Sufi books and periodicals can be found in the Sufi Library in The Hague, Holland and in the Garden of Inayat, Novato, California; incomplete in the British Museum. Inayat's collected works are normally for sale in a recent edition. Abbreviations of books or periodicals which are cited more than once:

Chaubey: S. K. Chaubey, *Indian Music Today,* Kitab Mahal, Allahabad, 1945. Disciple: *Memories of Hazrat Inayat Khan,* by a Disciple (Sophia Saintsbury Green), Rider & Co, London, undated.

Durga Das: Durga Das, *India from Curzon to Nehru and After,* Collins, London 1969.

Forty Years: 1910-1950, Forty Years of Sufism, Sufi Movement, Geneva/The Hague, 1950.

Gayan: Hazrat Inayat Khan, *Notes from the unstruck Music from the Gayan.* Quotations from the fourth edition, Deventer 1936; recent editions Sufi Publishing Company, London.

Germain: André Germain, *La Bourgeoisie qui Brûle. Propos d'un Témoin (1890-1940),* Paris, 1951.

Gramont: Elisabeth de Gramont, *Souvenirs du Monde de 1890 à 1940,* Grasset, Paris, 1966·

Havelock Ellis: H. Havelock Ellis, *My Life,* Heinemann, London, 1940.

Minqar-é-Musiqar: Professor Inayat Khan, *Minqar-é-Musiqar,* Indian Press, Allahabad 1913. The manuscript was completed in Hydarabad, 1324 A. H., about 1906 A. D. Quotations from an anonymous translation with reference to the original pages.

Pages: Musharaff Moulamia Khan, *Pages in the Life of a Sufi. Reflections and Reminiscences,* 2nd, augmented edition, Sufi Publishing Company, London/Southampton 1971.

Nirtan: Hazrat Inayat Khan, *Nirtan or the Dance of the Soul.* Quotations from the fourth edition, see *Gayan.*

Overton Fuller: Jean Overton Fuller, *Noor-un-Nisa Inayat Khan* (Madeleine). Quotations from and references to the pages in the 8th augmented edition, East-West Publications/Barrie & Jenkins, Rotterdam/London, 1971.

Sengupta: Padmini Sengupta, *Sarojini Naidu,* Asia Publishing House, Bombay, 1966.

SM: The Sufi Message of Hazrat Inayat Khan, Barrie and Rockliff, London, 1960-1969. Twelve volumes collected works. In the notes a Roman numeral indicates a volume, an Arabic numeral the page. *SM* XII, 177 means *Sufi Message,* Vol. XII, p. 177.

St. Denis: Ruth St Denis, *An Unfinished Life,* Harrap London, 1939.

Van Stolk: Sirkar van Stolk with Daphne Dunlop, *Memories of a Sufi Sage,* East-West Publications, Rotterdam, 1967.

Subhan: John A. Subhan, B. A., B. D., D. D., *Sufism, its Saints and Shrines, An Introduction to the Study of Sufism with Special Reference to India and Pakistan,* revised edition, Lucknow Publishing House, Lucknow, 1960.

The Sufi: The Sufi, quarterly magazine, London 1915-1920, 1926-1939.

Sufism: Sufism, quarterly magazine, 1921-1925.

Sufi Record: Sufi Record, Golden Jubilee of the Sufi Message, 1910-1960, Headquarters, Geneva and Heijnis, Zaandijk, 1960.

Tagore: Rabindranath Tagore, *My Reminiscences,* Macmillan, London, 1917.

Vadan: Hazrat Inayat Khan, *The Divine Symphony or Vadan.* Quotations from the fourth edition, see *Gayan.*

Notes

Chapter I

1. Van Stolk, p. 24.
2. Govindbai H. Desai, *Visitor's Guide to Baroda*, p. 22. Another description of Baroda by the same author in *Forty Years in Baroda*, 1929, p. 9: 'In place of wide thoroughfares a few narrow streets, blind lanes and alleys, dusty in summer, muddy during the rains and filthy at all times.'
3. *Pages*, p. 46.
4. *Pages*, p. 4. The passport of Inayat's brother Maheboob Khan still said Yuskin caste. Because of their religion Moslems don't belong to the caste system, but it may be applied socially. The Persian translation of Yuskin or Yuzkhan – head of the clan – was Djamma Shah. This title Djamma Shah has given rise to misunderstanding. In some biographies of Inayat mention is made of a saint Jama Shah as the founder of the family. Probably the proper name Jama has been confused with the temporal title Djamma Shah, and the tradition regarding spiritual leadership. (Information given by Mahmood Khan).
5. *Pages*, p. 7 does not mention a holy man along the road, but a vision in Ajmer. This is understandable, as Ajmer played an important part in Inayat's own life. I have chosen the older version from Mehr Baksh's *Biography*.
6. Inayatullah Khan (son of) Rahematullah Khan. Inayat(ullah) means Favour (of God). Khan is a title and form of address, which cannot be omitted in the East. *In consultation with the family I am using only his first name in this book.* In the *Biography* by Mehr Bakhsh he is also referred to as Inayat. According to Paul Reps he scorned titles. Letters to his disciples are signed Murshid. The brothers called him at first Ustad, then Professor and later Hazrat. As a child at home he was Chhota-mian, the young master. Indians whom I met referred to him as Khan Sahib Inayat Khan, Sufi Inayat Khan, Pir Inayat Khan Sahib, Hazrat Pir Inayat Khan: W. D. Begg in the appendices to *The Big Five of India in Sufism*, Ajmer, 1972, p. 199 writes Pir-o-Murshid Hazrat Sufi Inayat Khan.
7. T. R. Pandya, *A Study of Education in Baroda*, 1915, pp. 95 and 117.
8. Indra Datt, Baroda, *a Study Constitutional and Political*, Lucknow, 1936, p. 50: 'He was weak in mathematics, in which he will have the honest sympathy of many of us.'
9. Tagore, pp. 36, 50 and 89.
10. *SM* XII, 131.

Chapter II

1. Chaubey, p. 9. *SM* I, 219; II, 13, 116, 137; X, 224. H. A. Popley, *The Music of India,* Calcutta, 1950, sec. ed., p. 17.
2. Durga Das, pp. 25, 27, 29 and 32, examples of co-operation between Hindus and Moslems and worship of each other's holy places. Krishan Chander, in his autobiographical novel *Mitti ke Sanam* (Beloved Soil), New Delhi, Asia Publishers, 1966, p. 166, tells how he and his brother, during their long journey on foot from Kashmir to Lahore, found an equally warm reception in Hindu and Moslem homes and villages on their way.
3. Information given by Professor Haroon Khan Shervani, Hyderabad.
4. *SM* V, 108. The elephants *SM* VIII, 32. The muni *SM* XII, 139.
5. Durga Das, pp. 28 and 36. E. E. Sullivan, *Education in Social Change,* Asia Publishing House, London 1968, pp. 1 and 4.
6. Tagore, p. 143.
7. *Sufi Record,* p. 13.

Chapter III

1. Inayat *Git Ratnavali, on the Poetry and Science of Songs,* 1903.
2. *Biography of the Author,* signed TSERCLAES, London, 1913; preceeds *A Sufi Message of Spiritual Liberty.* This oldest western biography has not been reprinted. The author is either Baron Ryclof de T'Serclaes (1873-1935) in England or Baron Alexandre de T'Serclaes in Paris (1846-1915), who belonged to the Parisian circle de scribed in Chapter VII.
3. *Songs of India,* rendered from the Urdu, Hindi and Persian by Inayat Khan and Jennie Duncan Westbrook, London 1918, p. 29.
4. The death of the third child, Karemat Khan, *Pages,* p. 10. The wedding, *Pages,* p. 46.
5. Information by the family in Europe and Baroda. The explanation concerning the objections given by Mahmood Khan.
6. Sir Stanley Reed, *The India I knew, 1897-1947,* Odham, London 1952, *passim.*
7. *SM* XII, 136. T'Serclaes (see note 2 above), p. 9.
8. Inayat Khan, 'The Music of India, a paper written for the Musical Conference at Baroda,' *The Sufi,* April 1916, pp. 8-18; reprinted in *Journal of the Oriental Institute,* MS University of Baroda, Vol. V, No 1, Sept. 1955.
9. Sarojini Naidu, *The Sceptred Flute, Songs of India,* Kitabistan, Allahabad, 2nd ed. 1946, p. 29.
10. It may have been the other great anniversary of 17 Rajab, which in 1903 was 1 st November.

11. Information given by Professor Haroon Khan Shervani, Hyderabad.
12. New outlook, wonderment *SM* X, 35, 83, 92 and 93. Meeting the Nizam, *SM* XII, 137; T'Serclaes, p. 10. The ring and title of honour are mentioned in both published biographies, but not the purse with the hundred golden ashrafis. Just as it is not done to mention the women of the family, so one does not talk money in front of strangers. The unpublished *Biography,* for the inner circle only, does mention the gift. The 'purse', a small burlap bag prosaically stamped in ink by the exchequer, is in the collection of Musharaff Khan. Inayat's eldest son Vilayat inherited the ring.

Chapter IV

1. *SM* XII, 146.
2. Information by Rayhane Behn Tyabji, daughter of a Barodan judge.
3. *The Sufi,* 1918, first issue, p. 4.
4. True and false masters, *SM* XII, 147. Meeting Murshid Madani, SM XII, 148. The ignorant neighbour *SM* VII, 259 and VIII, 284. Necessary qualities for spiritual training *SM* X, 74 and 78-80. The murshid's small talk *SM* I, 76, X, 79. 'Having had a modern education,' *SM* VI, 165. Puzzled by the blessing *SM* VI, 211 and XI, 84. Initial difficulties, *SM* IV, 141, 142, VI, 261 and *passim.* First lessons, *SM* IV, 256, VIII 45, 50, X, 35, 90, 99 and 108, XI, 161.
5. On physical control, *SM* IV, 57, 99, 126-132 and 152, VII, 208, 209, VIII, 51, 120, X, 40. On various methods, *SM* IV, 109, 124 and 179, VIII, 283. Self-observation and memory control, *SM* II, 232 and 233, IV, 233 and 234, VI, 90 and 120, VIII, 201, X, 90, XI, 196. Levels of consciousness, *SM* VIII, 201, X, 108. Training in empathy, *SM* VIII, 46

   The notebook *SM* II, 233, IV, 141, X, 79, 'Whom do you torture?' *SM* VI, 67, Ascesis being temporary, *SM* V, 24, VI, 58, VIII, 46. Breath, *SM* II, 142, IV, 100 and 194. VII, 102-109 and 142-144, XI, 197. On 'amusing'tests, *SM* IX, 235, X, 64-66, 81 and 96.
6. On various methods *SM* IV, 57, 95-103, 131, 165, 166, 236, VII, 262-266, X, 86. Rhythm and music, *SM* I, 209, II, 19, 46, 56, 102, 104, 108, 112, 144, and 151. IV, 20. On receiving and assimilating, *SM* X, 66 and 81. XI, 43. On word repetition, *SM* II, 108, 133, 159 and 172. Self-suggestion, *SM* IV, 287, VII, 108. Coué, *SM* II, 167, IV, 171, X, 259, XI, 73. Concentration, *SM* II, 102, 169, III, 15, IV, 122, 153-156, 169, V, 33, 149, X, 26, XI, 77. Tension and relaxation, *SM* IV, 162 and 166, VI, 156. Meditation, *SM* I, 97, IV, 138, VIII, 47, 133 and 135, X, 29 and 70. God realization, *SM* I, 44, 45, 76, 87, 145, 185, II, 132, IV, 287, VII, 139, VIII, 331, IX, 58, X, 28, XI, 201. On recognizing a mystic by his atmosphere *SM* IV, 133, 142 and 156.

7. 'God exists, Thou, you, I, we, etc., *Minqar-é-Musiqar*, p. 1. 'Walk cautiously,' p.2. 'Be through with it, you and this high talk,' p. 8. 'God in all shapes, p. 113. 'I am losing all my consciousness and knowledge,' p. 140. 'My name is "unknown",' p. 221.

8. The faqir who asked the way, *SM* VIII, 23, XII, 73. Love, *SM* I, 19, 23, 43, 72, 77, 150, 216, 232, 239, II, 133, 236, 237, III, 144, 243-250, 252, IV, 220, 221, 232, 234, 235, V, 17, 143-187, VI, 30, 46, VII, 11, 73-81, VIII, 22, 96, 100, 133, 149, 219, 220, 225, 226, IX, 19, 20, 57, 64, 261, X, 45, 46, 55, 75, XI, 104, 188-191, XII, 87 and 93. The disciple who had to fall in love, *SM* V, 180-181. VIII, 271. Telepathy, reflection, *SM* IV, 245, 260, 264, XII, 60-67. Curiosity *SM* V, 63, 65 and 75.

9. Books on Sufism in the Near East, among others, are: R. A. Nicholson, *The Mystics of Islam,* Bell & Sons, London 1914, and A. J. Arberry, *Sufism, An account of the Mystics of Islam,* Allen & Unwin, London 1950. Books on the Indian Sufis, in addition to Subhan, are Bankey Behari, *Sufis, Mystics and Yogis of India,* Bharatiya Vidya Bhavan, Bombay 1971, W. D. Begg, *The Holy Biography of Hazrat Khwaja Moinuddin Chishti of Ajmer,* Ajmer, 1960, and *The Big Five of India in Sufism,* Ajmer 1972. One of the latest and most comprehensive books is by J. Spencer Trimingham, *The Sufi Orders in Islam,* Oxford, 1971. Inayat on various Sufi-schools, *SM* II, 60, V, 21, VIII, 14 and 18.

10. Summing up the training, *SM* XII, 149. First results *SM* 85, 99, 100, 102. Relationship to the murshid *SM* I, 46, 48, 101, II, 170, 241, 244, IV, 131, 234, 235, V, 187 and 221, VI, 94, VIII, 284, IX, 115 and 235, X, 96, XI, 215 and 256, XII, 148.

11. Quoted *SM* II, 95 and 61. Different kinds of ecstasy *SM* I, 43, 91, II, 57, IV, 114, 119, 131, 202, V, 32, VI, 113, VII, 206, IX, 115, X, 70, XI, 191, XII, 68-75. Drugs *SM* V 86, VIII, 298.

12. Information by Mahmood Nizami, Delhi.

13. Collection of reviews and recommendations: 'Professor Inayat Khan's music every time gave a fresh pleasure to the heart and unlimited peace to the soul. There is no question about his most high attainments in music.'

14. *SM* V, 119.

15. Usually the words of Inayat's master are rendered as 'harmonize the East and the West with the harmony of thy music.' Some change 'harmony' into 'rythm,' because rhythm and melody are the elements of Indian music, whereas harmony in a western musical sense is scarcely used. There is a word 'ahangi' meaning harmony in a figurative sense (information given by Bishop Subhan). In *Minqar-é-Musiqar* one finds the images 'melody of the soul' and 'melody of existence.'

Therefore I choose to quote the rendering from *Sufi,* June 1919, p. 3, which says 'music of thy soul.'

Inayat's youngest brother Musharaff Khan lived with him in Calcutta, shortly after Murshid Madani's death. When addressing Sufi meetings he used to give a more colloquial rendering: 'You are gifted in music, you are gifted in philosophy, combine these two, go abroad and bring better understanding between East and West.'

Chapter V

1. Leaving Hyderabad, *SM* V, 71. Wandering route, *Forty Years,* p. 33.
2. *The Confessions of Inayat Khan, Short Biography* by Regina Miriam Bloch, London 1915, end of the fourth chapter; this passage is omitted in the *SM* edition (XII, 126-163). Remarks in the same vein *SM* V, 78 and X, 89. For R. M. Bloch see Chapter VIII.
3. The dervishes in Ajmer *SM* I, 153, VI, 142, XII, 140-143. Ajmer in general, *SM* II, 203 and X, 66.
4. The wrestler, *SM* IV, 144. The telegraph clerck, *SM* IV, 172 and VI, 114. Holy men in disguise *SM* VII, 114, VIII, 209, 212, 283, 291, X, 106, XII, 143-145. *Pages* p. 66.
5. *Pages,* p. 65, *The Sufi,* 1915-1917 *passim.*
6. Princes, *SM* X, 221 and *Music of India* (see Chapter III, note 8). In the unpublished *Biography* there is a passage on flatterers, convention, and the princes not understanding the changing world.
7. *Pages,* p. 67.
8. The Pathan soldier, *SM* VI, 50.
9. F. S. V. Donnison, *Burma,* Benn, London 1970, p. 86-92.
10. In reply to my questions Professor Premlata Sharma gave me the following quotation from a discussion on the value of music: 'Music is very valuable... Contrary references relate only to those people who make music their living.' From: Maharana Kumbha, *Sangitaraja,* part I, ed. Dr Premlata Sharma, Benares 1963, p. 10. Compare with this *SM* II, 104, 105 and 139 and X, 177.
11. Memories of Burma, *SM* VI, 55 and XII, 35.
12. The title of honour Tansen was still used in 1911 in America. The musical section of Benares Hindu University has a collection of old gramophone records; there is one by 'Inayat Khan (Tansen) Pathan.' Gopika Romon Roy, raja of Sylhet, says in a letter of recommendation 'Inayat Khan, the modern Tansen, has given me very great pleasure by his music.' A society Bhawaniput Sangit Sammilani in Calcutta wrote: 'We have learnt to look upon you as the morning star of Indian musical revival.' Other old Indian reviews refer to Professor Khan Pathan.
13. *Pages,* p. 53 and 55.
14. *SM* XII, 138.

Chapter VI

1. First impressions New York SM XII, 151. Statue of Liberty, *SM* IX, 205.
2. It is sometimes said they went hungry. According to Mahmood Khan the brothers were sent money from home, but they shuddered at western food, so that Ali Khan started to cook their meals; many Indians in the West do their own cooking. Compare *Pages*. p.95.
3. St Denis, pp. 58, 59 and 210. *Pages,* p. 80.
4. The oldest western recommendation is by Cornelios Rybner, Head of the Department of Music, Columbia University: 'We were not only interested in the effective way in which oriental music expressed emotions, but in the thorough, systematic and scientific way in which tone and relationship were worked out. It was a great treat to hear the Veena, the sacred instrument of India, played so as to present the quarter tones and florid passages of Hindu music in a medium which could not be possibly interpreted by notation. I most heartily command the musical presentation as being worthy of serious attention.' Other recommendations are signed by the directors of Cailmut Organ School and Teacher's College, New York 17 and 23 February 1911. There is a newspaper cutting of 27-2-1911 (Chicago) and another dated 21-3-1911 (Denver); compare route sheet below, note 9.
5. *The Musician, for Teacher, Pupil and Lover of Music,* New York, volume for 1911, pp. 152 and 158.
6. *SM* II, 104 and 193.
7. *Sufi Record,* p. 40.
8. See also *SM* XII, 160.
9. St Denis, p. 139, on her tour in the spring of 1911. Without naming him she answers Inayat's objections to her fancy imitation. Route sheet of this tour in Christena Schlundt, *The Professional Appearances of Ruth St Denis and Ted Shawn,* New York 1962; performances in Chicago, February 19, 21-26 and 28, March 1-4, St Louis, March 5, 7, 8-11, Springfield, March 13, Milwaukee, March 14, Davenport, March 15, Des Moines, March 16, Kansas City, March 17, Topeka, March 18, Denver, March 20 and 22-25, Pueblo, March 27, Colorado Springs, March 28, Salt Lake City, March 30, 31 and April 1, San Francisco, April 3-8 and 10-15. After this date Inayat went a different way.
10. *Theatre Collection* of the *Robinson Locke Collection,* R. St Denis, V, 417 P 64 NAF Rt, New York Public Library. Ruth's so-called Sufi described in *Los Angeles Graphic,* April 29, 1911.
11. Murshid Madani's 'I am sorry', *SM* XII, 21. See further Chapter VIII note 17 and Chapter XI note 4.

12. Maheboob Khan had been in school with one of Vinoba Bhave's elder brothers. This school friend could offer him a position as a court musician with the maharaja of Jamnagar in Kathiawar, but Maheboob Khan did not leave his brother.

13. *Letters of Edward Fitzgerald,* ed. W. A. Wright, London, Macmillan, 1910, 2 vol. His arrogant and melancholy remarks on Omar and other Persians mostly in his letters to Cowell: Vol. I, pp. 294, 304, 306, 311, 312, 316-322, 324, 325, 327, 330, 332-335, 337, 342-346, 348; Vol. II, pp. 4, 5, 26, 27, 29, 44, 45, 54, 62, 101, 102, 153, 155, 216, 263. Norton in the *American Review* is quoted in *Life's Echo, a Possible Elucidation of the Mysteriously Cryptic 'Tessalations' made mostly by Byron, Fitzgerald, and others, from Omar Qayyam's 'Ruba'iyat,'* by 'Tis True,' 1923. The anonymous author of this luxurious edition was acquainted with 3 manuscripts and satirized the mystical interpretation. The battle is still raging. A. J. Arberry discovered a fourth and older manuscript, but also believed in a scoffing anti-religious Omar. In 1967 Robert Graves and Omar Ali-Shah (*The Rubaiyyat of Omar Khayaam, a new translation,* Cassel 1967, Penguin ed. 1972) published a list of forty manuscripts, which have always been known in the East; one of these dates from the original period. These authors demonstrate Fitzgerald's faults and reject Arberry's interpretation. The much disputed Omar Khayyam is not the most important Persian poet. Hafiz, Rumi and Saadi are the great ones.

14. C. H. A. Bjerregaard, *The Inner Life and Tao Teh King,* p. 80 (found by William Foley).

15. William Foley noted the same thing in Bjerregaard's other books.

16. Freedom of the soul, *SM* II, 79, VII, 180-197, VIII, 15. Freedom in other senses, *SM* VII, 164, 193, VIII, 223 and V, 34. Combined, *SM* VI, 155, VII, 171, 183.

17. *Pages,* p. 101.

18. Walter Lord, *A Night to Remember,* Bantam book 1956, p. 48.

Chapter VII

1. A. H. Fox Strangways, *The Music of Hindustan,* Oxford 1914, reprinted 1965.

2. *The Journal of the Royal Asiatic Society of Great Britain and Ireland,* 1915, 2nd vol. p. 578. On p. 595 their friend in the RAS, Yusuf Ali, remarks how fortunate it is that the society no longer occupies itself only with the past, but also pays attention to modern problems and has arranged lectures on music.

3. Nirad C. Chaudhuri, *The Continent of Circe,* Chatto & Windus, London 1967, pp. 280-302, 'The Dominant Minority.'

4. Sengupta, p. 82, Mrs Naidu addressing Gokhalé in top hat: 'Where

is your rebellious turban?' Inayat's sympathetic Englishmen, *SM* XII, 154.

5. Gramont. p. 182, the Persian balls. Marcel Dietschy, *La Passion de Claude Debussy,* A la Baconnière, Neuchâtel 1962, Persian ballet music, pp. 222 and 262, project for an Indian drama, pp. 115, 207, 268, on eastern music, pp. 192 and 195. Sacha Guitry, *Lucien Guitry, sa Carrière et sa Vie,* Argenteuil 1930, p. 105. Robert Mallet, *Paul Claudel et André Gide, Correspondance 1899-1926,* Gallimard, Paris, 16th ed., pp. 214, 226 and 361. Valéry Larbaud, *Lettres à André Gide,* Stols, Paris/The Hague, pp. 84, 86 and following.

6. *Gil Blas,* 25th October 1912. On Bailly: V.-E. M. Michelet, *Les Compagnons de la Hiérophanie,* Dorbon, Paris, pp. 65-78.

7. *L'Illustration théatrale,* Vol. IX, 1st February 1913, contains E. Knoblauch, 'Kismet, Conte Arabe,' translation by Jules Lemaitre. From the list of characters: 'Le chanteur hindou − M. Inayat Khan; Orchestre Royal Hindou sous la direction de M. Inayat Khan; Hindous conduits par M. W. de Sylva; musique de M. Furst et de M. Chr. Wilson.'

8. Sam Waagenaar, Mata Hari's biographer (*The Murder of Mata Hari,* Appleton-Century, New York, 1965) brought this concert to my notice and kindly provided me with details from Mata Hari's scrapbooks. Paul Olivier's commentary in *Le Journal de l'Université des Annales,* Vol. VI, Part. II, pp. 593 and 639.

9. Table-talk, *Disciple,* p. 20; D'Annunzio in Gramont, pp. 255-258.

10. Gabriele D'Annunzio, *Notturno,* 1916, *Tutte le Opere,* Mondadori, pp. 153-155. Ilse is Baroness Deslandes. She and her room full of decorative animals are described by Germain, p. 108 and following. Alastair, pen name of a decadent poet, Germain p. 127 and following. 'Stilled the *owls;*' the original has 'screech owls and eagle-owls' with an untranslatable pun on flirts and dandies.

11. Angelos Cocles (D'Annunzio), *Cento e cento e cento e cento pagine del libro segreto,* Venice 1935, p. 234. Goethe has the story of Majnun and Leila in the *Westöstlicher Diwan;* I have not come across any other European translation.

12. Overton Fuller, p. 32.

13. Gramont, p. 260.

14. Marcel Dietschy, Debussy's biographer, has kindly supplied me with this quotation from an unpublished letter from the collection of Professeur Pasteur Valléry-Radot.

15. Léon Vallas, *Claude Debussy et son Temps,* Paris 1932, p. 332 and Guy Tosi, *Debussy et D'Annunzio,* Correspondance inédite, pp. 37 and 100, on the Indian drama that D'Annunzio was to write for Debussy.

16. *SM* II. 113. This was the reaction of a friend of the family, a Gujarati jeweller named Ibrahim Patèl. Tagore mentions a similar dislike for

some western singing. When in August 1914 the Khans hurriedly left Paris, they entrusted most of their possessions and trophies, among others the Indian gramophone records, to this friend Patèl. But he died during the war, his widow sold the contents of her house and departed. In this way almost all pre-1914 documents have been lost, with exception of a few trifles kept by Musharaff Khan.

17. *SM*. II, 138. Debussy, 'Musical Taste in Modern Times,' *Monthly Musical Record,* 1912, p. 261.

18. Sengupta, p. 84.

19. Collection of newspaper cuttings in the family: the veena described, *Daily News and Leader,* London 4-7-1913. 'A command of the Czar of Russia,' *Monthly Musical Record,* London, 1913. 'A young man of striking personality,' *Daily Citizen,* undated.

20. This first book, *A Sufi Message of Spiritual Liberty* has been reprinted in *SM* V, pp. 9-36, but much has been changed and even omitted, among other things the preface, quoted here.

21. On Russia in those days: E. J. Dillon, *The Eclipse of Russia,* Dent & Sons, London, 1918. M. Paléologue, *La Russie des Tsars, pendant la grande guerre,* Plon, Paris 1921. Margarita Woloschin, *Die grüne Schlange, Lebenserinnerungen,* Deutsche Verlag-Anstalt, Stuttgart, 1954. Felix Youssoupof, *Avant l'Exil,* Plon, Paris 1952. Konstantin Paustovsky, *Story of a Life,* Harvill Press, London 1965.

22. Some lines on Russia, *SM* XII, 155, *Pages* pp. 108 and 109.

23. Several legends have sprung up from this nightly sleigh-ride and the visit to the mysterious gathering of monks. One story mixed this up with the fact that Mr Balakin, for political reasons, advised the family not to go to India, and perhaps suggested for them to leave. Inayat's departure — at the end of May — is often depicted as a romantic flight through the snow with some type cast revolutionaries holding them up. Moscow in the spring of 1914 was quieter than usual, owing to prohibition (Paléologue).

The other legend centres around the Finnish doctor. His name and title are given fully in the *Autobiography,* but the brothers and the Begum remembered the stealthy invitation and something about monks. A mysterious monk, in the 1930's mentality, could only be Rasputin. Rasputin was no monk, and went about in a peasant's costume made of silk. Inayat may have spoken about Rasputin; his source was Prince Yussupov, Rasputin's murderer, who came to see the master in London in 1919 and became a mureed in secret. A few other conspicuous persons were secret mureeds; André Germain was one, and Grand Duke Ernst Ludwig von Hessen und bei Rhein (information by Mahmood Khan, confirmed by the present Landgraf Philip von Hessen). In addition to what Inayat learnt from Yussupov in 1919, he always kept himself informed about religious sects and pseudo-religions. One recognizes Rasputin's sect in a description of 'self-centred mystics who call themselves God or a part of God, and thus make an excuse for committing any licentious sins they like.' (*SM* XII, 161, where the word 'licentious' before 'sins' has been omitted).

Dr. E. W. Lybeck, the real host during the sleigh-ride and the mysterious talks is to be found in Atle Wilskman, *Skriftner utgivna av Svenska litteratursällskapet i Finland*, vol. CXXXVIII: 1. Year of birth, 1864; licentiated in philosophy, 1887, licentiated in medicine, 1890, doctor's degree, 1895; head of a private nerve clinic, 1896-1904; afterwards director of a sanatorium in Rouvesi and medical superintendant of the spa Kirvu. Ardent champion of natural healing methods. Married in Edinburg 1895, died 1919. Finland from 1809 to 1917 was part of Russia; especially after 1910 it was treated as a province. Another legend has it that Inayat had lived in the Kremlin with the Czar and that his baby daughter was nursed by the nurse of the Czar's children. The Czar did not reside in the Kremlin, but in Tsarskoje Selo near St Petersburg; the address of Inayat and his family in Moscou was: Belle Etage, Maison Abidinre à la Petrovka, Au coin de Krapivinsky, Pereoulsk; the nurse of princely babies was a Mrs Günst (Yussupov, p. 195) and Noor-un-Nisa was looked after by a Tartar woman. Three misinterpreted items may have given birth to the Inayat-in-Kremlin-legend: the London interview of summer 1913 (see page 125), a painted portrait of Inayat against a background of Kremlin-towers, and the fact that Moscow, later, became the capital of the Sovyet Union. Most Inayat legends are born about 1930 and bear traces of the idiosyncrasies of those years.

24. *Russkya Vedomosti* in Amsterdam, Internationaal Instituut voor Sociale Geschiedenis and Hoover Institute on War, Peace and Revolution, Stanford, Cal. Other reviews (undated cuttings) in *Now, Otro Rosseei* and *Raneie Otro*. A line from the latter: 'Professor Inayat Khan at the Imperial Conservatoire performed exceedingly original, brilliant, noble and modest music.'

25. Anarchists *SM* IV, 247, 268 and V, 73. His one time schoolmate who became an anarchist was Barendra Ghose, a younger brother of Aurobindo Ghose; he was detained and convinced for incendiary activity in 1908. As an early nationalist, in Baroda, he used to criticize the Khan family's European costume.

26. L. Ssabaneev, *Souvenirs de Scriabine,* Moscou 1925, pp. 171. 172.

27. Sarah Bernhard *SM* VIII, 234.

Chapter VIII

1. Havelock Ellis, pp. 406 and 416.

2. See Chapter VII, note 2.
3. In the catalogue of the British Museum there are two titles to her name. No other data found.
4. F.M.A., *Evening News*, 13-2-1915. 'Society to unite faiths ... ambitious,' *Pall Mall Gazette*, May or June 1915. Lakmé reviews, *Daily Telegraph*, 3-6-1915 and *Daily Chronicle*, 8-6-1915. Reviews of the lectures, *Manchester Guardian*, 26-6-1915, *Era*, 30-6-1915 and *South Wales Daily News*, 5-7-1915.
5. Years later this song has been taped, as sung by Musharaff Khan; the latter called it a swadeshi (freedom) song for India. Mahmood Khan heard from his father the story of the 'rebellious' singing in a meeting of compatriots and the subsequent cancelling of concerts for the front line troops. The story is borne out by outside data. There is a cutting from the *Daily Telegraph*, 6-7-1915, announcing a matinee of the Islamic Society in the New Theatre. After this date *The Sufi* does not mention any more large-scale public performances; for two or three years they had to restrict themselves to concerts on their own premises and a few poorly paid engagements Raden Aju Jodjana found for them. The original text runs as follows:
   Tum kiske putre kehelate ho,/ Kissi nam se jane jate ho,/ Hindu ho ya Mussalman ho/ Christi ho ya Parsi ho/ Jag mèn Hindu kehelate ho/ Ya tum sultan ya muflis ho./ Woh aan kehan, woh maan kehan?/ Woh shaan kehan, woh gyán kehan?/ Hanuman ki puja Rama kare?/ Yeh kaise dhara chalate ho.
6. *Gayan*, pp. 4, 29 *SM* I, 97, 99, VIII, 247 and X, 94.
7. True to one's principles, *Vadan*, p. 34. The Sufi does not prescribe principles, what is good for one, may be bad for another *SM* VIII 21, *Gayan*, p. 36, SM II, 28, 29, V, 127, VI, 250, VII, 198-201, IX, 78 and 180. People want to make things rigid *SM* VIII, 171.
8. God-realisation, self-realisation, *Gayan*, p. 1. *The Sufi* 1915, Vol. I, number 1, p. 1. *SM* V 13 and 22 (Inayat's first book reprinted). *SM* XI, 15 (Inayat's last lectures)
   The current form of the ten Sufi thoughts and 3 Sufi aims in *SM* IX, 267; explanation, I, 13-22.
9. *SM* I, 209, II, 98, 126, 185, IV, 175, V, 20, 131, XI, 28; see further Chapter X, note 13.
10. Nowadays one can also hear the objection that Inayat's Sufis are not 'real' Sufis. This view is strengthened by certain political tendencies to isolate Islam and Islamic states. Inayat used to answer almost exasperated that no real mystic can speak of the mysticism of one religion and that anyone who stresses differences more than underlying unity is no real Sufi, i.e. mystic. Of the more than 200 places concerning this subject I refer to a few: *SM* I, 13-21, 45, 53, 72, II, 167, 172, IV, 118, V, 15, 23 ('that Sufism sprang from Islam or from

any other religion, is not necessarily true; yet it may rightly be called the spirit of Islam as well as the pure essence of all religions and philosophies'), 121, 122, 213, 214, 222, 248, VI, 137, 186, VII, 21, 27, 179, VIII, 13-23, IX, 148 ('The Sufi Message which is now being given is the child of that mother who has been known for so many years as Sufism. It connects the two lines of the prophetic mission, the Hindu line and that of Ben Israel, in order that they may become the medium to unite in God and truth both East and West. It is the same truth ... which the wise of all ages have held.'), IX, 236, 258, 264, X, 27 ('as God cannot be divided, so mysticism cannot be divided'), X, 253, XI, 146, XII, 134, 163.

Inayat himself could reach the spirit of the masters through any religion. In April 1923 he spoke in Leyden for Indonesian students on Mohammed; a few days later at the Roman Catholic University of Nijmegen on Christ. 'When he spoke on Mohammed, Mohammed was everything for him. When he spoke on Christ, Christ,' his companions wrote. Of course his layman's mystical exercises are child's play compared to a complete eastern training, but it was not his aim to make a 'world full of saints' (*SM* VI, 238) 'but to make it possible for people of the West... to obtain glimpses of the truth which the ancient mystics possessed' (II, 171). 'What the world needs is the mystical outlook' (XI, 186). The ideal of the members of his movement ought to be 'to invite humans to become members of humanity.' (VII, 179). Some of his disciples, though, did go through a full training and a few went to Ajmer; even now some of his son's and grandson's followers go there.

11. *SM* V, 201, VI, 12, 69, VIII, 227, XII, 118.
12. See Chapter III note 8.
13. Giving up his music *SM* II, Preface and XII, 152; music and meditation *SM* II, 77, 109, 136, 139, 152. It is paradise *SM* II, 104. See further Chapter IV, note 6.
14. Impossibility of expressing the essence in words, *SM* I, 86, V, 214, VI, 197, VIII, 231, 272, IX, 137, 265 and XI, 167.
15. Disciple, p. 65.
16. *Gayan,* p. 65. These headquarters not made for our rest, *The Sufi,* November 1915, p. 70.
17. Warnings against occultism and spiritualism, *SM* II, 122, 183, 260, V, 70, VI, 163, VIII, 25, X, 68, XI, 141, 147, 205 and XII, 117.
18. *NRC/Handelsblad,* Amsterdam, Rotterdam, 16-10-1971.
19. *The Soul Whence and Wither, SM* I, 107-185. The war lectures *SM* 41-78.
20. Havelock Ellis, p. 509.
21. *SM* V, 63-65 and 75.
22. *De Samenleving,* 1910-1911, pp. 285, 295, 315 and 329.

23. Edinburg answers, *The Sufi,* June 1919. Reprinted, but corrupted, in the third person and without the introductory and final words quoted herein *SM* I, 25. 'If there is anything in my philosophy' *SM* II, Preface. When should one become an initiate, *Sufi,* April 1918, pp. 6, 7.

24. *Sufi,* April 1918. India Office Records, Jud. and Publ. Dept. Register, 1920, file 1797.

25. Compare with this information given by R. A. Jodjana *SM* I, 87 and II, 87.

26. Inayat made spelling mistakes, for instance he wrote 'speack' instead of 'speak' and one wonders how old were the English text books in Baroda High School. Some of his deviant spelling was a play with words and sounds, but many actual mistakes through lack of experience with the written language. In the quoted text he also spelled 'thay' for 'they' and 'to critisise.' In another letter one finds 'strugle' for 'struggle' and 'repeatition' for 'repetition.' 'Good buy' for 'good bye' is probably a pun on western priorities. He certainly did not know the etymology of this word (God be with you), he evaluated words with his ears.

It was a great drawback that he learnt his English very late. For an Indian to speak impeccably he has to start young; there are very few consonants sounding more or less the same in English and Urdu. In 1915 Inayat still needed some help (information given by R. A. Jodjana) when addressing his public. Later he spoke with ease and very clearly. The printed text of his lectures is doctored a bit, some of the flavour of his straight soul-to-soul spoken language got lost in the more correct but less lively English of the editors. For instance 'Now one may ask' — a reaction to an unspoken question of a listener — is nearly always omitted.

Chapter IX

1. *Forty Years,* p. 17. *SM* X, 32

2. *Forty Years,* p. 49.

3. *SM* VI, 159.

4. *The Sufi,* October 1920, p. 4 and 5.

5. Not only harmonizing East and West, but all antagonistic groups, *Sufism* May 1921, p. 11, March and June 1923, p. 15. *SM* VIII, 20 and X, 21. The wrong application of a right priciple, *SM* IX, 14. Russia and Germany, *SM* VI, 106. Future *SM* VIII, 216. Enthusiasm in India 1921, Sengupta, p. 164. The world is ill, *SM* X, 264. Pre-ecumenical groups, *Sufi,* 1917-1920, *passim;* compare *The Problem of the Day, SM* X, 241-270. Thousands of such societies not enough, *Sufism,* May 1921, p. 15. Optimist with open eyes, *SM* VI, 81.

6. The battlefield, Disciple, p. 62-64. The Italian sea captain, Van Stolk, p. 68. Not to teach but to tune, *SM* II, Preface, X, 73; Van Stolk, p. 62.

7. Leo Uittenboogaard, *De wereld een verbijsterend avontuur,* part II, pp. 198-201, The Hague 1949. On my checking his source Mr Uittenboogaard answered that he did know who Inayat Khan was, but had not read his works. Immediately after visiting the underground café he had jotted down the quotations and he was pleased to hear that they tallied with original sayings of Inayat.

8. *Sufism,* March and May 1921.

9. *The Bogeyman, SM* XII, 173-193.

10. Psychology in the East, *SM* II, 46, 167, XI, 73. Coué, see Chapter IV note 6. The use of vanity *SM* I, 76, III, 220, VI, 57 and 98; *Gayan*, pp. 41, 42. One can be wisely selfish, wrong and right egoist *SM* IV, 117, VII, 271. Feeling of guilt *SM* VIII, 201. False self-denial *SM* VI, 155. Self-pity, *SM* III, 205, IV, 51, VI, 83, 100, 168 and 178; *Gayan*, p. 23. Self-analysis *SM* VI, 272 and 273, 19, 20. Emotional people are not always loving people, *SM* VIII, 280. The urge for too much perfection, *SM,* X, 67. Subconscious, *SM* XI, 49, 123. Psychosomatica in Health, *SM* IV, *passim*, V, 78. Inayat's definition of psychology, *SM* XI, 73.

11. The 'practical' books are mostly reprinted in *SM* III and VI. Warnings against making things rigid and against personal adoration *SM* VI, 250, VIII, 171; *Gayan* p. 32; *Sufism,* September 1922, report of the anniversary. See also Chapter VIII, notes 7 and 10. Not superbeings, but fuller life... to bring about better conditions, *SM* VII, 238, 246, VIII, 179, X, 248, 270. Inner life not only a spiritual development, but also the culture of humanity, *Sufism,* September 1923, p. 6 and *SM* X, 75. Praying without a sense of brotherhood no good, *SM* X, 264, 265, 87; the so-called thought-culture, *SM* III, 76, 77, *SM* VI, lll.

12. Katwijk, Disciple. p. 73. New Forest, Diciple, p. 86. Compare *SM* VII, 41.

13. Paderewski, *SM* IV, 153. Two people of the same thought meeting, *SM* X, 265.

14. Seasickness, *SM* IX, 53. Omitting the invocation, *Forty Years,* p. 15. The invocation described, Van Stolk, p. 17.

15. Nyogen Senzaki, 'Sufism and Zen,' *The Japanese American,* 11-5-1923, reprinted in *On Zen Meditation* by Nanshin Okamoto, 1936.

16. *SM* II, 44, 93, lll and VI, 109; in *SM* X, 230 a passage on jazz in factories is omitted. The original text in *Yesterday, Today and Tomorrow,* Luzac, London, p. 95.

17. *San Francisco Chronicle* 27-4-1923. Lack of materiality, *SM* VIII, 222, 223. On one-sided tendencies, *SM* III, 236, IV, 237.

18. In Moscow the classicist Professor F. E. Korc, 1843-1915, member of the Academy; in London Henry M. de Léon, sécretaire de la Société internationale de philologie, sciences et beaux-arts.

19. J. S. Trimingham, *The Sufi Orders in Islam*, Oxford, Clarendon, 1971, p. l. Al-Haqq, Truth or the Real is the Sufi term for God. Inayat on the fear of the name, X, 194, XII, 11 and 13. See further Chapter X, note 7. On division of labour *SM* X, 246. Labour conditions, *SM* III, 188. Respected businessman *SM* X, 31. Socialism and capitalism have the same god, *SM* VII, 247. It is the human relation that counts, *SM* X, 75. Like tuning a piano to one note, *SM* IX, 22.

NB. The numbers 74, 43, 90, 65, 33, 8, 16, 92, 79, 100, 11, 36, 48, 9 and 21 from the collection-Smit-Kerbert have been used for this chapter.

Chapter X

1. Quoted for the title, *Nirtan,* p. 28. The laughing madzub *SM* VIII, 298 and X, 124. To say little, *SM* I, 118, IV, 108, X, 25.

2. Germain, pp. 244 and 277.

3. For Gide and Tagore see Chapter VII, note 5.

4. A grown-up among children, *SM* I, 74, 78, VI, 83, X, 23.

5. Gramont, pp. 16, 21, 57, 118, part II, pp. 49 and 50.

6. Disciple, pp. 78 and 80.

7. Different ideas about God and religion, Vadan, p. 105 *SM* I, 118, II, 97, VII, 212, VIII, 37, 118, IX, 27, 29, 56, 250, X, 62, 250, 255, 256, XI, 161, XII, ll, 18 and 32. Church authorities failed, *SM* VI, 260, X, 243, XII, 105. 'Religion only for simple people,' *SM* IX, 71. Causes of unbelief: loss and sorrow, *SM* IX, 71, 162; fear X, 139; injustice and misuse *SM* IX, 21, 162, X, 150, VIII, 272. The materialist *SM* X, 139; the intellectual *SM* V, 124, VII, 262, IX, 54, X, 50, 257, XII, 23. The agnostic *SM* V, 201. A mystic not a dreamer *SM* X, 13 and 14. Unnecessary complexity *SM* X, 25 and 26. A long face, *SM* I, 78. A freethinker among the religious *SM* V, 22.

8. Headquarters created, *Sufism* 1923. Report autumn assembly 1924, *Monthly Record HQ,* May 1925.

9. Bengt Sundkler, *Nathan Söderblom, his Life and Work,* London, 1968, pp. 23, 44, 48, 66, 67, 68, 88, 97, 144, 155-160, 271, 272 and 321.

10. A book is a dead teacher, *SM* VII, 143. Rumi's books thrown out, *SM* X, 137, XII, 74; remarks in the same vein, *SM* I, 224, IV, 220, VI, 131, 192, VII, 30, VIII, 31, 329, XI, 17; compare note 17 of this chapter. One cannot explain anything subtle in words, *SM* V, 201, VI, 131, IX, 150, X, 73, XI, 145, 167, XII, 13 and 18; also Chapter VIII, note 13. Definition of religion *SM* IX, 267: 'There is one religion... progress in the right direction (i.e. towards God, the source).'

11. Prof. Dr. M. C. van Mourik Broekman, *Geestelijke stromingen in het Christelijk cultuurbeeld,* Meulenhoff, Amsterdam 1949, p. 110 and following.

12. Samuel Lewis, later called Sufi Ahmed Murad Chishti. Part of Mrs Martin's pupils after her death became followers of Meher Baba (1894-1969); this group took the name of Sufis Reoriented.

13. Avicenna, *SM* IV, 43, X, 13, 259. Vibrations *SM* I, 209, II *passim,* XI, 25-33, 58, XII, 118. Light *SM* XI, 136, electricity *SM* IV, 175, V, 91, radio *SM* II, 182, 260. Comparing science and mysticism *SM,* I, 127, VI, 226, VII, 210. Combining old and new medicine: Hakim Ajmal Khan, Gandhi's doctor, did. Many do, nowadays, in China.

14. Quotations from respectively: *The American,* Boston 21-12-1925, *New York Evening World,* 9-12-1925, *New York Post,* 26-12-1925, *Globe,* Boston, 27-12-1925. Sorbonne in *New York World* 18-12-1925, *New York Sun,* 19-12-1925, *Globe,* 27-12-1925.

15. *Gayan,* p. 53/4.

16. Professor Froissard *SM* XII, 118. Dr Abrams, *SM* II, 107, IV, 34. The scientist who asked for mysterious tricks *SM* VII, 231, XI, 221. The scientist who had discovered the soul, *SM* II, 128.

17. Study of life, SM I, 224, V, 212, VI, 104, 106, VII, 30, 31, X, 30, 89, 137, XI, 212. *Sufism,* December 1923, p. 13 records that somebody asked what the third Sufi-idea, ('There is one holy book... the sacred scripture of nature') meant. The answer was: 'Life.' Van Stolk, p. 40, describes the difficult exercise of observing and judging different types.

18. See note 7 above. Belief and authority, *SM* VI, 210, IX, 54, Following like sheep, *SM* VII, 174, IX, 55. Eternal matter *SM* IV, 41, XI, 67.

19. Duality and unity, *SM* II, 151, V, 13, VI, 252, VIII, 25, 100, IX, 196. Personal and abstract God, *SM* VI, 252, X, 14. First limited then broad, *SM* IX, 68, XI, 242, *Vadan,* p. 73. Compare note 10 above.

20. Compare Erich Fromm, *The Art of loving,* Bantam ed. pp. 59, 65 and 91. Ideal a means, *SM* VI, 252. No unity without love, *SM* V, 182.

21. Silence in the Waldorf Astoria Hotel, *New York Telegram,* 26-12-1925. The unrobed bishop, *Baltimore News,* 12-1-1926. Interview with Ford, *Detroit News,* 7-2-1926. The radio speeches, *Soufisme* 1926/7), January, p. 25, March, p. 25.

22. *SM,* V, 169, *Vadan,* p. 89. Final quotation, *Nirtan,* p. 25.

Chapter XI

1. *SM* XII. 107. Even a saint is not perfect, *SM* VI, 68, X, 67, 105, XII, 274. Compare *Gayan* 47, 65/6, *Vadan* 70.

2. Memoirs of disciples used for this chapter: 41, 67, 86, 19, 1, 2, 6, 8, 9, 12, 14, 15, 25, 26, 27, 33, 38, 47, 54, 62, 66, 70, 79, 90, 44, 16, 43, 77, 48, 72, 81, 13, 29, 37, 67, 61, 92, 45.

3. *SM* IX, 24, X, 264.
4. *SM* XII, 163. Ascesis limited, *SM* V, 24, VIII, 46, 299, X, 18, VI, 96. Life's trials enough, *SM* VI, 58. Compare Chapter IV, p. 58. Combining work and meditation *SM* XII, 105. Warnings against occultism, Chapter VIII, note 17.
5. *SM* IV, 133, XI, 35. All questions gone, *SM* XI, 214; Forty Years, pp. 16 and 58; Van Stolk, p. 39; *Nirtan*, p. 22/23. Balance *SM* IV, 17, 237, VI, 36, XI, 255. *Vadan* p. 84.
6. Detachment, *SM* I, 74, 78, V, 123, VI, 120; *Vadan*, p. 101.
7. Overton Fuller. pp. 36, 40, 41, 45. Inayat on Montessori, *SM* III, 36. For all, *Gayan* pp 39, 85, *SM* VII 227, 228.
8. Van Stolk, p. 81. All nations, *Sufism* 1921-1923, *passim; SM* IX, 248, X, 270, XII, 51. Also emphatic information by B. S. Beorse. The healed child, collection Smit-Kerbert 44. Several healings, see note 2 above. Zanetti's Amazement, *Forty Years*, p. 18. Compare *Vadan*, p. 90 (the bringers of joy) p. 131 (deepest dephts) and *Gayan* pp. 57, 59. *Vadan*, p. 31
9. Van Stolk, p. 40.
10. *SM* XII, p. 179 and following.
11. On him Martin Lings, *A Moslem Saint of the Twentieth Century*, Los Angeles, 1961. He was in Paris, because a mosque was opened there.
12. Romain Rolland, *La Vie de Ramakrishna*, Stock, Paris, 1929, p. 52/53. Sir Francis Younghusband, *Modern Mystics*, Murray, London 1935, pp. 68, 82, 270-273. Compare W. D. Begg, *The Holy Biography of Hazrat Khwaja Muinuddin Hasan Chishti*, Ajmer 1972, p. 69, and *The Big Five of India in Sufism*, Ajmer 1972, p. 89: several saints married after a prophetic dream, because 'marriage is incumbent upon every Muslim.'
13. *The Sufi*, July 1937, 'In Memoriam Miss Goodenough.', p. 108.
14. On democracy in general, *SM* III, 155, VII, 170-175, IX, 30. Spiritual democracy, *SM* VII, 176-179, IX, 121, 126, X, 65, 82, 245. For all, see note 7 above. Every creature loves freedom, *SM* VII, 180. Every group has a leader, *SM*, VII, 223, IX, 127. Nobody considered as inferior *SM* I, 154, III, 246, VI, 47, 54/55, VII, 172, 223, X, 245, XII, 35. Democracy misused *SM* VII, 223. Aristocracy misused, *SM* IX, 121.
15. Master-pupil relationship, *SM* II, 170, VII, 226, VIII, 171, 284, IX, 245, X, 63/4, 98-114, XI, 140, 256, XII, 84, 104, 115-117.
16. *SM* XII, 191. India poem not published.
17. *SM* XII, 214. Before you judge, *Nirtan*, p. 29. This poem has been set to music by Shaikh-al-Mashaikh Maheboob Khan.
18. *SM* V, 137. *Vadan*, pp. 79, 89.

Chapter XII

1. Apart from the letters quoted and information given by the family, most data for this chapter are supplied by Kismet Stam; she wrote down her memories in 1926, and answered my questions and corrected some points 1970-1973. Like Raden Aju Jodjana Miss Stam is still vigorously active in spite of her age; she plays the viola in the municipal orchestra of Palma, Mallorca.
2. Subhan, pp. 129-131.
3. *SM* V, 119.
4. Durga Das, pp. 118, 122 and following. Sengupta, p. 91.
5. Musharaff Khan, *The Sufi,* 1936, 'An Indian Pilgrimage' II, p. 74.
6. Durga Das on Swami Shraddhanand, pp. 33, 37, 68, 89, 124; on Hakim Ajmal Khan, pp. 71, 78, 96, 107, 124. When Musharaff Khan was in Baroda in 1943, he lectured on Inayat's work in the West before the Arya Samaj.
7. Syed Idries Shah, *Oriental Magic,* London 1956, p. 72. Fifth and last stage of the Sufi mystic: the saint returns to the world to guide people.
8. Idries Shah, p. 65. Subhan, p. 197. *SM, passim.*
9. Uncle Pathan's reply arrived next summer.

Glossary and Personal Notes

ADVAITA. Literally non-duality, all is one; monism.

AGRA. Town in Northwest India, on the bank of the Yamuna, 250 Km southeast of Delhi. Important historical monuments, TajMahal, etc. Note: All Indian cities mentioned in this list are also centres of commerce, industry, learning and railway traffic.

AJMER. Town in northwest India, on the Delhi-Bombay railway line. Important place of pilgrimage.

AKBAR, JALALUDDIN, 1542-1605. Great Moghul emperor. Improved government, promoted agriculture and commerce, protected learning and art and tried to create unity among the different religions, including Christianity.

ALI KHAN, PIR-O-MURSHID Mohammed, 1881-1958. Cousin of Hazrat Inayat Khan, well-known as a singer and a healer, also outside Sufi circles. Was head of the Sufi Movement from 1948-1958.

ALIGARH. Town in Northwest India; has a well-known Moslem University.

AMINA BEGUM, PIRANA SHARDA. Indian titles and names of Inayat's wife, Ora Ray Baker, q.v. Begum is a title and form of address.

ANGELICO, DA FIESOLE, FRA GIOVANNI, 1387-1455. Italian painter, famous for his frescos in the monastery of San Marco, Florence.

BAHAI. Religious movement, originated in Iran, seceded from the older Babism (1868). Universal, optimistically progressive.

BAKER, ORA RAY, 1892-1949. Inayat's American wife, daughter of Erastus Warner Baker, lawyer. See Overton-Fuller, pp. 30-32 and *passim*.

BALANCED ROCK. Valley of the Gods, Colorado. A large rock balancing on a small point. Favourite spot for excursions in the beginning of this century.

BANGALORE. Capital of the district Bangalore, Mysore State.

BANNERJI, SIR GURUDAS, born about 1850. Judge at the High Court from 1888. First Indian Vice-Chancellor of a university (Calcutta 1890-1892).

BARODA. Now part of Gujarat State, Northwest India, formerly one of the independent princedoms of the Mahrati confederation, q.v. Population mainly Hindu. Prominent in the field of education and modification of the caste system. Fertile plain, various kinds of agriculture and industry, many temples. The capital is also called Baroda. Inayat was born there. See further Gaekwar.

BENARES. The sacred city in Northeast India, in a bend of the Ganges. The river is 550-570 M. wide there, the north bank is much higher than the south bank and one gets a magnificent view from there. The actual Indian name is Varanasi, now used officially.

BENGAL. Originally, Bengal stretched from the Himalayas to the south-

290

east coast. In 1906 it was divided into East and West Bengal. Bangla Desh was formerly East Bengal. The Bengalis were the first to learn English and western science and consequently became the first nationalists; they still occupy many leading positions.

BERNHARDT, SARAH, 1844-1923. The greatest French actress of her day, internationally famous. Her mother was Dutch.

BHATKANDE, PUNDIT VIDVAN, 1860-1936. Well-known Indian musicologist; music director in Baroda 1920-1958. He abolished Maula Bakhsh's system of notation and introduced his own, probably a variation of the former.

BLAVATSKY, HELENA PETROVNA, née HAHN, 1831-1891. In 1875 she and Col. H. S. Olcott founded the Theosophical Society.

BUDDHA (the Enlightened One). Siddartha Gautama, lived from about 653 - 580 BC. Prince Siddartha left the world to find a solution to the problem of human suffering.

BUDDHISM. The teachings of Buddha, including liberation from suffering by giving up desire. The highest attainment is nirvana, perfect peace, without desire; this state can be reached in this life. The Buddha preached his first sermon at Benares. Under the emperor Ashoka his teachings flourished in India, but eventually they were superseded by Hinduism again. Buddhism spread to Ceylon, Burma, Indochina, China, Japan and temporarily to Indonesia (Borobudur): many forms developed. Since the nineteenth century its influence has been felt in the West.

BOMBAY. Large commercial city, capital and port, on islands in the Northeast, off the Arabian Ocean coast. Gate of India from the West.

BRAHMA. The god of creation, in popular religion depicted as a person.

BRAHMAN. Neuter of Brahma, the primeval principle of everything, the everlasting. In philosophical religion superhuman, immanent.

BRAHMANA, BRAHMIN. Member of the highest caste, q.v.

BRAHMO SAMAJ. One of the religious reform movements, social and progressive. Founded in 1828 by Ram Mohan Roy (1772-1833). One of the aims: to bring the different religions closer together. Opposed to the theory of reincarnation and the burning of widows, etc. In 1842 Debendranath Tagore, father of Rabindranath, became the leader. In 1857 and 1878 splits occurred, respectively more socially and more rationally inclined.

BROEKMAN, PROF. M. C. VAN MOURIK, 1878-1954. Liberal Protestant theologian, religious philosopher, interested in ethics and parapsychology.

BURBANK, LUTHER, 1849-1926. American horticulturist; improved garden-produce, and grew things like stoneless plums and thornless cacti.)

BURMA. State in Southeast Asia, bordering on Tibet, China, Bengal and the Bay of Bengal. Kingdom, from 1895-1948 under British rule.

CALCUTTA. On the east coast. Capital of West Bengal. From 1773-1912 the British capital in India.

CARUSO, ENRICO, 1873-1921. Italian singer, most famous tenor of his time.

CASTE. Hindu society is divided in four principal castes and thousands of subcastes. 1. Brahmana caste, originally priests, scholars and musicians. 2. Kshatriya caste, warriors and rulers. 3. Vaishya caste, merchants. 4. Sudra caste, manual workers. Apart from these are the casteless, the parias, Gandhis harijan. In the North the caste system is less rigidly applied than in the South.

CEYLON. Large island off the extreme southeastern tip of India, in the Ramayana and other epics referred to as Lanka, and now, as an independent republic, again called Sri Lanka.

CHALIAPIN, FJODOR, 1873-1921. Russian singer, most famous bass of his day.

CHURCHILL, LADY RANDOLPH, née Jennie Jerome, 1855-1921. American, mother of Sir Winston Churchill.

COUÉ, EMILE, 1847-1926. French psychotherapist, known for his-method of healing by autosuggestion.

D'ANNUNZIO, GABRIELE, 1857-1936. Italian poet and politician, Lived in France between 1910 and 1915, because of debts in Italy. Promoted Italy's joining the Allies in the First World War and took part in it as an active pilot. Later he associated himself with fascism, as a result of which he lost his *fin de siècle* popularity abroad.

DELHI (better Dehli). Old and new city on the west bank of the Yamuna, in the centre of Northern India; capital of divers kingdoms and empires for thousands of years.

DERVISH (Persian). Religious mendicant, sometimes a renunciate.

DHRUPAD. Northern classical music, influenced by the Moslem conquerors. The variations are adornments, singing demands a very large vocal range.

DILRUBA. String instrument with four strings and seven sympathetic strings, played with a bow.

DRAVIDIANS. Collective name for the original population of South India.

DONIZETTI, G. D. M., 1797-1848. Italian composer.

DULAC, EDMOND (later EDMUND), 1882-1953. Well-known English illustrator of French descent.

DUNCAN, ISADORA, 1880-1927. American dancer of Irish descent, inspired by Greek art, danced barefoot instead of on the toes in ballet shoes. Many schools in France, Russia and America.

DUNSANY, LORD EDWARD J. M. D. P., 1878-1957. Irish novelist and playwright.

ELLIS, HENRY HAVELOCK, 1859-1939, English cultural philosopher, one of the first to write about the psychology of sex.

FAQIR (Arabic). A humble or poor man, a beggar, a mystic. The western association of acrobat or juggler is incorrect.

FROMM, ERICH, 1900-... . Cultural psychologist, originally German psychoanalyst, 1934-1948 at various American institutes, 1951 professor in Mexico.

GAEKWAR. Family name of the maharajas of Baroda; the word means cowherd, hence it became 'the Gaekwar.' Between 1847 and 1875 two princes in succession exerted themselves in intrigues, fratricide, extravagances, cruelties and misrule. Therefore Maula Bakhsh could not bear staying in Baroda at first. But Shri Sayaji Rao III Gaekwar, 1862-1939, was as excellent a ruler as his predecessors were reprehensible. As a boy of twelve he was brought from his village and from three descendants of the founder of the dynasty he was chosen as the most suitable. Much has been written about him, e.g. P. S. P. Rice, *Life of Sayaji Rao*, 1931, 2 vols and Ph. W. Sergeant, *The Ruler of Baroda*, Murray, London, 1928.

GALERIES LAFAYETTE. Department stores in Paris.

GARÇONNES. Thin, Eton-cropped girls who, about 1925, shocked people by their outward show of emancipation.

GAYAN. Literally a song, music. Abbreviated title of Inayat's first book of aphorisms. Gayan and its sequels *Vadan* and *Nirtan*, unlike Inayat's other work, were not dictated, but composed of spontaneous ideas, jotted down and rewritten by Inayat on scraps of paper. The contents are varied: ideas formulated, advice, answers, prayers, reactions to the writer's experiences, and expressions of his mystical search and attainment.

GAYANSHALA. The music academy Maula Bakhsh founded in Baroda.

GHAZAL (*Persian*). Short poem of at most fifteen couplets.

GHOSE, SRI AUROBINDO, 1872-1950. Circa 1895 professor of English literature in Baroda; after 1906 nationalist leader; later founder of an ashram and a community, Auroville.

GOANESE. Inhabitant of Goa, until 1961 Portuguese enclave in India.

GOKHALE, GOPALKRISHNA, 1866-1915. One of the great Indian leaders before Gandhi.

GOLCONDA. Old fortress-town, now in ruins, five miles northwest of Hyderabad. In the sixteenth century famous for its diamond industry, in the twentieth century still the treasury of the Nizam.

GOPIS. The milkmaids to whom Krishna appeared. When he danced with them all, each girl was left with the impression of being his only partner.

GUITRY, LUCIEN, 1860-1925. Famous French actor and director, father of Sacha Guitry.

GUJARAT. Plains north of Bombay.

GUJARATI. The language of Gujarat and surroundings, one of the fourteen languages in the Indian Constitution. Moslims and Parsis use more Arabic and Persian words than belong to standard Gujarati. It has a long literary tradition. Inayat's language in childhood was Gujarati.

GULBARGA. Town in Mysore, South-India.

GURU *(Sanskrit)*. Spiritual teacher. Identical with the Persian word Murshid.

GWALIOR. Town, formerly princely state in Northeast India with many historical places, temples, rock sculpture and a famous fortress.

HANUMAN. Commander of the monkey army, the auxiliary troops in the epic Ramayana.

HARIJAN. Children of God, name given to the parias by Gandhi. See caste.

HAZRAT *(Arabic)*. Very reverent form of address and title of saints. The word means presence, he is present.

HINDI. Vernacular language of North India, spoken by the Hindu people; it is applied to the various dialects, as well as to the literary language, usually called High Hindi.

HINDU. In America, France and Russia every Indian was called Hindu, among other reasons because 'Indian' meant Red Indian. For an Indian a Hindu is one who belongs to the complicated socio-religion known as Hinduism.

HINDUISM. The religious and social institutions and traditions of the Hindus. It includes high philosophy and mysticism as well as simple idol-worship, is tolerant, has many sects and a great power of assimilation.

HINDUSTANI. A confusing term, used by some to indicate Urdu. A mixed language, understood in most of Northern India.

HYDER ALI, 1722-1782. Resisted the British on a large scale and successfully. Had French artillery troops in his service. Originally from the Punjab, he became the ruler of Mysore.

HYDERABAD. The fourth largest city in India, on the right bank of the river Musi, in South India. Founded in 1589. There is another Hyderabad in the Northwest, now in Pakistan, formerly the capital of Sind.

INAYAT KHAN. Family name of the descendants of Inayat Khan. He had four children:

1. *Noor-un-Nisa,* 1914-1944, See p. 135 and Overton Fuller.

2. *Vilayat,* 1917-... Studied philosophy and psychology in Paris and at Oxford. 1940-1945 officer in the British Navy. Later he was a journalist and in the diplomatic service of several Asian and North African countries. The Bourguibas, both father and son, offered him a government post in Tunesia, which he refused to do what pupils asked of him: continue his father's work (since about 1952). He has one son, Seraphiel, born in 1971.

3. *Hidayat,* 1918-... Musician, was violinist in the Haarlem orchestra

(Holland). In his compositions he seeks to link eastern and western music. He has one daughter, Mrs. Carlberg, and two sons; the eldest son, Fazal, see below.

4. Khair-un-Nisa, now called Claire, Mrs Harper, 1919-... She has one son and one grandchild.

There are, to date, five grandchildren, one of whom is:

Fazal, 1942-... Was trained in the USA as a computer specialist. About 1965 he was invited to continue the work of his grandfather and great-uncles. He has three sons and one daughter.

There are, to date, eleven great-grandchildren.

INDRA. Hindu god of power in nature (thunder) and of rain.

ISLAM. Surrender, peace; the religion founded by Mohamed.

IVANOV, WJATSJESLAW IVANOVICH, 1866-1949. Russian poet, leader of the symbolists. Had a leading salon in St Petersburg from 1905-1911, later in Moscow. Emigrated to Rome in 1924.

JAIPUR. Capital of Rajasthan, formerly of the princely state Jaipur, 223 Km southwest of Delhi.

JAINS. Members of a sect, separated from Hinduism; they follow an extreme principle of non-killing.

JALTARANG. Percussion instrument, consisting of twelve porcelain bowls filled with water at different levels. When tapped they produce different notes.

JAURÊS, A. M. JEAN, 1859-1914. Most important figure in European socialism at the beginning of the century. In July 1914 he tried to make the French Government pacify the Russians, was therefore branded as a bribed puppet of the Germans, and murdered by a nationalist on 31st July.

JODJANA, RADEN MAS, 1890-1972. Javanese prince and court dancer, brought the Javanese art of dancing to the West, His Dutch wife, Raden Aju Jodjana — Khurshid de Ravalieu in 1915 — was one of Inayat's first disciples.

KAMA. Desire, passion. Also a god of love, a beautiful youth whose vehicle is a parrot, and who wounds with arrows.

KHAN-DE KONINGH, MRS W. S. MUSHARAFF. Widow of Inayat's youngest brother. She was the principal of the Municipal Dalton High School for girls at the Hague. She collects and arranges historical Sufi material.

KHAJURAO. Was a village in Madya Pradesh with eighty-five temples, of which twenty remain. The best known is the Kandarya Mahadeo, dating back to about 1000 BC. It depicts the mountain Meru, which unites heaven and earth. This is symbolically expressed in the sculpture of many couples in various kinds of embrace.

KHWAJA MOINUDDIN CHISHTI, circa 1140-1236. Best-known saint of the Chishti order, founded by Abu Ishaq Shami.

KRISHNA, eighth incarnation of the Hindu god Vishnu. In the Bhagavad Gita he is identified with the Supreme.

KSHATRIYA. See under Castes.

KU KLUX KLAN. A secret political society in the USA, powerful terrorists after the Civil War in the nineteenth century and after the First World War.

LAHORE. Capital of West Punjab, now in Pakistan.

LEAGUE OF NATIONS. Founded on 10th Januari 1920 to promote international co-operation and peace, the first draft was made by President Wilson of America. In the end the United Stated did not join. After 1940 the League of Nations was practically eliminated, in 1946 it was officially dissolved and succeeded by the United Nations.

LUCKNOW. Town on a tributary of the Ganges, formerly capital of the then province Agra-Oudh. After the decline of the rulers in Delhi, Oudh became a cultural centre. There is a new town and an old one, the latter having many historical remains.

MADANI, MURSHID SYED MOHAMMED ABU HASHIM, died in 1907. Inayat's spiritual teacher. Syed: descendant of Mohammed; Abu Hashim: father of Hashim; Mohammed is the murshid's own first name; Madani is the family name, meaning that they came from Medina. Though there are hundreds of Syeds, it is considered important for a spiritual teacher to be a descendant of Mohammed, because it implies uninterrupted passing on of inner wisdom.

MADRAS. Capital of the state Madras, third largest city in India, on the Bay of Bengal. According to Durga Das, p. 103, this was the most Indian part of India, where even councillors went barefoot, and Hindus, Moslems and Christians dressed alike.

MADURAI. Town in Madras State, cultural-religious centre, featuring Shiva temples with colourful, sculptured steeple gates and among other things a hall with a thousand pillars. It was in Madurai that Gandhi wore a loin-cloth and shaved his head for the first time.

MAHARAJA. Hindu prince or ruler. Also form of address for leading Hindus.

MAHEBOOB PYARUMIR KHAN, SHAIKH-UL-MASHAIKH, 1887-1948. Inayat's younger brother. Musician, also trained in western music. Composer, was working on music that would link East and West, put many of Inayat's poems to music. Was leader of the Sufi Movement from 1928-1948. Married Miss G. C. S. van Goens, daughter of Rycklof van Goens and the Hon. M. J. F. van Beyma, in 1924. One daughter, Rahimunnisa, born in 1923 and one son:

MAHMOOD KHAN YOUSKINE, SHAIKH-UL-MASHAIKH, 1927-... Studied history of music and history at Leyden University. His uncle Pir-o-Murshid Ali Khan had originally appointed him as his successor in the Movement. Eventually the succession was so arranged that

296

Vilayat Inayat Khan became the head of the London-based Sufi Order, Fazal Inayat Khan of the Geneva-based Sufi Movement and Mahmood head of the family. He occupied an honorary post at the Pakistan Embassy in The Hague, and is now connected with the Policy Bureau for Technical Assistance at the Dutch Ministery of Foreign Affairs. Has two daughters and two sons.

MAIN STREET. Book by Sinclair Lewis, portraying life in an American provincial town.

MALABAR. District in the Southwest of Madras State, centre of South Indian culture.

MANTRAS. Holy words and formulas used in chanting.

MAHRATTAS. Militant Hindu people, who successfully resisted the Moghul conquerors towards the end of the seventeenth century. They formed a confederation of states towards the end of the eighteenth century and fought Tipu Sahib as well as the British.

MAHRATI. The language of the Mahrattas, central Indian language.

MATA HARI. Margaretha Geertruida Zelle, 1876-1917. Was known in the beginning of the century for her so-called oriental dances and as a courtesan. She was executed as a spy by the French. According to Sam Waagenaar's book *The Murder of Mata Hari* this was an injustice.

MINQAR-É-MUSIQAR. (The singing bird). Inayat's most important work in Hindustani and Persian. The contents of the book are descriptions of ragas and dances, as well as explanation of their inner meaning. The poems are by various Indian poets and some by Inayat himself. Written in Hyderabad 1903-1906, printed in Allahabad 1913.

MOGHULS. Turko-Mongolian ruling dynasty in India, 1527-1857. Their golden age was under Akbar, q.v.; zenith of culture was reached under Shah Jehan, 1628-1659. The rulers came under British protection in 1805, and were dismissed in 1857.

MONTESSORI, DR MARIA, 1870-1952. Originally physician and professor of anthropology. She designed a pedagogic system for mentally defective children, which was later elaborated upon for normal children. Principles: child's own working tempo, own type of activity, development of spontaneity, dedication and self-confidence.

MOSCOW. Today the seat of government of the Soviet Union. In 1914 the capital was St Petersburg, but Moscow was the recognized spiritual and cultural centre of Russia.

MAULA BAKHSH, 1833-1896. Original name Chole Khan (son of) Ghise Khan (son of) Enver Khan. *Seventieth Anniversary,* College of Indian Music, Dance and Dramatics. Baroda, 1956, pp. 23 and 24. Also C. R. Day, *The Music and Musical Instruments of Southern India and the Deccan,* pp. XVI and 173.

MUREED, murid (*Persian*). Disciple, the same as *chela* in Sanskrit.

MURSHID (*Persian*). Spiritual teacher, the same as *guru* in Sanskrit.

MUSÉE GUIMET. Centre for oriental art in Paris, Place d' Iéna. Founded by the industrialist Guimet.

MUSHARAFF MOULAMIR KHAN, PIR-O-MURSHID, 1895-1967. Inayat's youngest brother, leader of the movement from 1959-1967. In 1935 he wrote lively memories of Baroda, which were reprinted in 1971, augmented from conversations and answers to questions. He, too, was a singer and musician, and he gave concerts in Europe for many years.

MYSORE. State in South India, original capital Mysore, later Bangalore. Flourished most under Hyder Ali, q.v. From 1831-1881 under direct British rule. Mysore was restored as a Hindu princedom in 1881.

NAIDU, SAROJINI, 1879-1948. Poetess, freedom fighter, member and president (1924) of the Congress party. Fought for the emancipation of women.

NAINI TAL. Town and district in Uttar Pradesh. Sanatorium. European schools, military barracks; lake, mountain streams, woods.

NAOROJI, DADABHAI, 1825-1917. First great political leader, 'the grand old man of India.' In *Sufi* 1916 occurs a poem about the need of India, by the American Edmund Russell, and dedicated to Naoroji. He was a philosopher and a businessman, 'more concerned about the prestige and welfare of his country than about profit.' (P. K. Gopalakrishnan).

NEPAL. Independent kingdom in the Himalayas; more or less under British protection from 1816-1917.

NEWBOLT, SIR HENRY, 1862-1938. Naval officer and poet. British naval historian.

NIRTAN. Inayat's third book of aphorisms and poems, written between 1925 and 1927. See *Gayan*.

NIZAM OF HYDERABAD, MIR MAHEBOOB ALI KHAN, ASAF JAH, 1867-1911. Descendant of a Tartar soldier, Asaf Jah, 1713. The title is derived from an Arabic word meaning order, government. The Nizams were supposed to be the richest rulers in India. Nawab (nabob) is one of the twentyfive or thirty words that constitute his complete name and titles.

NIZAMUDDIN AULIA, HAZRAT, 1237-1325. Mystic in the Chishti school. One of his disciples was Amir Khusro, the first Hindustani poet. The tombs of both are in Hazrat Nizamuddin (old name Ghiatpur), now part of New Delhi.

OUR TOWN. Play by Thornton Wilder, depicting life in an American provincial town.

PADEREWSKI, IGNATIUS, 1860-1941. Polish pianist, composer, politician, first president of Poland after its restoration in 1918.

PUNJAB. (Land of five rivers). Borders on Afghanistan, now partly Indian, partly Pakistani. Large melting-pot of nationalities and races. The people are energetic, and many occupy leading positions in India.

PARSIS. Followers of Zarathustra in India. Descendants of Persians who emigrated to India in the eight century, when their country was conquered by the Arabs. An active group, industrialists, etc.

PHRENOLOGY. An obsolete science whereby mental qualities, capabilities, etc. are judged from the shape of the skull.

PIR. (*Persian*), Spiritual teacher, Pir-o-Murshid can be translated as senior and guide, a great master.

QAWWAL. Singer of songs that arouse ecstasy.

RAGA. The theme or mood of a piece of music, a given melody of at the maximum seven notes. The singer or player varies and elaborates on the theme, but is restricted by certain rules. Each raga has its own particular time and atmosphere, for instance: 'early morning, quiet,' or 'early morning, passionate,' 'evening, love, happiness,' or 'evening, calm and mysterious.' Nobody will want to sing or listen to a morning raga in the evening or a daytime raga at night.

RAHEMAT (ULLAH) KHAN (SON OF) BAHADUR KHAN (SON OF) NYAMAT KHAN, 1843-1910. Inayat's father, a singer, hailed from Sialkot in the Punjab. See Chapter I, note 4.

RAMA. One of the manifestations of Vishnu; the ideal man.

RAMAKRISHNA (GADADHAR CHATTERJI), 1834-1886. Mystic and religious leader. The Ramakrishna Mission, well-known outside India too, was founded by his disciple Vivekananda.

RANGOON. Capital of Burma.

RASPUTIN (the profligate), GRIGORII JEFIMOVICH NOWIJ, 1863-1916. A farmer's son. He led a wild life, appeared to have supernormal powers, and joined one of the many Russian sects, one that interpreted the idea of 'salvation though repentance' as 'make sure that you sin, then you will be forgiven.' The idea of mystic union, too, Rasputin interpreted physically. Result: orgies. In 1907 Rasputin was called to the Court to heal the heir to the throne, who suffered from haemophilia. The czarina especially came under his influence. Whether he was used by certain parties or was himself the conductor, is not certain, but any person whom he named was appointed or dismissed. Normal government became impossible. He was generally considered a source of evil in Russia, only the czarina's immediate circle believed in him. He certainly had magnetism. Y(o)uss(o)upov (*Avant l'Exil*, p. 237) was once hypnotized by him and found that he could not move, but could continue to think without Rasputin being aware of this. He imposed his will, but could not 'reflect', receive the thoughts of others.

REINCARNATION. Teaching of the transmigration of souls, adopted from the Hindus by the theosophists; the belief that after death the soul will return in another body, in better or worse conditions, according to good or bad behaviour in life.

RISHI. Holy hermit, mystic living in isolation.

RUMI, JALALUDDIN. d. 1273. Most important Persian Sufi poet. Inayat quotes more than thirty of his poems.

RUMMEL, WALTER M., 1887-1953, German componist and composer, one of the notable foreigners in the Paris art world of pre-1914, a friend of Isadora Duncan.

SAADI, SHAIKH MUSLIHUDDIN d. 1283. Important Persian Sufi poet. Inayat quotes about twenty five of his poems.

SAMADHI *(Sanskrit;* WAJAD in Arabic and Persian). Peace, the highest state of being of the mystic. Excited ecstasy is a state of transition.

SARI. Women's garment, a length of material nearly six times as long as it is wide. It is wrapped round the waist, pleated in front and the remainder thrown across the shoulder so that it hangs down at the back, and can be used to cover the head.

SCOTT, CYRILL, 1879-... English composer and poet, influenced by eastern philosophy.

SCRIABINE, ALEXANDER NICOLAIEVICH, 1872-1915. Russian composer, who had a grand plan for a religious play, uniting all forms of art. There has been a renewed interest in him recently; during his life he was very famous and rather proud.

SHAIKH-UL-MASHAIKH. See Maheboob and Mahmood Khans. The spiritual title of the family was Mashaikh at first, since 1924 Shaikh-ul-Mashaikh.

SHERPAS. Tribe of small farmers on the slopes of the Himalayas in Nepal, notable as guides and porters.

SHIAS. Moslim sect, originally political; came into being in the time of Mohammed's son-in-law, Ali.

SHIVA (MAHADEV). The god of destruction, but also of purification, transformation and fertility. He is often depicted in his cosmic dance, destroying monsters. He is worshipped in a primitive as well as in a monotheistic, philosophical way, as are all Hindu gods.

SIKHS. Followers of a religion without caste, seceded from Hinduism; monotheistic. Founder Guru Nanak, 1469-1533. Active, militant group of people.

SHRUTIS. Gliders, transitional notes, incorrectly called quarter tones.

SUFISM. Historically a collective name for several mystic movements in Islam. The origin of the word is not known, though it is probably derived from the Arabic word *suf,* meaning wool. Inayat emphasizes that Sufism means mysticism in general and that it already existed before Mohammed. In the East, too, one may find his definition 'Sufism is not a religion, church, or sect, but an attitude to life.' Inayat was anxious not to found a sect. See further Chapter IV, note 9 and Chapter VIII, note 10.

SÖDERBLOM, NATHAN, 1866-1931. Swedish theologian, founder of the oecumenical movement. Received the Nobel prize in 1930.

SUNNIS. Group within Islam, more orthodox than the Shias. For that reason they needed mystical schools as a complement.

SUFFRAGETTES. Conspicuous women fighters for votes for women, in the beginning of this century.

TABLA. Percussion instruments: one drum with a clear tone, often accompanied by a larger drum with a deeper tone. Used to accompany singing and string instruments.

TAGORE RABINDRANATH, 1861-1941. Bengali writer and poet. He wrote much more than is known in the West, for instance the Indian national anthem. Worked for harmonious relations between East and West. Received the Nobel prize in 1913. Maula Bakhsh knew his father and elder brothers.

TAJ MAHAL. Mausoleum of the wife of Shah Jehan, one of the most famous monuments in the world.

TANEIEV, SERGEI IVANOVICH, 1856-1915. Russian composer and pianist, famous educationist.

TANJORE. Two hundred Km south of Madras. There is a palace dating back to 1550, with a large library and a temple dating back to the eleventh century.

TANSEN, 1560-1605. Historical musician and composer about whom legendary stories are told. One of the 'nine gems' at Akbar's court.

TARANA or TELLANA. Musical language, used in drumming. Also a type of song consisting of disconnected syllables, tarana sounds.

TARTARS, Tribes of horsemen on the Asian plains, conquered by Genghis Khan in 1202, assimilated by the Mongols. They occupied Russia between the thirteenth and the sixteenth century and then were assimilated by the Russians. Only Moslem groups remained; they have now been organized into autonomous Soviet Republics. Some aristocratic Russian families, for instance the Yussupovs, were proud of their Tartar descent.

TILAK, BAL GANGADHAR, 1856-1920. Scholar and nationalist, orthodox Hindu, leader of the extremist wing of the Congress Party.

TIPU SULTAN, 1759-1799. Sultan of Mysore, son of Hyder Áli; fought the British, as did his father. Tipu's sons were taken to Calcutta by the conquerors, his uncle, the brother of Hyder Ali, became the head of the 'Mysore Tipus.' It is believed that Casimebi, the first wife of Maula Bakhsh, descended from him (Information given by Mahmood Khan).

TUTHANKHAMEN. In 1923 his tomb was excavated by Carter and Carnarvon, the only royal Egyptian tomb that, after three thousand years, was found undamaged. A Tuthankhamen vogue followed.

UNIVERSITÉ DES ANNALES. Institute for the cultural education of young girls; courses in literature, history of art, sociology were given, and examinations conducted; the school arranged concerts and lectures also.

URDU. Indo-Aryan language, spoken by Moslems and others in Northern India. Mixed with Persian and Arabic words, while Hindi is mixed with Sanskrit; therefore those who speak Urdu and those who speak Hindi cannot always understand each other easily.

USTAD. Teacher; a music teacher of the old school, who would only teach his own sons or chosen pupils.

VADAN. Inayat's aphorisms and poems, composed between 1921 and 1925. See *Gayan*.

VEDANTA. System of philosophy, way to liberation of the soul. Principle: the one-ness of the individual soul with the universal soul of Brahman, See *Advaita*.

VEENA (VINA). String instrument with two soundboxes, four melody strings, and three sympathizing strings, and twenty two frets. The notes are made with the left hand and the strings plucked with the right. The microtonal nuances are obtained by deflection of the strings, whole passages being played by a lateral movement of the left hand, without fresh plucking. There are several types of vinas.

VISHNU. Hindu god, the preserver.

YAMUNA. One of the great rivers springing from the Brahmaputra, largest sister river of the Ganges.